The American Frontier

Other books in the Turning Points series:

Turning | Points
IN WORLD HISTORY

The American Frontier

James D. Torr, *Book Editor*

Daniel Leone, *President*
Bonnie Szumski, *Publisher*
Scott Barbour, *Managing Editor*

Greenhaven Press, Inc., San Diego, California

Library of Congress Cataloging-in-Publication Data

The American frontier / James D. Torr, book editor.
    p. cm. — (Turning points in world history)
    Includes bibliographical references and index.
    ISBN 0-7377-0785-2 (pbk. : alk. paper)—
ISBN 0-7377-0786-0 (lib. bdg. : alk. paper)
    1. Frontier and pioneer life—United States. 2. Frontier and pioneer life—West (U.S.) 3. United States—Territorial expansion. 4. West (U.S.)—Discovery and exploration. 5. West (U.S.)— History. I. Torr, James D., 1974– II. Turning points in world history (Greenhaven Press)

E179.5 .A472 2002
978'.02—dc21   2001033514
                                                          CIP

Cover photo: Bettmann/CORBIS

© 2002 by Greenhaven Press, Inc.
10911 Technology Place, San Diego, CA 92127

Printed in the U.S.A.

Contents

Chapter 2: Destiny and War

Chapter 3: Gold Fever

Foreword

Certain past events stand out as pivotal, as having effects and outcomes that change the course of history. These events are often referred to as turning points. Historian Louis L. Snyder provides this useful definition:

> A turning point in history is an event, happening, or stage which thrusts the course of historical development into a different direction. By definition a turning point is a great event, but it is even more—a great event with the explosive impact of altering the trend of man's life on the planet.

History's turning points have taken many forms. Some were single, brief, and shattering events with immediate and obvious impact. The invasion of Britain by William the Conqueror in 1066, for example, swiftly transformed that land's political and social institutions and paved the way for the rise of the modern English nation. By contrast, other single events were deemed of minor significance when they occurred, only later recognized as turning points. The assassination of a little-known European nobleman, Archduke Franz Ferdinand, on June 28, 1914, in the Bosnian town of Sarajevo was such an event; only after it touched off a chain reaction of political-military crises that escalated into the global conflict known as World War I did the murder's true significance become evident.

Other crucial turning points occurred not in terms of a few hours, days, months, or even years, but instead as evolutionary developments spanning decades or even centuries. One of the most pivotal turning points in human history, for instance—the development of agriculture, which replaced nomadic hunter-gatherer societies with more permanent settlements—occurred over the course of many generations. Still other great turning points were neither events nor developments, but rather revolutionary new inventions and innovations that significantly altered social customs and ideas, military tactics, home life, the spread of knowledge, and the human condition in general. The developments of writing, gunpowder, the printing press, antibiotics, the electric light, atomic energy, television, and the computer, the last two of which have recently ushered in the world-altering information age, represent only some of these innovative turning points.

Each anthology in the Greenhaven Turning Points in World History series presents a group of essays chosen for their accessibility. The anthology's structure also enhances this accessibility. First, an introductory essay provides a general overview of the principal events and figures involved, placing the topic in its historical context. The essays that follow explore various aspects in more detail, some targeting political trends and consequences, others social, literary, cultural, and/or technological ramifications, and still others pivotal leaders and other influential figures. To aid the reader in choosing the material of immediate interest or need, each essay is introduced by a concise summary of the contributing writer's main themes and insights.

In addition, each volume contains extensive research tools, including a collection of excerpts from primary source documents pertaining to the historical events and figures under discussion. In the anthology on the French Revolution, for example, readers can examine the works of Rousseau, Voltaire, and other writers and thinkers whose championing of human rights helped fuel the French people's growing desire for liberty; the French *Declaration of the Rights of Man and Citizen*, presented to King Louis XVI by the French National Assembly on October 2, 1789; and eyewitness accounts of the attack on the royal palace and the horrors of the Reign of Terror. To guide students interested in pursuing further research on the subject, each volume features an extensive bibliography, which for easy access has been divided into separate sections by topic. Finally, a comprehensive index allows readers to scan and locate content efficiently. Each of the anthologies in the Greenhaven Turning Points in World History series provides students with a complete, detailed, and enlightening examination of a crucial historical watershed.

Introduction

In 1763 England's King George declared all land west of the Appalachians off-limits to colonial settlers. For the American colonists, however, the lure of the West greatly outweighed the decrees of a far-off king. By the time the American Revolution began, roughly thirty thousand settlers had crossed the Alleghenies in Pennsylvania to farm the area along the Ohio River near what is now Pittsburgh.

The settlement of the Ohio River valley established a pattern that would be repeated throughout the nineteenth century. It represented the triumph of the frontiersman and proof that America was a "land of opportunity." The Ohio River valley settlers, through courage and hard work, were able to make new lives for themselves in a new land.

The settlement of the Ohio River valley also exemplified a less pleasant reality. King George had issued his 1763 proclamation in an attempt to appease the Indians living in the region. Earlier that year an Ottawa chief named Pontiac had led a rebellion in which the Indians took over British forts and burned colonists' settlements in the area. The way in which Americans ignored their government's promise to the Indians set a precedent for relations between white settlers and Indian natives that was repeated again and again in the conquering of the American frontier.

In the nineteenth century the American frontier was pushed back from the Appalachians to the Mississippi to the Rockies, then South to Mexico, then finally all the way to the Pacific. The two themes of opportunity and conquest were present in almost every aspect of frontier expansion. Whether in the fur trade of the Rocky Mountains, the gold rush of California, or the cattle kingdoms of the Southwest, the frontier presented seemingly unlimited opportunities for the pioneer. But the land was not simply there for the taking: war, with both Indians and Mexico, was a major part of westward expansion. Although it wasn't coined until 1845, the term used to describe this concept of "conquering the frontier" is "Manifest Destiny."

A Growing Nation

At the turn of the nineteenth century—less than two decades after the end of the Revolutionary War—the United States was a fledgling nation of about 3 million. But the United States was growing. In the 1790s, Vermont, Kentucky, and Tennessee were added to the original thirteen states. Strictly in terms of land, however, the Northwest Territory was the greater acquisition. This territory southwest of the Great Lakes, northwest of the Ohio River, and east of the Mississippi was wrested from the Indians in the 1780s and 1790s. Its acquisition prompted Congress to pass the Northwest Ordinance of 1787, which laid the groundwork for how new states would be admitted to the Union. Ohio was the first state to emerge from the Northwest territory, followed by Indiana, Illinois, Michigan, and Wisconsin.

By 1801 it was clear that U.S. territory extended to the Mississippi, but there were several obstacles to further frontier exploration. In the South, Spain controlled Florida and Mexico, which at the time included both Texas and much of California. France had claimed the Louisiana Territory— roughly defined as the area between the Mississippi and the Rocky Mountains, north of Texas, and south of the Columbia River—but had transferred its claim on the territory to Spain in 1762. In the north Great Britain controlled Canada, and was supporting the Indians of the Great Lakes region in their efforts to maintain control of their lands.

Despite all these obstacles, President Thomas Jefferson, who took office in 1801, had grand plans for the American frontier. He was deeply curious about the land west of the Mississippi and spoke of an "empire of liberty" that would span the whole of North America. Jefferson biographer Joseph Ellis writes that "for Jefferson, more than any other major figure in the revolutionary generation, the West was America's future."[1] "As early as 1784," writes historian Gerald F. Kreyche, "Jefferson conferred with George Rogers Clark, the American Revolutionary War general and surveyor, about exploring the land west, even though the United States had no claim to it."[2]

The Explorers' Frontier

As Jefferson took office, events in Europe dramatically altered the official status of Louisiana and thus the American frontier. Napoleon Bonaparte had risen to power in France in 1799, and in 1800 he invaded and defeated Spain and dictated a peace treaty that made Louisiana a French possession again. This meant that the French would control the important port of New Orleans, although the official transfer would not take place until 1803, at which time Jefferson sent delegates to France to negotiate for the port's purchase. But by that time Napoleon had experienced serious setbacks in his military campaign to build a French empire. In need of finances, Napoleon offered to sell the United States all of the Louisiana Territory rather than just the port of New Orleans. The shocked American delegates agreed, and "for the small price of $15 million," writes historian Sanford Wexler, "the United States acquired 828,000 square miles of territory, which doubled the size of the nation."[3]

Jefferson was now free to make public the transcontinental expedition he had been planning since he took office in 1801. A month before his inauguration Jefferson had appointed army captain Meriwether Lewis as his private secretary, and together they had begun planning an expedition to find a water route to the Pacific—the fabled "Northwest Passage." Jefferson also emphasized the importance of mapping the territory, discovering the natural resources the land had to offer, and making contact with the Indian tribes of the area. As co-captain of the Corps of Discovery, as it was to be called, Lewis chose William Clark, a fellow Virginian who had served under him in the army.

"On May, 14, 1804," writes Kreyche, "the intrepid Lewis and Clark began a journey that would take them to the delta of the mighty Columbia River on the Pacific Ocean."[4] Lewis and Clark failed to find an all-water route to the Pacific, but they revealed much about the thousands of miles of unexplored territory west of the Mississippi and greatly strengthened America's claim to the Pacific Northwest. In the minds of the American people, writes historian Bernard DeVoto, the Lewis and Clark expedition "satisfied desire and it created desire: the desire of a westering nation."[5]

Other explorers added to interest about the West. Zebulon Pike, for example, explored the upper Mississippi River and later the headwaters of the Arkansas and Red Rivers, where he discovered Pike's Peak. Stephen H. Long also explored the area around what is now the Texas panhandle and the Great Plains. On his maps, however, Long called the latter the "Great American Desert," which discouraged further exploration of the area for several decades.

The Fur Trappers' Frontier

One of the most significant contributions of these explorations was to raise interest in the Rocky Mountain fur trade. Upon returning from his journey in 1806 Lewis wrote that the upper Missouri River was "richer in beaver and otter than any country on earth."[6] The fur trade soon became the principal economic opportunity drawing Americans to the frontier until 1840.

The European demand for furs from the New World had existed since the seventeenth century, with Indians selling beaver and other furs to traders who in turn sold them in Europe, where they were very fashionable. Not until after the Louisiana Purchase, however, did white settlers begin fur trapping in an organized fashion. One of the first to do so was Manuel Lisa, a Spanish trader. Lisa and George Drouillard, who had been in the Corps of Discovery, mounted one of the first organized commercial fur-trapping expeditions in 1807. In 1808 Lisa founded the Missouri Fur Company along with William Clark, but in its first expedition the company was attacked by Blackfeet Indians. (As always, there was competition between whites and Indians for natural resources on the frontier.) John Jacob Astor had more success with the American Fur Company, also founded in 1808.

These initial ventures were for the most part lucrative, but the outbreak of the War of 1812 put a temporary halt to commercial fur trapping. Then in 1821 the fur industry was revitalized with the founding of the Rocky Mountain Fur Company by General William Ashley and Major Andrew Henry. Ashley issued a call for "enterprising young men" in a St. Louis *Missouri-Gazette* advertisement well-known to historians of the American West:

> To ENTERPRISING YOUNG MEN: The subscriber wishes to engage ONE HUNDRED MEN, to ascend the river Missouri of its source, there to be employed for one, two or three years. For particulars enquire of Major Andrew Henry near the Lead Mines, in the County of Washington, (who will ascend with, and command the party) or to the subscriber at St. Louis.
> —WM. H. ASHLEY[7]

Among the men who answered this call were now-legendary frontiersman and folk heroes such as Kit Carson, Jedediah Smith, Jim Bridger, Jean Baptiste Charbonneau (the son of Sacagawea), and the notorious boatman and brawler Mike Fink. These and other "mountain men," as they came to be known, contributed greatly to the development of the trans-Mississippi West from 1820 to 1840. Jim Bridger, for example, discovered the Great Salt Lake, and Jedediah Smith was the first American to travel to and from California using an overland route. "The fur frontier had the most powerful effect of all the frontier experiences," writes Mary Ellen Jones in *Daily Life on the 19th-Century American Frontier*, "the fur trapper as explorer amassed vast knowledge about geography, animals and plants, and about the Native Americans."[8]

The "Permanent" Indian Frontier

While some Indian tribes were hostile to white fur trappers, many mountain men were able to peacefully coexist with and learn from the Indians. The mountain men, after all, were only interested in trapping wildlife. The situation was much different between Indians and farmers, who were after the land itself.

In the period of prosperity following the War of 1812, thousands of settlers had moved into the fertile plains of the

Mississippi Valley and the Great Lakes. These lands had previously been designated as Indian territories, and the hostilities that followed the rush of settlers into the region presented the U.S. government with a problem. The solution the government offered was the Indian Intercourse Act of 1834, which marked the beginning of an Indian removal policy that would dominate U.S. Indian policy for the rest of the century. Tribes east of the Mississippi were to cede their lands and move west of the river. Frontier historian Ray Allen Billington sums up the situation:

> While Missouri and Arkansas were filling with land-hungry easterners, other migrants from across the Mississippi moved into the area just west of those two states. The newcomers were driven to the frontier not by the hope of economic gain, but by the bayonets of federal troops. They were the eastern Indians who, uprooted from their tribal lands, were forced to settle on unwanted reservations far from the haunts of white men.[9]

In fact the area these tribes had been forced to was the region Stephen Long had dubbed the "Great American Desert" and Zebulon Pike had said was "wholly unfit for cultivation."[10] This Indian territory was granted to the Indians for "as long as the grass grows and the rivers run."[11] White settlers were not to encroach on lands west of the ninety-fifth meridian, and thus the "Permanent Indian Frontier" was established.

Texas and Mexico

The government's attempt to solve "the Indian question"— to avoid war between Indians and whites—by restricting white settlement past the Mississippi was only a temporary solution. Americans' desire for new land and new opportunities was as strong as ever. Eventually, once the concept of Manifest Destiny really took hold, the government broke its promise to prohibit white settlement in the Indian territory, and war followed. But for roughly a quarter century, at least, most white settlers sought lands outside the Indian territory. As Billington explains, "The adventurers who continually sought homes on the fringes of civilization found that they could no longer drift ahead to adjacent lands as their fathers and forefathers had done. Instead they must either hurdle the Indian reservations and the Great American Desert to seek farms in the fertile valleys of the Pacific coast, or forsake their native land for the alien soil of Texas."[12]

The latter course was possible because in 1821, Mexico, which had been a Spanish colony for over a century, gained its independence. Under Spanish rule foreigners had been forbidden in Mexico, as had trade with the United States. Soon after Mexico declared its independence, Missouri trader William Becknell opened trade with Mexico via the Santa Fe Trail. That trail saw the first use of wagon trains and other practices that future settlers would depend on as they traveled the Oregon Trail two decades later.

Also in 1821, the Mexican government granted Stephen Austin permission to settle three hundred families in the Mexican region known as Texas. Fifteen years later, in 1836, the Republic of Texas would declare its independence from Mexico, with Sam Houston as its president.

"Oregon Fever"

While one group of American pioneers struggled for control of Texas, another group looked west. The Pacific Northwest had captivated the imagination of many easterners ever since Lewis and Clark's journey. "Oregon had been so widely publicized that Americans everywhere looked upon it as a great land of fortune,"[13] writes Thomas D. Clark in *Frontier America: The Story of the Westward Movement*. Boston school teacher Hall J. Kelly, for example, became an advocate for settlement of Oregon after reading the Lewis and Clark journals. For the rest of his life Kelly published pamphlets promoting the territory and lobbied Congress to colonize the region. The federal government was particularly interested in Oregon because England had a partial claim to it. In 1827 Great Britain and the United States agreed to "joint occupancy" of Oregon for an indefinite period of time—which in practical terms meant until Americans settled the area.

By the early 1840s "Oregon fever" had taken hold in the

East. Yet despite a growing clamor for "All Oregon or None," Congress was hesitant to provoke war with England by asserting an official claim over the territory. In the "great migration" of 1843, almost two thousand settlers crossed the two thousand miles from Independence, Missouri, to the Williamette Valley. In 1845 another migration of three thousand almost doubled the population of the region.

Destiny and War

Public pressure to annex both Oregon and the independent Republic of Texas was one of the key issues in the U.S. presidential election of 1844, and Democrat James K. Polk won the election by promising to achieve these two goals. With his victory, an expansionist fervor swept the country. This expansionism was given a name in 1845 when Democratic magazine editor John L. O'Sullivan proclaimed the United States' "manifest destiny to overspread the continent allotted by Providence for the free development of our yearly multiplying millions."[14] Soon other Democrats and proponents of westward expansion had taken up the cry of Manifest Destiny.

Manifest Destiny clearly had a religious connotation—that God intended for Americans to "overspread the continent." It also represented a political belief, inherited from the ideology of the Revolution, that American principles of democratic liberalism were destined to be adopted by people everywhere. "Finally, underlying other assumptions about Manifest Destiny was a persistent and widespread racism," write scholars James W. Davidson, William E. Gienapp, Christine Leigh Heyrman, Mark H. Lytle, and Michael E. Stoff in *Nation of Nations: A Narrative History of the American Republic*, "the same belief in racial superiority that was used to justify Indian removal under Jackson, to uphold slavery in the South, and to excuse segregation in the North also proved handy to defend expansion westward."[15]

Of course, all of these beliefs about frontier expansion had been present in America before the 1840s. The difference now was that the United States was willing to go to war to achieve its "destiny." In 1845 the United States annexed

Texas, and war with Mexico followed. After a two-year struggle that cost 13,000 American and nearly 50,000 Mexican lives, U.S. troops occupied Mexico City and forced a surrender. Under the Treaty of Guadalupe-Hidalgo, the United States paid Mexico $15 million for what is now the Southwest—California, New Mexico, Nevada, Utah, and Texas above the Rio Grande. Along with the June 1846 Oregon Treaty, in which Great Britain agreed to give up its claims below the 49th parallel, the boundaries of the contiguous United States were almost complete. (In the Gadsden Purchase of 1853 the United States also acquired much of present-day New Mexico and Arizona for $10 million.)

The Miners' Frontier

California officially became a U.S. territory with the signing of the Treaty of Guadalupe-Hidalgo on February 2, 1848. Just nine days earlier—unbeknownst to the treaty's negotiators in Mexico City or to anyone else outside California—gold had been discovered on the property of John Sutter, near present-day Sacramento. For the next two years the California gold rush represented the latest and greatest opportunity the frontier had to offer. In *Westward to the Pacific*, Billington describes the initial excitement:

> The discovery was made on 24 January 1848; a few diggers drifted in over the next months, but not until May did the mania begin. Then, suddenly, all California went mad as carpenters dropped their hammers, farmers their plow-handles, and preachers their Bibles, to rush to the "diggings." The infection reached the East much later. On 5 December President Polk devoted a portion of his annual message to Congress to the American River's riches. "The accounts of the abundance of gold in that territory," he reported, "would scarcely command belief were they not corroborated by the authentic reports of officers in the public service." That word from on high was enough. All the nation, and much of the world, succumbed to the gold fever.[16]

As a result of the rapid influx of "49ers," California's population soared and it achieved statehood in October 1850, a remarkably short time.

The California gold rush was only the first of many frontier mineral strikes over the next three decades. Two of the most important were the Pike's Peak, Colorado, gold strike of 1858 and the "Comstock Lode" silver strike near Virginia City, Nevada, in 1859. Other mineral strikes were made in Idaho, Montana, and Arizona in the late 1850s and early 1860s, and in the 1870s additional discoveries were made in Arizona, Colorado, and the Black Hills of the Dakota Territory. The Alaska Purchase of 1856 paid off with the Klondike gold rush of 1898 long before oil was discovered in the region. As in California, each new strike transformed the local economy. Boomtowns grew up around the mines, and when the rush was over, many of the newcomers stayed in their new homes. As Robert W. Richmond and Robert W. Mardock conclude, "the mining industry greatly accelerated settlement of the West. By 1869 the political boundaries of the Western states and territories had been largely defined, a permanent mineral industry had been established, and the demands of the mining regions for improved transportation had spurred the building of a transcontinental railroad."[17]

The Cowboys' Frontier

New York City merchant Asa Whitney had made the first public proposal to build a transcontinental railroad in 1844, when "Oregon fever" still gripped the nation. After the California gold rush, federal surveys were conducted to determine possible routes for a railroad, but disagreements between Northerners and Southerners kept Congress from funding construction on any specific route. Only after the Confederate states seceded at the start of the Civil War was Congress able to pass the Pacific Railroad Act of 1862. This act chartered the Union Pacific Railroad to be built westward from Omaha and for the Central Pacific Railroad to be built eastward from San Francisco. The two lines were joined at Promontory, Utah, in May 1869. Other transcontinental railroads followed, including the Santa Fe line that stretched to Los Angeles and the Northern Pacific that reached Puget Sound.

One of the most important railways in the settling of the frontier was the Kansas Pacific, which, when it reached to Abilene, Kansas, marked the beginning of the cattle trail frontier. Cattle driving had existed in Texas since the 1830s. Herders would drive their cattle to New Orleans, and in some cases north to Missouri, where the animals were valued for leather as much as beef. After the Civil War, the North experienced an acute beef shortage. The new western railroads provided a means to get this beef to the Northern markets: In the "long drive," Texas cowboys drove thousands of cattle up the Chisholm Trail to the railroad terminus at Abilene. "So began the era of the long drive and wild cowtowns, the gunslinger and boot hills, which won such a prominent place in the fact and fancy of American history,"[18] write Richmond and Mardock.

Indeed, the era of the "long drives"—which lasted little more than two decades, from the 1860s to the 1880s—is the one most associated with the "Wild West." Cattle towns such as Abilene, Wichita, and Dodge City experienced a certain level of lawlessness as normally hard-working, sober cowboys caroused for a few days at the end of a drive.

The North American Indian Wars

In addition to wild cattle towns, another prominent theme in modern caricatures of the "Wild West" is the rivalry between cowboys and Indians. A series of ferocious wars between whites and Indians did break out in the 1860s and continued for the next thirty years. In *Indian-Fighting Army*, historian Fairfax Downey reports that from 1869 to 1875, "there were some 200 pitched battles between the Army and the Indians."[19] Kreyche writes that "From the end of the Civil War to the last fight between soldiers and Indians at Leech Lake, Minnesota, in 1898, there were 938 fights."[20] But rather than cowboys, it was the railroads and the white farmers they brought that presented the greatest threat to the Indians.

With the flood of white settlers onto the Great Plains, it was clear to both whites and Indians that the federal government would not keep its promise to keep the "Great

American Desert" an Indian territory. Since the creation of the "Permanent Indian Frontier" in the 1830s, U.S. policy on settlement of the Great Plains had gradually shifted from prohibition to active encouragement. As a result, the army was called to put down various Indian uprisings and raids throughout the 1860s and 1870s, and both sides committed atrocities. In the Sand Creek Massacre of 1864, Colorado militiamen slaughtered nearly 500 Cheyenne in cold blood; in the Fetterman Massacre of 1866, 82 troops were ambushed and killed while trying to aid a group of woodcutters under attack by the Sioux. Several tribal chiefs declared war. The Sioux won a famous victory against General George Custer at the Battle of Little Big Horn in 1876, but were confined to reservations by 1881. The Nez Percé of the Pacific Northwest suffered a similar fate.

The most devastating blow to the Plains Indians was the destruction of the vast buffalo herds that once roamed the Midwest. Railroad track-laying crews slaughtered thousands of the animals for food, and professional hunters killed millions more for their hides or simply for sport. The animals had no cover on the plains and did not run from the report of gunfire, making it easier for one armed, mounted man to kill dozens of buffalo at a time and hundreds in the course of a few days. Hunters killed an estimated 3 million buffalo per year between 1872 and 1874. The U.S. Army also contributed to the slaughter, for as army colonel Richard Dodge reasoned in 1867, "every buffalo dead is an Indian gone."[21] In 1883 a museum expedition seeking specimens found less than 200 buffalo in all the West. The animal that had been the Plains tribes' primary source of both food and shelter was all but extinct.

The Farmers' Frontier

The biggest factor drawing settlers to the Great Plains was the railroads. While starting a new life on the frontier was still difficult and full of risks, at least getting to the frontier had become easier. Another factor was the promise of free land. Under the Homestead Act of 1862, all heads of families and males over twenty-one could claim 160 acres of the public domain, provided they cultivated the land for five years. More land was given away in 1889, when the federal government opened the Indian territory of Oklahoma up to homesteaders. Billington notes that "between 1870 and 1890 more land was occupied and more land placed under cultivation than in all the nation's previous history."[22]

"[The] peculiar environmental conditions of the plains areas worked an unusual hardship on the American frontiersmen,"[23] writes Clark. For example, since wood was scarce on the Plains, homesteaders often lived in sod houses—dwellings made entirely from the hard prairie sod. They also faced harsh winter blizzards and plagues of insects. Finally, the process of dry farming was necessary to make cultivation of the Great Plains possible. Dry farming required the farmer to plow to a depth of seven to ten inches just before the winter rains and snows fell, then to harrow the soil after each rainfall. This was arduous work, and Great Plains farmers were called "sodbusters" for this reason.

The Closing of the American Frontier

The farmer's frontier was the last frontier. By the 1880s the flood of settlers helped put an end to the great cattle drives, as farmers fenced off the land with barbed wire. Eventually the farmer's frontier also came to an end once all the free land was snatched up and the best parts settled. As the federal government reported after the census of 1890: "Up to and including 1880 the country had a frontier of settlement. . . . But at present the unsettled area has been so broken into by isolated bodies of settlement that there can hardly be said to be a frontier line."[24]

Some Americans entertained hopes of opening new frontier beyond the continental United States. In 1898 the United States not only annexed Hawaii, it also went to war with Spain over the independence of Cuba and ended up acquiring Guam, Puerto Rico, and (briefly) the Philippines. Theodore Roosevelt, for example, likened the Filipinos to American Indians and argued for colonization of the United States' new acquisitions. However, these imperialist ambitions never really captivated the public; the frontier movement as a nationally shared experience ended with the nineteenth century.

The closing of the frontier was greeted with apprehension. Since the nation's founding the frontier had represented, above all else, opportunity. This idea was first formalized by the historian Frederick Jackson Turner at an 1893 meeting of the American Historical Association. In what became known as the Turner thesis, he argued that in taking advantage of the opportunities the frontier offered, the nation's pioneering fur traders, miners, ranchers, and farmers had done more to shape the American character than any leaders in the East. "The true point of view in the history of this nation is not the Atlantic Coast, but the Great West,"[25] he declared.

Yet Turner rejected the idea that opportunities for Americans would vanish along with the frontier. "In place of old frontiers of wilderness," he argued, "there are new frontiers of unwon fields of science."[26] This sentiment was echoed in 1959 by historian Thomas D. Clark:

> There are frontiers today, but they are not free land frontiers. Whether in expanding city limits, opening new power and irrigation projects, combating debilitating diseases, . . . or staring at the moon as a possible new place for colonization, the ebullient American accepts his new problems as a frontier challenge. Spiritually the frontier survives in the American outlook, in the language, in the sense of space, and most of all in the basic national confidence of its resourcefulness.[27]

Many historians have challenged some of the more sweeping claims of the Turner thesis. But, as Wexler concludes, "there is no disagreement that the nation's expansion over nearly 3,000 miles of wilderness has left an indelible mark on American history and on the American character."[28]

Notes

1. Quoted in Robert V. Hine and John Mack Faragher, *The American West: A New Interpretive History.* New Haven, CT: Yale University Press, 2000, p. 134.

2. Gerald F. Kreyche, *Visions of the American West.* Lexington: University of Kentucky Press, 1989, p. 8.

3. Sanford Wexler, ed., *Westward Expansion: An Eyewitness History*. New York: Facts On File, 1991, p. 37.

4. Kreyche, *Visions of the American West*, p. 13.

5. Quoted in Hine and Faragher, *The American West*, p. 143.

6. Quoted in Hine and Faragher, *The American West*, p. 143.

7. Quoted in Arthur King Peters, *Seven Trails West*. New York: Abbeville Press, 1996, p. 35.

8. Mary Ellen Jones, *Daily Life on the 19th-Century American Frontier*. Westport, CT: Greenwood Press, 1998, p. 53.

9. Ray Allen Billington, *Westward Expansion: A History of the American Frontier*. New York: MacMillan, 1967, p. 469.

10. Quoted in Wexler, ed., *Westward Expansion*, p. 87.

11. Quoted in Wexler, ed., *Westward Expansion*, p. 88.

12. Billington, *Westward Expansion*, p. 474.

13. Thomas D. Clark, *Frontier America: The Story of the Westward Movement*. New York: Charles Scribner's Sons, 1959, p. 496.

14. Quoted in Don Nardo, ed., *Turning Points in World History: North American Indian Wars*. San Diego: Greenhaven Press, 1999, p. 53.

15. Quoted in Nardo, ed., *North American Indian Wars*, p. 54.

16. Billington, *Westward to the Pacific: An Overview of America's Westward Expansion*. St. Louis, Missouri: Jefferson National Expansion Historical Association, 1979, p. 66.

17. Robert W. Richmond and Robert W. Mardock, eds., *A Nation Moving West: Reading in the History of the American Frontier*. Lincoln: University of Nebraska Press, 1966, p. 191.

18. Richmond and Mardock, eds., *A Nation Moving West*, p. 283.

19. Quoted in Kreyche, *Visions of the American West*, p. 212.

20. Kreyche, *Visions of the American West*, p. 212.

21. Quoted in Hine and Faragher, *The American West*, p. 317.

22. Billington, *Westward to the Pacific*, p. 101.

23. Clark, *Frontier America*, p. 733.

24. Quoted in Hine and Faragher, *The American West*, p. 493.

25. Quoted in Wexler, *Westward Expansion*, p. 281.

26. Quoted in Hine and Faragher, *The American West*, p. 494.

27. Clark, *Frontier America*, p. 762.

28. Wexler, *Westward Expansion*, p. 281.

Chapter 1

The Opening
of the West

Turning
Points

IN WORLD HISTORY

Lewis and Clark's Journey Across the Continent

Gerald F. Kreyche

In the following essay Gerald F. Kreyche describes Meriwether Lewis and William Clark's groundbreaking expedition up the Missouri River, across the continental divide, and west along the Columbia River to the Pacific coast of what is now Oregon. Lewis had been appointed by President Thomas Jefferson to find a Northwest Passage—an all-water route to the Pacific—which they hoped would lead to rich trade with the Orient. Although they found no such route, writes Kreyche, Lewis and Clark's expedition remains remarkable. In their two-and-a-half-year journey, the men ventured into unknown lands and befriended Indians from many tribes. Most importantly, they returned with eight volumes of notes on what they had seen, vastly increasing their fledgling nation's knowledge of what lay beyond the frontier. Kreyche is a professor of philosophy at DePaul University and an editor of *USA Today* magazine.

Every society has a need for heroes who serve as role models. The U.S. is no exception and has produced its share of them—President Abraham Lincoln, aviator Charles Lindbergh, civil rights leader Martin Luther King, Jr., and the astronauts, to name a few. Heroes belong to the ages, and we can refresh our pride and patriotism by recalling their deeds.

In the early 19th century, two relatively unsung heroes, Meriwether Lewis and William Clark, braved the perils of a vast unknown territory to enlarge knowledge, increase commerce, and establish a relationship with unknown Indians. Their journals produced eight detailed volumes of data

From "Lewis and Clark: Trailblazers Who Opened a Continent," by Gerald F. Kreyche, *USA Today* magazine, January 1998. Copyright © 1998 by the Society for the Advancement of Education. Reprinted with permission.

ranging from maps, climate, geography, and ethnic observations to the discovery of new species of plants and animals.

Thomas Jefferson's Corps of Discovery

In the late 18th century, America's western border was constituted first by the Allegheny Mountains and later the Mississippi River. Little was known of the geography immediately beyond the Father of Waters, and less yet of what lay west of the Missouri River. This was to change, however, for President Thomas Jefferson had an unquenchable yearning for such knowledge and did something about it.

As early as 1784, he conferred with George Rogers Clark about exploring this uncharted area. In 1786, he hired John Ledyard, a former marine associate of British explorer James Cook, to walk from west to east, beginning in Stockholm, Sweden. The intent was to traverse Russia, Alaska, the western Canadian coast, and thence across the Louisiana Territory. Ledyard walked from Stockholm to St. Petersburg, Russia, in two weeks. The Russians stopped him at Irkutsk, Siberia, and Jefferson was disappointed again. Undaunted, Jefferson made plans for Andre Michael to explore the area, but this, too, failed.

After being inaugurated in 1801, Jefferson had the power to make his pet project a reality. He appointed as his private secretary Meriwether Lewis, a wellborn young army captain. In January, 1803, in a secret message to Congress, the President asked for funding to realize his exploratory project of what lay between the Missouri River and the Pacific Ocean. The sum of $2,500 was appropriated. (The project eventually was to cost $38,000, an early case of a governmental cost overrun.)

Jefferson asked Lewis to head the project. Lewis had served under William Clark (younger brother of George Rogers Clark) in earlier times and offered him co-leadership of the expedition, designated The Corps of Discovery. Clark accepted Lewis' offer to "participate with him in its fatigues, its dangers and its honors." Clark, no longer on active army status, was told he would receive a regular army captaincy, but Congress refused to grant it.

Nevertheless, Lewis designated Clark as captain and co-commander; the expedition's men so regarded him and the journals so record it.

A Complementary Pair

Lewis and Clark were scientist-explorers and singularly complementary. Although both were leaders of men and strict disciplinarians, Lewis was somewhat aloof, with a family background of bouts of despondency; Clark was more the extrovert and father figure. Lewis had great scientific interests in flora, fauna, and minerals, and Clark's surveying and engineering skills fit well with the demands of the expedition. While Lewis tended to view Indians fundamentally as savages, Clark, like Jefferson, saw the Indian as a full member of the human race and child of nature. At all times, the two soldiers were a team, each leading the expedition every other day. No known quarrel between them ever was recorded, although on a few occasions they thought it expedient to separate, probably to cool off and get out of each other's hair.

To prepare for their journey into the unknown, Lewis stayed in the East to study astronomy, plant taxonomy, practical medicine, etc., and to gather equipment from the armory at Harper's Ferry, Virginia. The supplies would include trading goods such as awls, fishhooks, paints, tobacco twists, Jefferson medals, whiskey, and a generous amount of laudanum (a morphine-like drug). Lewis supervised the building of a 22-foot keelboat needed to take them up the Missouri to a winter quartering place. Additionally, he had his eye out for recruits for the expedition.

Clark went to St. Louis to recruit "robust, helthy, hardy" young, experienced, and versatile backwoodsmen. All were single. The captains needed interpreters, river experts, and hunters able to live under the most demanding conditions. Also sought were men with multiple skills who could do carpentry and blacksmith work and follow orders. With the exception of a hunter-interpreter, George Drouillard, if they were not already in the army, they enrolled in it. Privates received five dollars a month; sergeants, eight dollars. Both leaders and the sergeants kept journals.

The Trip Upriver

On May 14, 1804, the regular group of 29 men, plus a temporary complement of 16 others, set off from the St. Louis area for Mandan, in what is now North Dakota, the site of their winter quarters. With them came Lewis' Newfoundland dog, Scannon, and Clark's body-servant, a black man named York. Clark's journal entry reads, "I set out at 4 o'-clock P.M. in the presence of many of the neighboring inhabitents, and proceeded under a jentle brease up the Missourie." Little did they know it would be some 7,200 miles and nearly two and a half years before their return.

The trip upriver was backbreaking, as spring floods pushed the water downstream in torrents. Hunters walked the shores, while the keelboat men alternately rowed, poled, sailed, and rope-pulled the boat against the current. Wind, rain, and hail seemed to meet them at every turn in the serpentine Missouri. Snags and sandbars were everywhere. Bloated, gangrenous buffalo carcasses floated downstream, witnesses to the treachery of thin ice ahead. Often, for security reasons, the expedition party docked at night on small islands, some of which floated away as they embarked in the morning.

Ambassadors of goodwill, they stopped at major Indian villages, counseling peace instead of internecine warfare as well as distributing gifts. At the same time, they questioned the Indians about what lay ahead. Generally, such information was reliable. Tragedy struck at Council Bluffs (now Iowa), where Sergeant Charles Floyd died, probably of a ruptured appendix. He was the only member of the Corps to lose his life. After a proper eulogy, the captains wrote in their journals, as they were to do many times, "We proceeded on." Today, an obelisk marks the general location.

The Myth of Sacajawea

On Nov. 2, 1804, they reached a river confluence about 30 miles north of present-day Bismarck, North Dakota, and settled in with the Mandan Indians, who welcomed them as security against Sioux attacks. They met Toussaint Charbonneau, a 40-year-old trapper wintering there, who, although ignorant of English, spoke a number of Indian languages. Equally important, he had a teenage wife, Sacajawea, a Shoshone who had been captured and traded by the Hidatsa (Minitari). Her tribe were horse-people and lived near the headwaters of the Missouri, two facts that enticed Lewis and Clark to hire Charbonneau and, as part of the deal, arrange for her to accompany them to the area. It would prove burdensome, though, for she delivered a baby boy, Baptiste, who would go with them. Clark took a liking to him and nicknamed him Pompey, even naming and autographing a river cliff prominence (Pompey's Pillar) after him. Later, Clark was to adopt the boy.

A myth of political correctness tells of Sacajawea being the guide for the expedition. Nothing could be further from the truth, as she was six years removed from her people and, when kidnapped, had been taken on a completely different route than that followed by the explorers. She did know Indian herbs, food, and medicine, though, and her presence and that of her child assured others that this was no war party.

Various factors of luck augured the party's success, such as Clark's flaming red hair and York's black skin and "buffalo hair." These would be items of curiosity to upriver Indians. The Corps also had an acrobat who walked on his hands, a one-eyed fiddler, and an air gun that made no explosion when fired. Some Indians previously thought that sound, not the rifle ball, killed, and could not understand this magic. Lewis' dog always was viewed with larcenous eyes, as Indians used dogs for hauling, camp guards, and eating.

Parts Unknown

On April 7, 1805, the now seasoned expeditionary force left the village and went northwest for parts unknown. Their vehicles were six small canoes and two large pirogues [dugouts]. The extras who accompanied them to the fort returned home with the keelboat. Aboard it were samples of flora and minerals, as well as "barking squirrels" (prairie dogs) and other hides and stuffed animals unknown to the East, such as "beardless goats" (pronghorn antelope). Lewis noted, "I could but esteem this moment of departure as among the most happy of my life."

They entered country that was increasingly wild and where white men had not penetrated. Grizzly bears proved to be a considerable threat, but food was plentiful as buffalo abounded. Frequent entries record that "Musquetoes were troublesum." For a time, they were plagued by the ague, dysentery, and boils. Clark drained a half-pint of fluid from one carbuncle on his ankle. The change of diet from meat to camas bulbs to fish didn't help. They laboriously portaged about 16 miles around Great Falls (now Montana), and reached the three forks of the Missouri River, which they named the Jefferson, Madison, and Gallatin. They were but a short distance northwest of what is now Yellowstone National Park.

Lewis followed the Jefferson fork, as Clark and Sacajawea lingered behind. Seeing some Indians, Lewis tried to entice them with presents to meet him, rolling up his sleeves and pointing to his white skin, calling out, "Tabba-bone." Supposedly, this was Shoshone for "white man," but a mispronunciation could render it as the equivalent of "enemy."

The Shoshone feared this was a trick of their hereditary enemies, the Blackfeet, as they never had seen white men. They scarcely were reassured when Clark, Sacajawea, and the rest of the party caught up with Lewis. However, Sacajawea began to suck furiously on her fingers, indicating she was suckled by these people. She also recognized another woman who had been kidnapped with her, but had escaped. When a council was called, she recognized her brother, Cameawhait, a Shoshone chief. This helped the Corps in trading for needed horses to cross the Continental Divide.

The explorers were disappointed, for they had hoped that, by now, they would be close to the Pacific. This could not be so, though, as these Indians knew no white men, and the salmon (a saltwater fish) they had were from trade, not the Indians' own fishing. Staying with the Shoshone for about a week, during which his 31st birthday occurred, Lewis wrote introspectively that he regretted his "many hours . . . of indolence [and now] would live for mankind, as I have hitherto lived for myself."

Across the Continental Divide

They hired a Shoshone guide known as "Old Toby" and his sons to cross the treacherous Bitterroot Mountains, the Continental Divide. After doing yeoman's service, the Indians deserted the party without collecting pay near the Clearwater and Snake rivers. The reason was the intention of the explorers to run ferocious rapids that seemed to swallow up everything in their fury. The Corps were able to run them without serious consequence, though. They proceeded on and came upon the Flathead Indians. One Flathead boy knew Shoshone, and a roundabout process of translation was established. Clark spoke English, and an army man translated it to French for Charbonneau. He, in turn, changed it to Minitari, and Sacajawea converted it to Shoshone, which the Flathead boy rendered in his language.

The group pursued the Clearwater River, which met the Snake River. This flowed into the Columbia, which emptied into the Pacific Ocean. Numerous Indian tribes inhabited the Columbia—Clatsop, Chinook, Salish, to name a few. Most were poverty-stricken and a far cry from the healthy Plains Indians. Many were blinded by age 30, as the sun reflecting off the water while they were fishing took its toll. Clark administered ointments and laudanum. Most didn't improve healthwise, but the Indians felt better for the drug and any placebo effects.

Lewis and Clark were overjoyed to find some Columbia River Indians using white men's curse words and wearing metal trinkets. Both only could be from ships' crews that plied the Pacific shores. The Corps were nearing the western end of their journey and, on November 7, 1805, Lewis declared, "Great joy in camp we are in view of the Ocian." They constructed a rude Fort Clatsop (now rebuilt) by the Columbia River estuary near Astoria, in what today is Oregon, and sent parties in all directions to gather information. There was great excitement when reports of a beached whale reached the fort. Sacajawea, who continued with the expedition, insisted on seeing this leviathan, and she was accommodated. The men busied themselves hunting, making salt, and preparing for the journey home. (The salt cairn is reconstructed and preserved not many miles from the fort.)

The Corps entertained the hope that they might make contact with a coastal ship to return them home, and one ship, the Lydia, did arrive, but, through a communication failure or lying by the Indians, the captain believed the Corps already had left over land.

On March 23, 1806, after a rainy and miserable winter, the expedition left Fort Clatsop and, along the way, split into three groups hoping to explore more territory. They felt duty-bound to learn as much as they could and agreed to meet at the confluence of the Yellowstone and Missouri rivers. They traded beads and boats for horses and faced the worst kind of pilfering, even Scannon being nearly dog-napped.

Lewis, whose route took him through the territory of the fierce Blackfeet, invited a small party into his camp. One of them tried to steal soldier Reuben Field's gun and was stabbed for his efforts; another stole a horse and, losing all patience, Lewis "at a distance of thirty steps shot him in the belly." Fearing a large war party might be nearby, they traveled the next 60 miles nearly non-stop.

On the way to meet Clark, Lewis and a one-eyed hunter, Peter Cruzatte—both dressed in elkskin—went into the brush to hunt. Lewis was shot in the buttocks by Cruzatte, who apparently mistook him for an elk. The wound was painful, but no vital parts were damaged, although Lewis privately wondered if the shooting was deliberate.

Downriver, Lewis' party met two Illinois trappers searching for beaver. When they learned about the Blackfeet incident, they backtracked and accompanied Lewis to the rendezvous. There, with the captains' permission, they persuaded John Colter, who later discovered Yellowstone, to leave the party and to show them the beaver areas.

Having rendezvoused with the others, all stopped at the Mandan village in which they had spent the previous winter. Here, Toussaint Charbonneau, Sacajawea, and Baptiste (Pompey) parted company. The trapper was paid about $400–500 for his services.

A Heroes' Welcome

Upon their return home, all the men received double pay and land grants from a grateful Congress. Several of the men went back to trap the area from which they had come, commencing the era of the mountain men. One became a judge and U.S. Senator, and another a district attorney. Others returned to farming. Clark had some sort of fallout with York, and the latter was reduced to a hired-out slave, a considerable fall from the prestigious body-servant status. Eventually, though, he was freed by Clark.

Lewis was appointed governor of the Louisiana Territory, but ran into personal and political problems. He suffered severe bouts of depression, began to drink heavily, and had to dose himself with drugs more frequently. To clear his name, he set off for Washington, but grew increasingly suicidal. He attempted to kill himself several times and finally succeeded on the Natchez Trace, at Grinder's Stand in Tennessee in 1809. Nevertheless, Meriwether Lewis should be remembered not for the circumstances of his death, but for his life of duty, leadership, and love of country.

Clark was appointed governor and Indian agent of the Missouri Territory. He also was given the rank of brigadier general in the militia—not bad for a bogus captain! He married Julia Hancock, a childhood friend, and named one of their children after Lewis, his comrade-in-arms. After Julia's death, Clark married her cousin, Harriet Kennerly.

Sacajawea died a young woman around 1812 at Ft. Union near the Missouri-Yellowstone confluence. Although she was rumored to die an old lady at Ft. Washakie in Wyoming—indeed, a large gravestone with her name is engraved there on the Shoshone-Arapaho Reservation—the evidence for the Ft. Union death is more compelling. Clark adopted young Pompey, who later became a famous linguist and toured Europe in the company of royalty. Eventually, he became a mountain man.

William Clark died in 1838, a good friend of the Indians and, like Meriwether Lewis, a genuine American hero.

The Significance of the Lewis and Clark Expedition

National Park Service

The following essay is excerpted from the introduction to *Lewis and Clark: Historic Places Associated with Their Transcontinental Exploration*, a guide to the modern-day Lewis and Clark trail published by the National Park Service. In it, the authors claim that the Lewis and Clark expedition spurred other pioneers to explore the lands west of the Mississippi River. The maps they prepared were the most immediately useful product of the expedition. Fur trappers were particularly attracted by Lewis and Clark's reports of Rocky Mountain wildlife. Launched in 1804, the Lewis and Clark expedition can be seen as the first step in the settlement of the American frontier, a process that would not be completed until the end of the nineteenth century.

The Lewis and Clark Expedition was one of the most dramatic and significant episodes in the history of the United States. In 1804–6 it carried the destiny as well as the flag of our young Nation westward from the Mississippi across thousands of miles of mostly unknown land—up the Missouri, over the Rocky Mountains, and on to the Pacific. This epic feat not only sparked national pride, but it also fired the imagination of the American people and made them feel for the first time the full sweep of the continent on which they lived. Equally as important, the political and economic ramifications of the trek vitally affected the subsequent course and growth of the Nation.

It its scope and achievements, the expedition towers

From *Lewis and Clark: Historic Places Associated with Their Transcontinental Exploration, 1804–1806*, vol. 13 in The National Survey of Historic Sites and Buildings series, edited by Robert G. Ferris (Washington, DC: U.S. Dept. of the Interior, National Park Service, 1975).

among the major explorations of the North American Continent and the world. Its members included the first U.S. citizens to cross the continent; the first individuals to traverse it within the area of the present United States; and the first white men to explore the Upper Missouri area and a large part of the Columbia Basin as well as to pass over the Continental Divide within the drainage area of the two rivers.

Opening the Trans-Mississippi West

Before Lewis and Clark, the trans-Mississippi West was largely a virgin land. British, Spanish, and French explorers and traders had barely penetrated it. Apart from a tiny fringe of French-American settlement in the St. Louis area and elsewhere along the Mississippi and small Spanish colonies in the Rio Grande Valley of New Mexico and in California, the region was virtually uninhabited by whites. For the most part enveloped in rumor, fantasy, and mystery, it was almost as strange as outer space would be to the later generation that was first to orbit the earth and put a man on the moon.

The men of the expedition made their way through this vast land, living mainly off its resources and superbly adapting themselves to the new conditions it imposed. They encountered alien tribes and menacing animals. On foot, on horseback, and by boat, they pushed over jagged mountain ranges, across seemingly endless plains, through tangled forests, against powerful currents and raging waters. Under two determined captains and three hardy sergeants, the explorers met danger as a matter of course and suffered hunger, fatigue, privation, and sickness. . . .

The expedition was as astutely conceived as it was efficiently conducted. President Thomas Jefferson organized it in 1802 because he foresaw the continental destiny of the Nation. At that time, the United States had been independent from Britain for only 19 years and depended to a large extent for its very survival on the conflicts generated by imperial rivalry among Britain, Spain, and France. Furthermore, the Union consisted of only 16 States, the Original Thirteen plus Vermont, Kentucky, and Tennessee. Although some settlers had reached the Mississippi, most parts of the western portion of the national domain were not settled at all and most of the remainder was but sparsely populated. In 1803 Ohio came into the Union, and the United States purchased from France the Louisiana Territory, a huge and ill-defined block of territory west of the Mississippi. . . .

Jefferson was continuing the centuries-long search for a Northwest Passage to the riches of the Orient—an all-water or nearly all-water route from the Atlantic to the Pacific through or around northern North America that would obviate the need for U.S. and European ships to make the long voyages around South America and Africa. In 1778 the English explorer Capt. James Cook had made an inconclusive search for the passage along the Pacific coast of the continent, but in 1792–94 the Vancouver Expedition had demonstrated that for all practical purposes an all-water route through the continent did not exist. Jefferson hoped that the Lewis and Clark Expedition might still find a nearly all-water passage, but it made no such discovery. As a matter of fact, the pathway it charted was not even economically feasible because of the long portages required and serious navigational problems.

If Lewis and Clark did not discover the Northwest Passage or a practicable transcontinental channel of commerce, their other accomplishments were formidable. The significance of their exploration extends over a broad and interrelated gamut—in geopolitics, westward expansion, and scientific knowledge. From the standpoint of international politics, the expedition basically altered the imperial struggle for control of the North American Continent, particularly the present northwestern United States, to which the U.S. claim was substantially strengthened.

The Initial Spur to Westward Expansion

The westward expansion that ensued in the wake of Lewis and Clark would provide substance to that claim. The wealth of detailed information they acquired about the climate, terrain, native peoples, plants, animals, and other resources of the princely domain they had trodden represented an invitation to occupy and settle it. In their footsteps, came

The Beginning of Western Expansion

Any evaluation of Lewis and Clark's Voyage of Discovery must note its major disappointments: it confirmed that there was no Northwest Passage, thus putting an end to Jefferson's long-cherished dream. And despite Lewis and Clark's brilliant personal and logistical triumph, their difficult northerly, watery route would never attract many followers since it did not permit the wagon-train traffic essential for homesteading emigrants.

But such disappointments, grave as they seemed at the time, were outshone by the light of the expedition's many accomplishments. It had recorded a dazzling number of "firsts." The corps was the first party of whites to cross the continental United States to the Pacific. (Alexander Mackenzie's zigzag crossing via the Arctic in 1793 had occurred in present Canada.) Sacagawea, a Native American, became the first woman known to have crossed the continent from the Missouri to the western ocean. Her infant son, Jean Baptiste Charbonneau, was the first child to do so. Clark's slave, York, was the first black man to cross the continent. In addition, and of greater significance, Lewis and Clark's records constitute the first serious anthropological observations of western Indian tribes, the first comprehensive collection and description of western flora and fauna, and the first maps of the Northwest based on celestial navigation and on-site notations.

Above and beyond all these achievements, the success of the expedition assumed a vital geopolitical dimension by reinforcing United States claims in the Pacific Northwest vis-à-vis the British, Russian, and Spanish interests. By heightening American awareness of the Far West and its commercial potential—especially the fur trade—the expedition stimulated the notion of western expansion that would mature, for better and for worse, as the powerful concept of Manifest Destiny.

Arthur King Peters, *Seven Trails West*, 1996.

other explorers, as well as trappers, traders, hunters, adventurers, prospectors, homesteaders, ranchers, soldiers, missionaries, Indian agents, and businessmen. They filled in the map, blazed the trails, traded in furs, mined the depths of the earth, tilled the soil, grazed stock, constructed railroads and roads, created towns, founded industries, and formed Territories and States. Ever moving westward, they conquered the land and carried civilization to the shores of the Pacific.

Many of these people followed for part of the way the Missouri River route that Lewis and Clark had pioneered— a waterway that became one of the major westward routes, though the complications of traveling it by steamboat restricted the flow of traffic to its lower reaches and rendered it less useful than the major overland trails.

The initial spur to westward expansion was the news the explorers brought back about the rich potentialities of the western fur trade, which were concentrated in the Upper Missouri-Yellowstone River-Rocky Mountain area. This trade was the first means of exploiting the resources of the newly discovered land. Trappers and traders were the first to penetrate it in detail, and these mountain men laid the groundwork for the miners and settlers who followed.

Reacting to newspaper and word-of-mouth accounts of the reports of Lewis and Clark to Jefferson and others of the wealth in furs and a natural all-water route of access, the Missouri, adventurers and trappers flocked to St. Louis in the winter and spring of 1806–7. But, as in the later days of the mining rushes, most of those who chose to operate independently were to meet frustration. They were forced to confine their activities to the Lower Missouri or join one of the large and well-organized companies that soon sprang up and monopolized the Rocky Mountain fur trade. Only they possessed the necessary capital to finance the long journeys necessary to reach the hunting grounds and send out parties of sufficient size to ward off Indian attacks.

But such hostilities, mainly limited to spasmodic outbreaks of the Teton Sioux, Arikaras, and Blackfeet, were undoubtedly far less severe than they might have been were it not for the reservoir of goodwill the expedition had left with nearly all the western tribes. This reservoir, which Clark deepened during his long and distinguished post-expedition career as Superintendent of Indian Affairs in St. Louis, contributed to the success of the early westward movement. . . .

Lewis and Clark as Scientist-Explorers

The Lewis and Clark Expedition also made major contributions to the fields of geography-cartography, ethnography, and natural history. Scientists were kept busy for a long time digesting the mass of raw information, studying plant and animal specimens, analyzing descriptions and translating them into the appropriate technical language, and classifying and correlating data.

Neither of the two leaders were trained scientists by the standards of their day. Many of their geographic calculations were faulty because they often relied on dead reckoning and did not properly adjust their chronometer and other instruments. Their descriptions of plants and animals lacked professional nomenclature and polish. But, considering the time in which they lived and the circumstances they faced in the field, they demonstrated remarkable competence.

Except in cartography, Lewis was primarily responsible for most of the scientific contributions. He was better educated than Clark and during 2 years of residence with President Jefferson prior to the expedition had enjoyed access to his fine library and been able to draw on his extensive knowledge of zoology and botany. Lewis had also enjoyed the benefit of a cram course in science at Philadelphia and Lancaster that Jefferson arranged for him.

The geographical findings were in themselves of outstanding significance. Lewis and Clark determined the true course of the Upper Missouri and its major tributaries. They discovered that a long, instead of short, portage separated it from the Columbia, which proved to be a majestic stream rivaling the Missouri itself rather than a short coastal river. Neither the Missouri nor the Columbia was found to be navigable to its source, as many had believed. The explorers also learned that, instead of a narrow and easily traversed mountain range, two broad north-south systems, the Rockies and the Cascades, represented major barriers.

Passing for the most part through country that no Americans and few white men had ever seen, the two captains dotted the map with names of streams and natural features. Some of the designations that have survived to this day include the Jefferson, Madison, Gallatin, Milk, Marias, and Judith Rivers, Beaverhead Rock, Rattlesnake Cliffs, White Bear Islands, York Canyon, and Baptiste Creek. Unfortunately, many other names that were bestowed have faded out of existence.

Clark made his scientific mark primarily in the field of cartography, for which his training consisted mainly of some experience in practical surveying and a limited amount of Army mapping. Yet his relatively crude maps, prepared under field conditions, enriched geographical knowledge and stimulated cartographical advances. . . .

Ethnography and Natural History

The second scientific field on which the Lewis and Clark Expedition exerted a major impact was ethnography. Although the two captains' comprehensive descriptions of the natives and their way of life contained some errors and misconceptions, as a whole they were so astonishingly accurate and complete that they provided a basic document for western ethnologists.

Previously, almost nothing had been known of the Indians westward from the Mandan villages, in present North Dakota, to the Upper Columbia. Native groups residing in that area, whom the explorers were undoubtedly the first white men to encounter and describe, included the Northern Shoshoni, Flatheads, Nez Perces, Cayuses, Yakimas, and Walla Wallas. Although the expedition did not meet any Crows, their presence was noted.

The final category of scientific knowledge that the exploration enriched was natural history. Usually based on their own observations but sometimes on Indian information, the two captains described hundreds of species of fishes, reptiles, amphibians, mammals, birds, plants, trees, and shrubs. Some were completely new to the world of science; others had never previously been encountered in North America; or earlier descriptions were sketchy and inadequate. In these categories, among mammals alone, are the pronghorn (antelope), bighorn sheep, mountain beaver, black-tailed prairie dog, white weasel, mountain goat, grizzly bear, coyote, and various species of deer, rabbit, squirrel, fox, and wolf. In addition to their descriptions, Lewis and Clark also sent back a large number of zoological specimens, including a few live ones as well as skins, bones, skeletons, teeth, talons, and horns, and in addition a diversity of botanical items.

East of the Mississippi: The Agricultural Frontier

Thomas D. Clark

For several decades after the United States was formed, the land between the original thirteen colonies and the Mississippi River was considered frontier territory. While explorers, traders, or trappers ventured farther across the continent—west to the Rocky Mountains or southwest to Mexico—the majority of pioneers were farmers who settled the thousands of miles of fertile but untamed territory that would become Kentucky, Tennessee, Ohio, Indiana, Illinois, and Michigan. Historian Thomas D. Clark describes the experiences of these pioneer families who, in the period between 1815 and 1840, pushed the American frontier back by building farms, communities, and eventually states. Clark is the author of numerous books on nineteenth-century America, including *Emerging South*, *History of Kentucky*, and *Frontier America: The Story of the Westward Movement*, from which the following essay is excerpted.

As settlements [along the frontier] increased, roads were opened and it became possible to use wheeled vehicles. The first settlement of Kentucky, Tennessee and Ohio was accomplished largely by use of the pack horse and the flatboat. There was almost no significant use of wagons, carts and carriages, and it was not until state governments were organized in these territories that effective public attention was given to roads. With the second phase of settlement, however, the wagon became a basic vehicle of westward expansion. . . .

Before the wagon could be used with any satisfaction, the numerous pioneer trails had to be widened, bridges and ferries established, and state legislatures created. In the middle of the eighteenth century the Conestoga wagon was introduced in the country around Lancaster, Pennsylvania. It was a heavy and clumsy vehicle with wide tires, massive running gears, and box bodies which sloped down from either end to prevent the loss of cargo on hilly roads. Traditionally the gears of these wagons were painted blue and the boxes red with scenic panels on the sides. Flexible wood staves were bowed across to support canvas coverings, which in turn were pulled tight with drawstrings front and rear. After 1800, settlers moved into new country with wagons and carts. The boats floating down stream were laden with these vehicles. In many instances it was possible to drive through the forest during dry seasons and to ford streams without benefit of roads and bridges.

The advent of the wagon was a necessity before the agricultural frontier could make any material advancement. Only a limited number of settlers at best could secure ready access to streamside farms and the easy transport of their products. Not only did the wagon speed up folk and crop movement, but the manufacture of these vehicles created a new frontier industry. Many towns had their wagon works, and it was not at all unusual for country blacksmiths to make wagons on the side. . . .

Steamboats plied all the western streams wherever there was water enough to float them. Some reckless pilots said they asked only for heavy dews to speed them on their way across country. Lower decks of these vessels were crammed with freight: animals, wagons, plowtools, furniture, and household plunder in general, millstones, stocks of peddlers' goods, clocks, gadgets, and even coffins. Settler, merchant, Yankee speculator, land hunter, preacher, European traveler and government official all were going westward. As [nineteenth-century reverend and writer] Robert Baird wrote:

> Whilst above, in the deck cabin, there is everything that may be called human—all sorts of men and women, of all trades, from all parts of the world, of all possible manners and habits. There is the half-horse and half-alligator Kentucky

flatboatman, swaggering and boasting of his prowess, his rifle, and his wife. One is sawing away on his wretched old fiddle all day long; another is grinding a knife or razor; here is a party playing cards; and in yonder corner is a dance to the sound of a jew's harp; whilst few are trying to demean themselves soberly, by sitting in silence or reading a book. But it is almost impossible—the wondrous tale and horrible Indian story they are telling; the bottle and the jug are freely circulating; and the boisterous and deafening laugh is incessantly raised, sufficient to banish every vestige of seriousness, thought and sense.

Into Indiana Territory

Amidst this confusion, and even in the minds of those lank and laconic men who sat astride piles of freight leaning their chins forward on long, bony, calloused hands, there worked the silent factor of the great American dream. Whether drifting down the wild current amidst snags and sandbars, obeying the navigational instructions "to keep well over to the right shore, round the head bar of the island," or struggling overland in rickety carts and covered wagons, or rushing headlong aboard crowded and explosive steamboats, floating hells of gamblers and sharpers, everybody who claimed to be a settler dreamed of the rich lands of the West. Up the White, the Wabash, the Embarrass, the Miami, the Mississippi and hundreds of lesser streams they came. In that rich center band of Indiana Territory which stretched across from Illinois on the west to Ohio on the east, there were the outlines of almost forty counties by 1830. An exuberant contemporary author boasted that there was "not a finer district of country of the same extent in the United States. . . . Almost every part of it possessed a fine soil, covered in its natural state with heavy forest of oak, poplar, walnut, hicory, ash, sugar maple, beech, wild cherry, honey locust, coffee tree, hackberry, cucumber tree, linden, etc., etc., with dogwood, iron wood, spice bush, and other small underwood." This was the new Wabash Eden over which white men and Indians had fought on a November morn just two decades before. The land was black, rich and level, and as further proof of its desirability there were the towering forest trees. In keeping with an old frontier adage which prevailed across the timber belt, big trees meant good land.

Almost 275,000 square miles of fertile land, a staggering total of 175,000,000 acres, awaited the axe, torch and plow of the lonely settler pushing westward with herd, field and garden seeds, and family. Here in the great territory between the rivers and south of the lakes was an empire twice the size of the British Isles and almost twice as fertile. When the plow was dragged through much of the soil, it turned up black as coal dust. To eyes that had grown old staring into the red furrows of Virginia and the Carolinas this was too good to be real. After 1800, the census-takers recorded their fabulous stories of population increases in this vast northwest country. In thirty years Ohio had increased from 45,365 persons in 1800 to 937,903 in 1830, and ten years later there were 1,500,000. Where a straggling population of 5,000 held on to the fringes of Indiana in 1800, there was a comfortable backlog of 343,031 in 1830 and twice that many in 1840. In the three decades from 1810 to 1840 Illinois' population expanded from 12,282 to 476,183, and Michigan grew from 4,776 to 212,267 in the same period. Population poured into these new northwestern areas from the great feeder states of the eastern seaboard and all but prostrated the joyful contemporary statisticians by such phenomenal growth. In 1850 New York had sent 24,310 people to Indiana, 133,756 to Michigan, 83,975 to Ohio, and 67,180 to Illinois. In the same years Virginia fed over the mountains 24,756 to Illinois, 85,975 to Ohio, 1,504 to Michigan, and 41,819 to Indiana. The New England states emptied their towns into Michigan, Indiana and Illinois. . . .

Building Communities

Families that moved with the frontier made their own social patterns as they went. Backwoods towns, churches and schools gave some distinct cultural tones to the communities, while courthouses and jails, village groggeries (euphemistically called groceries), political speakings, militia musters, square dances, house-raisings and logrollings left a more indelible imprint on social life. Fundamentally there was little difference, North or South, in the actual social structures of the communities. Everywhere the problems were those of wresting cleared land from the towering forests, breaking the rough virgin soil, building county site towns, erecting watermills and tiny factories, and opening seminavigable streams to flatboat and steamboat travel. Whether one planted corn, cotton, hemp, tobacco or wheat, the economic problems were much the same. . . .

Life, of course, was uncertain on the frontier. However, it was a timid soul indeed who held back because he was afraid to take his chances in the new land. A surprisingly large number did escape death from accidents and epidemic diseases. Everywhere the contemporary travelers turned in the Northwest, they found people either prospering or poised ready to enjoy the fruits of the land. Where the forests were largely unbroken by settlement, there was an astounding amount of game: passenger pigeons, turkeys, ducks, geese, bear, deer, elk, squirrels, and rabbits. Land produced corn in vast quantities and other field crops in like proportions. Proof of the fertility of the soil was to be seen in the river commerce. Timothy Flint described the procession to market of the farmers and manufacturers from the new states. Kentuckians, Ohioans, Indianians, Missourians and "Suckers" from Illinois were to be seen in the huge fleets of flatboats that rode the currents southward. At the famous New Madrid eddy, Flint saw flatboats from almost every settled point on the Ohio and Mississippi and their tributaries. There were Kentuckians with hemp, tobacco, grain, meats, whisky and cloth from their farms. Ohioans came with farm produce and manufactured Yankee notions, produce from Indiana, cattle, horses, grain and meat from Missouri and Illinois. "Some boats," wrote the minister-observer,

> are loaded with corn in the ear and in bulk; others with barrels of apples and potatoes. Some have loads of cider and what they call cider royal, or cider that has been strengthened by boiling and freezing. There are dried fruits, every kind of spirits manufactured in these regions, and in short, the products of the ingenuity and agriculture of the whole

upper country of the West. They have come from regions thousands of miles apart. They have floated to a common point of union. The surfaces of the boats cover some acres.

Added to the hubbub of farmers' boats on their way to market were merchants' boats loaded with Yankee notions, and settlers drifting down to the Mississippi before they turned their faces northward to western Illinois and Missouri. The whole scene was one of ceaseless activity. Across the older settlements spread the news of the amount of corn and wheat produced on an acre, of the color and texture of the soil, of the availability of land, and of the freedom which was promised in the new country.

No population booms in this nation's history received more publicity than did this era of frontier expansion after 1815. Travelers from abroad and along the eastern seaboard came to view the process, the Yankees and seaboard travelers to do missionary work, to look for markets for their goods, and to find new homes; the foreigners to view the operation of American democracy in its greatest moment of flux, to see the natural sights, to ride the steamboats, to ask thousands of inane questions, to find land for prospective emigrants, and to compare the raw American frontier civilization unfavorably with that of Old England and Europe. These visitors have left behind a vast and variegated record of fact, gross misrepresentation, exaggeration of what they saw, and overdrawn accounts of their experiences. Some wrote understandingly and truthfully of the scene before them, appreciating the fact that what they saw and experienced was only a beginning, not the maturity, of a fresh spread of American society. . . . Guidebook editors presented much objective material in the form of statistics, but their textual matter was often too favorable to be wholly dependable.

Agents of the Future

The democratic process on this part of the frontier was to be seen in almost every aspect of human relationships. Noticeable was the fact that the deeper the Americans penetrated into the continent the less apt they were to tolerate any significant amount of immediate social stratification. Human relationships were gauged in terms of immediate personal needs, and a man was not only ready but obligated by community custom to assist his neighbor along no matter who he was. Poverty was a matter of the moment for many people; the land held out the same promise to everybody for the future. Competition for wealth would grow with the economic refinements of permanent settlement. False modesty was left behind with the discarded furniture and the property accumulations which came with sedentary life in older communities. More sophisticated and discriminating travelers often commented on men and women undressing before each other in the same room, on strangers of mixed sexes conversing with each other while still abed, and on small bedrooms crowded with sleepers of both sexes. All of this occurred without any appreciable amount of promiscuity. The informalities of political campaigning, militia musters, and the holding of courts intrigued visitors who were used to the fancy-uniformed and bewigged dignity of foreign military men and judges. In fact the whole process of social organization was geared to the needs of the moment and place. All in all the most noticeable characteristic of this restless throng of people moving on with the receding frontier was the self-inspired sense of destiny. Most frontiersmen regarded the present moment as a necessary interval of time passage; certainly they looked little to the past. They were agents of the future who built houses, farms, towns, counties, states and personal fortunes.

The Opening of Texas and the Santa Fe Trail

Dale Van Every

One major turning point in the opening of the American frontier was the Mexican movement for independence from Spain in the first quarter of the nineteenth century. Prior to that time the Spanish government in Mexico had rigidly prohibited Americans from settling in the region. Historian Dale Van Every explains that as the Spanish became preoccupied with Mexican rebels, they allowed Stephen Austin to set up a small American colony in Texas, which was then a region of Mexico. After the August 24, 1821, Treaty of Córdoba ended Spanish rule in Mexico, American pioneers such as William Becknell seized the opportunity to open trade in the Southwest via the Santa Fe Trail. That trail saw the first use of wagon trains and other practices that future settlers would depend on as they set out across the frontier. Dale Van Every is the author of a four-volume history of the American frontier.

Since the first Americans had crossed the Mississippi to what was then Spanish soil, they had nursed an interest in Texas born of the frontiersman's predisposition to consider any distant land surely more attractive than any land he yet knew. . . . In 1812 Lieutenant Augustus Magee of the United States Army, whose current duty was the maintenance of order along the Louisiana-Texas boundary, resigned his commission for the purpose of organizing . . . an American invasion of Texas under pretense of assisting Mexican patriots then revolting against royalist Spain. He was joined by more than 800 Americans, some interested primarily in loot

From *The Final Challenge*, by Dale Van Every. Copyright © 1964 by Dale Van Every; renewed 1992 by Frances Van Every. Reprinted by permission of Harper-Collins Publishers, Inc.

but many regarding the expedition as an opportunity to acquire grants of Texas land. Magee died early in the campaign but the invasion met with an initial success that extended to the capture of San Antonio. The filibusterers appeared for a time to have seized effective control of Texas 32 years in advance of its eventual annexation by the United States. At the Battle of Medina, August 18, 1813, however, the invaders were overwhelmed by a reinforced royalist column. Of the Americans engaged only 93 were known to have escaped back across the border.

The First American Settlement in Texas

For more than a century Spanish authorities had been painfully aware of the continuing menace to Mexico represented by the population vacuum in Texas. Sporadic efforts to promote any appreciable immigration of Mexican or European settlers to so remote a region had invariably failed. Its isolation, distance from markets, lack of communications, and the fierce hostility of its Indians posed difficulties from which all ordinary colonists recoiled. In 1820, the Spanish Cortés [the representative assembly that governed the colony], harassed by the ten-year-long Mexican revolution, decided as a choice among many evils to permit the entry under certain circumstances and careful regulation of a limited number of American settlers in the hope that they might assist in the control of Indian belligerence while at the same time providing a counterweight to the activities of Mexican patriots and a possible bulwark to the intrusion of unauthorized Americans. Moses Austin, whose fortune gained in a Missouri lead mine operation had been lost in the post war depression, was the first American to recognize the new opportunity. Making the 800-mile journey on horseback accompanied only by a black servant, he reached San Antonio in December 1820, to petition the Spanish governor for permission to settle 300 American families in Texas. After many rebuffs and delays he gained a hearing by making the point that he was not actually an American but a Spanish citizen and a Catholic by virtue of allegiances he had accepted when taking residence in Missouri in 1797. Overtaxed by his exertions, he died June 10, 1821, before learning his petition had been granted. Responsibility for organizing the colony devolved upon his 27-year-old son, Stephen, an obligation which was discharged with patience, sagacity, resolution, and history-making success.

The task confronting Stephen Austin upon his return to the United States to recruit colonists appeared formidable. . . . His colony's site in Texas . . . was a remote and little known region, plagued by hostile Indians, and separated from the nearest American frontier by 200 miles of wilderness. . . . The colonists must renounce their allegiance to the United States, subscribe to Catholicism, become residents of a country that had for 12 years been disrupted by bloody revolution, and accept the prospect of living henceforth under a changing government whose future policies were totally unpredictable. . . .

Austin's Colony

[Nevertheless,] Austin was deluged with more letters applying for admission to his projected colony than he could find time to answer. He wrote the Spanish governor of Texas that he could as readily bring 1500 families as 300. The postwar depression had stimulated the response by giving many who might otherwise only have been tempted a valid excuse to make a new start. Public land in the United States was priced at $1.25 an acre while in Texas 4000 could be had for the equivalent of $200. But economic pressure did not provide an explanation accounting for the enthusiasm of the response. Men were not subjecting their families to such hazards for the sake of acres or dollars. Almost without exception the applications were from the frontier districts of Kentucky, Tennessee, Missouri and Arkansas Territory. They were from men who had been long conditioned to the esoteric satisfactions associated with being first in a new country and in whom the inclination to continue to venture had become a compulsion.

Austin's first families began arriving on the Brazos in December of 1821, some coming across the Gulf by schooner, others overland with wagons. . . .

In the earlier years of the colony the Indian danger posed the most demanding problem. During the century since Spain's first penetration, the Indians of Texas had gained less respect for white antagonists than had Indians farther north who had had always to deal with American frontiersmen. Spanish provincial governors had seldom been provided the military resources to punish Indian offenses. The few Mexican settlers, most of them unarmed, had courted safety by constant appeasement. A principal consideration leading to the Spanish and Mexican governments' decisions to permit American immigration had been the hope that the Americans might assume the burden of suppressing the Indian menace. This hope was justified as the newly arrived settlers promptly built stockades, invariably pursued raiders, and continued practicing the aggressive defense measures with which they had so long been familiar. When the initial Indian hostility became an acute emergency, they did not hesitate even to mount and arm their slaves. Other early problems were crop failures due to drought and the frequent horse-stealing inroads of Mexican and American outlaws from the no man's land along the international boundary. Still, in the face of so many widely reported disadvantages and perils, new American settlers continued to arrive. Each year the stream thickened. By 1830 the population of Austin's colony alone had increased to 4200. Again the frontier people had come to stay.

The Lure of Trade with Mexico

Since Americans had first crossed the Mississippi the lure of Texan land had been more than matched by the lure of Mexican silver. From the days of [the 16th-century explorer Hernán] Cortés' conquest the fabled riches of Mexico had gripped the imagination of the world. The northernmost Mexican town associated in the public mind with silver production was Santa Fe. But it was separated from the mouth of the Missouri by a 900-mile expanse of wild and desolate country which stretched across the most arid section of the plains and the hunting ground of the predatory Comanche. There was a secondary barrier even more forbidding than the distance, the terrain, and the Indians. Santa Fe had so far proved not the door to a market but the gate to a prison. The cornerstone of Spain's imperial policy was the rigid prohibition of trade between Spanish colonies and the people of other nations. . . . Parties that managed to reach Santa Fe were subjected to confiscation of their goods and imprisonment.

When American hunters and trappers first began to roam widely west of the Mississippi, they were drawn in the direction of Santa Fe as by a lodestone. The very name had a pleasant ring that summoned up exotic visions of Mexican treasure and Spanish women. The Kentuckian, James Pursley, whose career was reported in detail by [explorer Zebulon] Pike, was the first known to have reached his goal. After several adventurous years of trading and trapping during which he ranged from the Osage to the Mandan and then south again across the more distant plains, in June of 1805 he accompanied an Indian delegation to Santa Fe where he became a resident, supporting himself and prolonging his welcome by the practice of carpentry. Upon Pike's return from his congenial captivity [the explorer had been arrested near Mexico by the Spanish in 1807], his report on conditions south of the border had stirred added interest. Before 1810 Manuel Lisa had made a number of unsuccessful attempts to extend the trapping and Indian trading operations of his company to include trade with Santa Fe. In the great dispersal of free trappers during the Missouri Fur Company's 1810 withdrawal from the northwestern Missouri, Ezekiel Williams' party approached the borders of New Mexico and several members, including the recorded Joseph Philibert, visited New Mexican communities. It was becoming apparent that though official rejection of formal trade was still adamant the gregarious local inhabitants were privately disposed to welcome the random visits of individual American trappers.

Mexican Independence Leads to the Opening of the Santa Fe Trail

With the outbreak of the Mexican Revolution, alert Americans in Missouri began at once to anticipate the lifting of restraints on trade with Santa Fe. . . . It was Mexico's assumption of self-government in 1821 that finally opened the door to trade with Santa Fe. . . .

The trapper, William Becknell, was the first to reach Santa Fe and the first to achieve a complete and profitable transaction. After an organizing meeting at the home of Ezekiel Williams, he left Franklin September 1, 1821, with four companions and a small cargo of traps and trade goods borne on pack animals. He reached Santa Fe November 16th, precisely the right moment to take the fullest advantage of Mexican realization that they were at last winning the revolution, was welcomed by local officials, was able to sell his few goods at an exhilarating profit, and finished his business with so much dispatch that he could start his return home December 11th. His arrival at Franklin January 29, 1822, with rawhide bags bulging with silver dollars stirred intense excitement. The Santa Fe Trail had at last been opened.

Becknell himself was first to take advantage of the glittering new opportunity. He set out May 22, 1822, on his second Santa Fe venture with 21 men and 3 *wagons*. The ensuing first crossing of the plains by wheeled vehicles marked one of the greater milestones in the westward movement. The astonishing demonstration that the transport of heavy cargoes such distances over so forbidding a terrain was not only possible but practicable attracted hundreds of eager emulators. This was the sort of enterprise, combining novelty, danger, distance, and an incidental chance of quick, large gain, which most appealed to frontier inclinations. By 1824, 26 wagons were employed in the annual trek by 180 men who realized a combined profit of $190,000. The merchandise shipped in 1828 in 100 wagons was valued at $150,000 upon which a net return of 40 per cent was expected. More than personal profit was involved. The annual influx of silver had a striking effect on the economy of the American frontier where specie had formerly been almost unknown. And the inhabitants of the border, who mattered most, had discovered that the Great American Desert was not a serious barrier.

Like all frontier ventures, the Santa Fe trade imposed extreme demands upon those who sought its rewards. Distance, excessive heat, long stretches without water, and danger from Indians made each journey a physical feat. The Indian peril steadily mounted. The more distant Plains Indians, enraptured by the prospect of so much loot, stalked the caravans, seizing every opportunity to stampede grazing stock or cut off stragglers or attempt hit-and-run attacks in which men could be killed and wagons pillaged. . . . [The Santa Fe traders] rapidly developed remarkable self-sufficiency. Each year's caravan was composed of many small "proprietors," each of whom had his own stock of trade goods or of equipment with which he proposed to undertake trapping upon reaching the far southwest. These smaller parties assembled at Council Grove, 150 miles southwest of Independence, the terminus for Missouri River boat traffic. Here by the town-meeting procedures of frontier self-government officers were elected, camp and march regulations adopted, guard rosters drafted, and mutual defense measures agreed upon. The Santa Fe caravan was in effect a traveling frontier settlement, a projection across the plains and into a foreign country of the frontier experience, even to the circumstance that the ringed wagons at night duplicated the stockade in the defense of which all were mutually responsible. With characteristic frontier adaptability, these processes were continually improved in the light of experience. Traders soon discovered, for example, that for plains traffic mules were more serviceable than horses and that oxen were superior to either. In the management of Santa Fe wagon trains methods, skills, devices, and expedients were developed and perfected. Standards for plains travel had been established that were to prove of immeasurable advantage to the later immigrant trains upon whose success depended American occupation of Oregon and California.

Mountain Men: The Importance of the Fur Trade in the Opening of the West

William H. Goetzmann

Inspired by Lewis and Clark's reports of beaver inhabiting the Rocky Mountains, in 1808 and 1809 enterprising pioneers began arriving in the region. By the 1820s, the Rocky Mountain fur trade was in full swing, with several hundred men trapping beaver in the northern Rockies and selling the pelts in St. Louis, Missouri. As historian William H. Goetzmann explains, these men played an important role in westward expansion, blazing the trails that future pioneers would later follow on their way to California and Oregon. William H. Goetzmann is a professor of American studies and history at the University of Texas. He was awarded the 1967 Pulitzer Prize in history for *Exploration and Empire: The Explorer and the Scientist in the Winning of the American West.*

They numbered no more than a thousand and their heyday lasted less than twenty years, but the mountain men made their mark on American and world history. Since that time in the early-nineteenth century when, alone or in small groups, they ventured out across the wide Missouri into the trackless Rockies, they may have been cleaned up, their stories bowdlerized, their attitudes toward Native Americans and grizzly bears prettified, their exploits exaggerated or scaled down by the scientific scrutiny of historians; they may even have been mythologized all out of proportion (which many of them would have laughed about and liked), but they can never be forgotten or ignored. Theirs was a quintessentially unique

From "The Mountain Men," by William H. Goetzmann, *American West*, no. 4 (1978). Reprinted by permission of the author.

American experience of practical as well as symbolic significance. It is important to emphasize their uniqueness. No other country has produced such a creature—"critter" they would have said. There he stands, remote as Neanderthal man in some ways, with his rude costume of buckskin, his "possibles sack," his Hawken rifle and clanging beaver traps, peering alertly and intently out from under his low-crowned, wide-brimmed, feather-decked hat at some far horizon where destiny and opportunity and danger await—as alive today as he was yesterday.

Who were these mountain men and why should we remember them? First things first. They were, in [army general] William Ashley's words, "enterprising young men" who sought to make their fortunes in the hazardous occupation of beaver trapping in the Rocky Mountains, principally in the years between 1820 and 1840. Most of them were natural outdoorsmen in the tradition of Daniel Boone and the long hunters of Kentucky's dark and bloody ground. Like Boone, they preferred the solitude and adventure of the wilderness, and they proved equal to its challenges. But they were also different. They did not love the wilderness for its own sake, nor were they the outcast "romantic banditti" of Washington Irving's imagination. They were highly individualistic entrepreneurs who hoped to make a competence, if not a fortune, in the fur trade which was booming all over America and Europe as they entered the western wilderness. They were also self-conscious agents of American expansionism who saw endless possibilities in the West—once it was claimed from England and Spain and the indigenous red man. . . .

The Life of a Mountain Man

To pursue these ends, they deserted farms hacked out of forest clearings, jobs as storekeeper and frontier sheriff, even loved ones and families, to stake their lives and their meager fortunes on an expedition to the mountains. . . .

Their habitat was the Rocky Mountains where, gradually learning from the Indians, they were able to subsist off the rugged land and spend years out of sight of civilization. They made their own clothes or married Indian women who

made them for them. They lived on game of all kinds, pre-
ferring, of course, the buffalo—especially the hump ribs,
tongue, and liver, raw and warm and dripping with nutri-
tious blood. They also enjoyed deer, fish, mountain goat,
and an occasional dog. It was a lonely life, full of privation in
which self-reliance was at a premium never dreamed of by
Ralph Waldo Emerson when he addressed the young men of
Harvard. To find the right mountain hideaway out of the
withering cold winter winds, to build a proper hut out of
bent saplings and hides, to find game and clear water and
avoid hostile Indians were necessities, as were such mundane
things as knowing how to set one's own broken bones, how
to cauterize wounds, how to dose oneself for the ague,
rheumatism, pneumonia, and tainted food. To combat the
loneliness, the mountain men told tall tales of "scrapes" and
strange sights seen on distant journeys or sometimes read
well-worn copies of Shakespeare or the Bible. Kit Carson's
exploits appeared in the early dime novels, and Jim Beck-
wourth dictated his adventures to an "amanuensis," but by
and large, the mountain men lived on the hard side of the
American Dream. They were lucky if they were adopted by
a friendly Indian tribe.

The beaver seasons were fall and spring, especially spring
when the ice was just breaking up on the cold mountain
streams. There in the dawn's early light the trapper made his
rounds collecting his catch. In the evening he baited his
traps for perhaps the fourth or fifth time in the day. All day
long while he waited, he scraped the skins of his catch on a
scraping stone and stretched them over willow frames to dry.
The day's catch could not be allowed to lie around and rot.
In between times he hunted and smoked meat for the long
winter. Summer, however, was the payoff. Beginning in 1825
he headed for a grand *rendezvous* on a branch of the Green
River, whose valley lay at the heart of the Rockies. There he
congregated with all the other mountain men who had survived the season; swapped stories; fought; bet on horse races;
traded or gambled his furs away for outrageously-priced rot-
gut whiskey, powder and lead, more traps, trade goods, and
well-used Indian women. . . .

The *rendezvous* continued as an annual event from 1825 to 1838. Then it abruptly ended, as did the life of the free trapper.

Pathfinders and Trailblazers

If their lives were so buried in remoteness and the high noon of the free trapper lasted such a short time, why does posterity remember them so vividly? The reasons now seem clear. After Lewis and Clark, the mountain men were the first to penetrate and open up to Americans the vast mountain and basin country of the trans-Mississippi West. The Spaniards had posted a "rim of Christendom" in the arid Southwest and clung precariously to California. A few, notably Escalante in 1776, had penetrated far up into the Green River country and crossed over into the Great Basin of Utah. But Spanish *entradas* into the mountains were rare, and their knowledge was kept a guarded secret (which has led to so many tales of buried Spanish treasure). The British were late and hesitant in coming down from Canada. Thus, while the great European powers hung on the fringes of the West, the mountain men as harbingers of American civilization plunged boldly ahead on what became truly a transcontinental mission. Largely through their efforts the West was won for the United States in an imperial struggle with England and Spain.

They did not win the West by force of arms. Rather the mountain men served as pathfinders and then trailblazers for the thousands of emigrants who poured over the trails to Oregon and California. Moreover, the would-be settlers were awakened to the possibilities of these new lands by letters and reports sent back by the mountain men who looked at the West with a flexible eye—one as intent upon the possibilities for future American settlement as upon the likeliness of a good beaver stream. In 1830, for example, Jedediah Smith and his two partners, David E. Jackson and William L. Sublette, wrote a letter to the secretary of war extolling the virtues of Oregon and emphasizing the ease with which American settlers could reach it. This letter was published as an official government document and reprinted countless times. Similarly, Joshua Pilcher touted the Columbia Valley as a "paradise for farming, cattle raising and ship-building." He saw the site of Fort Vancouver (near present-day Portland, Oregon) as a place where "a great city . . . will eventually grow up." William Ashley called for federal troops to protect the mountain men and the emigrants who followed them. Clearly the mountain man saw himself as the vanguard of a great mass migration to the West. In his discovery of passes through the mountains and trails across the interior, he proved to be just that. But in succeeding he helped to end the wild, free life of the unfettered trapper. Nature's nobleman put himself on the path to ultimate extinction in practical terms, but because he epitomized "nature's nation" and the exotic, adventuresome self-reliance of the American, he lives forever in legend and history on both sides of the Atlantic. . . .

The Rocky Mountain Fur Company

The classic heroes of the Rocky Mountain fur trade were . . . those recruited by William H. Ashley. In February of 1822 he placed an ad in the Saint Louis, Missouri *Gazette and Public Advertiser* calling for "Enterprising Young Men . . . to ascend the Missouri to its source, there to be employed for one, two, or three years." This was the start of the Rocky Mountain Fur Company, which employed its men as free trappers under short-term contract. Clearly Ashley did this not out of altruism but because he hoped that by organizing his men and giving them the proper incentive he could himself become rich in a very short time and thus pursue the political career he had always wanted.

In the spring of 1823, Ashley and his partner, Andrew Henry, managed to establish a fort on the Yellowstone River despite the fact that one of their heavily laden barges sank in the Missouri destroying $10,000 worth of trade goods. But the river tribes were hostile, and in June the Arikara pinned down his best men on a sandbar in the Missouri under a withering barrage of rifle fire. Only the most skillful—Jedediah Smith, Edward Rose, Bill Sublette, Hugh Glass, and James Clyman—escaped. The whole affair, according to Clyman, "was more than I had contracted for and somewhat cooled my courage." . . .

In desperation Ashley and Henry decided to abandon the river and strike out overland for the mountains. This was the real beginning of the celebrated fur trade of the central Rockies.

Henry led one party, that was constantly harassed by Indians, to his fort on the Yellowstone. There he found his horses stolen and no furs. He moved his post upriver to its confluence with the Powder River and then over to the Bighorn. When all of this failed, he sent the main body of his men under John Weber over into the Wind River Basin, where they wintered with some friendly Crow Indians.

Discovery of the South Pass and the Great Salt Lake

On his trip to the mountains with Ashley's other brigade in 1823, Jedediah Smith had more than enough adventure. Somewhere in the Black Hills (a spur of the Rockies), Smith was attacked by an enraged grizzly. The bear grasped Smith's whole head in its jaw and began ripping and tearing his scalp. Before the bear was killed, Smith had lost most of his scalp and one ear, while his eye was turned queerly upward. In all this Smith never lost consciousness, and though bleeding profusely and doubtless in shock, he calmly ordered James Clyman to sew his scalp and ear back on. Clyman followed orders but without much hope. When the stitching was done, Smith mounted a horse and rode a mile into camp. Ten days later he had recovered enough to assume command, and the party pushed on. They reached the Wind River valley in late November, where they linked up with Weber's party in a bitterly cold encampment.

In February, Smith and his men attempted to quit the cold and the blizzards of the valley. The Indians showed them on a crude map a route south around the Wind River Mountains, which they traversed with great hardship including near starvation. But in rounding the Wind Rivers, Smith and his men located the famous South Pass of the Rocky Mountains, which thousands of argonauts would use on the trails to Oregon and California. It was the main gateway through the Rocky Mountains and comparable in American history to the Cumberland Gap, which took settlers in an earlier epic march over the Appalachians and into the great valley of the Ohio River.

Weber's party followed Smith, and when they reached the Green River he journeyed to Bear Lake while Smith headed south to the Uintas. Sometime during that winter or early spring a young mountain man, Jim Bridger, to settle a wager with his comrades, sailed down the Bear River in a bullboat and reached the Great Salt Lake. He tasted it and finding it salty, concluded that he had reached the Pacific Ocean. Later his friend James Clyman and three other mountain men sailed 'round the lake, assuring themselves it was not an arm of the sea. Bridger went on to many exploits, but his discovery of the Great Salt Lake must rank among his most spectacular.

The First *Rendezvous*

Many great mountain men assembled at the first *rendezvous* at Henry's Fork of the Green River in 1825, where they were greeted by General Ashley himself. Besides Bridger, there was Tom "Broken Hand" Fitzpatrick, who was soon to be part-owner of the Rocky Mountain Fur Company; Etienne Provost up from the south after *his* first look at the Great Salt Lake; Hugh Glass, soon to be famous as the man who, after being mauled by a bear and left for dead by his companions, managed to stay alive and crawl hundreds of miles to a friendly Indian village; and, of course, Jedediah Smith. Suffice to say that from the very beginning the *rendezvous* was the stomping ground of giants. . . .

Each year from 1825 onward the mountain men pursued their lonely trade, then gathered at the annual *rendezvous*. By 1827, Ashley had sold the Rocky Mountain Fur Company to Smith, David Jackson, and William Sublette and retired to Saint Louis a rich man. Over the next few years, the ownership of the Rocky Mountain Fur Company changed hands several times. It also had to face fierce competition from Canadian Hudson's Bay brigades coming east from Oregon under the able leadership of Peter Skene Ogden and Alexander Ross. The most dreaded competition, however, came from Astor's American Fur Company. . . .

Civilization Encroaches on the Rockies

The years 1832–1834 were momentous ones for the mountain men. In 1832 their ranks were severely decimated by a pitched battle with the Gros Ventre [Indians] at Pierre's Hole. In 1832, also, Kenneth McKenzie of the American Fur Company managed to secure the allegiance of the Blackfeet [Indians], and he established Fort McKenzie near the mouth of the Marias River in the heart of their country. And finally, in that same year, the steamboat *Yellowstone* made its first trip far up the Missouri to Fort Union. With this voyage, mechanization and organization and eastern capital began to take command.

In 1833, Captain Benjamin Louis Eulalie Bonneville of the U.S. Army mysteriously entered the fur trade. Allegedly on leave from the army for two years to try his hand at trapping, Bonneville always maintained he was on a mission for General Andrew Jackson. His every action seemed to suggest this. He reached the *rendezvous* at Green River and came off very badly at trading. Then he built a fort at Ham's Fork of the Green in a very exposed but also very strategic position. It was useless for fur trading but in a very good position to guard the Oregon Trail in the manner that Ashley had requested as long ago as 1825. Bonneville also reconnoitered as far as the Hudson's Bay posts on the Columbia but was turned back. Meanwhile he organized a crack crew of mountain men, placed them under the leadership of Joseph Reddeford Walker, and sent them to find an overland trail to California. Walker, a superb man in the wilderness, was perhaps Jedediah Smith's only equal as a mountain man and possibly his superior as a leader. In 1833–34, Walker led his men west from Great Salt Lake to the Humboldt River, then down that river to the Humboldt Sinks at the base of the California Sierra. Menaced by Indians, he and his men crossed over the Sierra on the watershed between the Merced and Tuolumne rivers. As they struggled down from the wintery peaks, they were the first Americans to see the great cliffs and misty, sky-high waterfalls of Yosemite. On his way home, Walker located what is now Walker's Pass around the southern end of the Sierra thanks to help from Indian guides. By the time he reached the *rendezvous* in 1834, Walker had laid out the primary emigrant trail to California. In just a few years it would be a main-travelled road with Walker himself helping to guide settlers over it. Washington Irving, trying desperately to write an "American book," celebrated the deeds of Bonneville and, most of all, Walker in his *Scenes and Adventures in the Rocky Mountains* (1837). Walker became for a time perhaps the most famous of all the mountain men back East.

The season of 1834 was momentous for more than Walker's return and the dissolution of the Rocky Mountain Fur Company. That year saw a Scottish baronet, Captain William Drummond Stewart of Murthly Castle, make his second visit to *rendezvous* and German Prince Maximilian of Wied-Neuwied return downriver aboard the *Yellowstone* from a scientific trip to Fort Union. In addition, Nathaniel Wyeth took a botanist, Thomas Nuttall, and an ornithologist, John Kirke Townsend, plus a missionary, Jason Lee, all the way to Oregon. The wild West of the mountain man had begun to be scientifically scrutinized, peopled by long trains of emigrants, and watched over by missionaries. The sober Prince Max and the fun-loving Captain Stewart—both veteran explorers, seemed to sense something was at an end. The Prince brought a young Swiss painter, Karl Bodmer, along to record the pristine scenes of wilderness life, while the raffish captain began to work on a thinly disguised fictional account of his life with the mountain men that would be published as *Altowan*. By 1837 he had employed the Baltimore painter Alfred Jacob Miller to capture what was left of the romantic freshness of the mountain man's life just as, even then, George Catlin was doing for the Indian. The fur trade itself never really died—not even when John Jacob Astor sold out his interests in American Fur in 1834—but by the mid-1830s the life of the mountain man had changed drastically. He, even more than the Indian, was a vanishing breed, and he began to look for other lines of work.

The Decline of the Mountain Man

It is customary to attribute the decline of the mountain man to the decline of the fur trade, and this in turn to the changing European fashions in men's hats. No longer did the London dandy stroll the Strand in a fashionable beaver-covered top hat, ergo the end of the fur trade, runs the explanation. It was certainly true that the mountain man had made his impact on European and American fashion, but the beaver hat was by no means the only impact. Furs continued to be used for coats, for trim, for gloves, and for sleigh and carriage robes. Hudson's Bay and even American Fur continued to do a big business well into the nineteenth century. Nor does the idea that the beaver were all trapped out of the mountains make perfect sense either. Less than a thousand mountain men could never have accomplished this in the face of ever-hostile Indians. The above may have been factors in the decline of the mountain man's world, but more immediate factors also must be considered. The uncertain financial conditions of Jackson's second term culminating in the Panic of 1837 placed the widely scattered individual entrepreneur-trapper at the mercy of the marketplace. As the price of furs dropped, the risk of trapping was not worth the mountain man's time. Even those optimists who believed that the price of beaver was certain to rise began looking for other occupations from wagon-train scout to farmer, rancher, or trading-post keeper. And these all related to their perception of a larger social process that was taking place—the mass migrations westward to Oregon and California. Civilization drove the mountain men out just as it had Daniel Boone from Kentucky. And the same irony prevailed. It was the lone hunter and the mountain man who made the westward migration possible. In a very real sense these heroic figures destroyed themselves by succeeding too well.

Chapter 2

Destiny and War

Manifest Destiny: Americans Embrace Expansionism

Ray Allen Billington

In 1844 several factors combined to convince Americans that the United States should annex all of Texas, California, and Oregon, even if it meant war with Mexico. First, frontiersmen in these far western territories wanted the protection of the federal government. Second, Americans feared that if the United States did not claim these territories, England or France would. Finally, as historian Ray Allen Billington explains, Americans claimed that the spread of American institutions would benefit Indians, Mexicans, and even the world. The phrase "Manifest Destiny" was coined to describe this ideology, and expansionism would dominate American frontier policy for the rest of the century.

A leader in the field of American frontier history, Ray Allen Billington wrote many books on the subject, including *America's Frontier Heritage*, *Westward Expansion: A History of the American Frontier*, and *The Far Western Frontier, 1830–1860*, from which the following essay is excerpted.

Eighteen forty-four was America's year of decision. Overnight the American people awakened to their role in the Divine Plan: the "area of freedom" embraced within the boundaries of their nation must be flung westward to the Pacific! As this realization dawned the timidity that had held them back in the past was forgotten. Earlier Presidents had hesitated to annex Texas lest war with Mexico follow; now popular opinion not only demanded—and secured—that land but all of California as well. Former statesmen had avoided offending mighty England as the two nations contested ownership of the Oregon Country; by the end of 1844 politicians and the people alike clamored for "All of Oregon or None" and happily prepared for the war that seemed inevitable. An overwhelming shift in public opinion was taking place, with expansion to the Pacific its foreordained result.

The Election of 1844

This expressed itself first in the election of 1844. The Whigs' perennial candidate, Henry Clay, was on record as opposing the annexation of Texas; such a step, he had declared, would not only lead to war with Mexico but would be "dangerous to the integrity of the Union." Although Clay hedged slightly before the election, the majority of the people viewed him as an opponent of expansion. The Democrats, on the other hand, met the issue squarely. Passing over the preconvention favorite, Martin Van Buren, because his antislavery principles led him to oppose annexing Texas, they chose a "dark horse," James K. Polk of Tennessee, as their standard bearer. Polk was an outspoken expansionist: "I have *no hesitation* in declaring," he wrote even before the convention, "that I am in favor of the Immediate Re-annexation of Texas." To win northern votes, the Democrats coupled a demand for Oregon with that for Texas. Boldly the party platform declared "that the re-occupation of Oregon and the re-annexation of Texas at the earliest possible period are great American measures, which this convention recommends to the cordial support of the Democracy of the Union."

The election that followed was no clear mandate for expansion. Polk received a majority vote in fifteen of the twenty-six states, and an electoral vote of 170 to Henry Clay's 105. Yet seven of the fifteen Democratic states were in the North, where Texan annexation was unpopular, while Clay carried such strongly expansionist states as North Carolina, Kentucky, and Tennessee. As is so often the case, the truth was less important than the impression created by Polk's victory. Both he and the nation believed that the people had spoken for expansion, no matter what the cost. From the day of his inauguration the new President was determined to give them what they wanted.

Why this shift in the climate of opinion? Why were Americans ready to risk war with powers abroad and conflict over the slavery issue at home to secure more territories when millions of acres within the country were still unoccupied? The answer can be found in the persistence of the westward movement, the reawakening fear of other nations, and the emergence of a new spirit that came to be known as "manifest destiny."

The Persistence of the Westward Movement

Certainly the relentless advance of the pioneer made expansion inevitable. Wherever he went, whether to Texas or California or Oregon, the frontiersman demanded that his country's protective arm be extended over him. Loyalty to the land of his adoption was unthinkable; he was an American and an American he would remain. "They seem," wrote one who lived among the pioneers of California, "to look upon this beautiful land as their own Canaan, and the motley race around them as the Hittites, the Hivites, and the Jebusites, whom they are to drive out." No extended reading of congressional debates is necessary to show that the statesmen of that day viewed expansion as inevitable, and believed that where the frontiersmen went the flag must follow. Possession, they felt, was nine points of the law. A New York editor only reflected public opinion when he wrote: "There is in fact no such thing as title to the wild lands of the new world, except that which actual possession gives. They belong to whoever will redeem them from the Indian and the desert, and subjugate them to the use of man." Here was justification enough for adding Texas and California and Oregon to the Union.

English and French Designs on Texas

But more was forthcoming, for scarcely a loyal citizen but believed these lands would fall to some foreign power if the United States did not act at once. Of these potential rivals, the most dreaded was England. Hatred of Britain had persisted since the days of the Revolution and the War of 1812.

In the 1840's this was heightened by British criticism of Americans as a "nation of swindlers" who had repudiated their just debts during the Panic of 1837, and by unfavorable reports of travelers who found little to their liking in the raw civilization of the United States. Charles Dickens, and others like him, hardly won favor when they painted the sturdy farmers of the Mississippi Valley as tobacco-spitting, eye-gouging, drunken, brawling, slave-beating semibarbarians. To make matters worse the two nations had been snarling at each other over American aid given insurgents in a rebellion

Young America

One of the groups interested in Manifest Destiny was led by young men who had not been old enough to participate in the Jacksonian reform movement of the 1830s, and who considered the drive for social and political equality in the 1840s either completed or irrelevant. As the nation turned its attention increasingly to the slavery issue during the latter decade, these men argued that slavery was unimportant when compared to the challenges of the West. Instead of worrying about the slaves, they urged, Americans should concern themselves with national needs and imperial destiny. Should they do this, North and South could unite in a crusade to bring American civilization to the Pacific instead of destroying each other in what the group considered a fruitless exercise of little consequence.

The group even had a name: Young America. . . . All spoke in glowing terms of the West; all were strongly anti-British, since Britain's control of the Oregon territory seemed the major barrier to the Pacific destiny; all were martial in tone and spirit, eager for a new war to prove America's worth.

Young America adopted Manifest Destiny as its slogan and the West as its utopia. Its leaders called upon Americans to go to the Pacific coast and establish America's claim for once and for all.

Robert Sobel, *Conquest and Conscience: The 1840s*, 1971.

that rocked Canada in 1837, and over a boundary dispute between Maine and New Brunswick.

With this background, rumors that England was working quietly to prevent the American annexation of Texas were enough to set indignation boiling. Nor were the rumors ill founded, for Britain was determined to keep the Texans independent by any means short of war. A strong Texas Republic would be an indispensable ally should the probable conflict with the United States develop, as well as a continuous brake on American expansion. Moreover both British capital and manufactured goods could find an outlet there; capitalists were wary of further investments within the United States since several states repudiated their debts following the Panic of 1837, while sellers were eager for a market in a tariff-free nation that could supply them with raw cotton for their textile mills. Humanitarians were also dedicated to preventing annexation. Fresh from their triumph in 1833, when all slaves in the British empire were freed, they were committed to a program of world-wide abolitionism. Texan union with the United States, they knew, would perpetuate slavery there, but an independent republic under British domination might be persuaded to adopt a program of gradual emancipation. Strategic, economic, and humanitarian goals all dictated that Texas must remain free.

These British designs profoundly influenced American opinion, especially in the South. Not a Southerner but believed that slavery was essential to cotton production, and cotton production essential to England's economy. Having freed its own slaves throughout the empire, Parliament must force every other cotton-growing land into abolitionism, for only in this way could competition continue on even terms. So Southerners reasoned as they watched every British move for confirmation of their thesis. Nor were these lacking. When a world's antislavery convention, held in London in 1843, declared that a free Texas would be "a perpetual incitement to murder, insurrection and outrage by the slaves of the Southern states," and when a slave rebellion in Cuba that autumn immediately followed a visit by English agents, nothing more was needed to show that slaves were being goaded into revolt everywhere. The Mississippi legislature spoke for most of the South when it declared: "The annexation of Texas to this Republic is essential to the future safety and repose of the southern states." Influential Whig planters who had hitherto opposed expansion leaped on the band wagon now, convinced that their way of life was at stake.

French designs on Texas aroused almost as much apprehension, and with some justification. Like England, France feared that annexation would deprive it of a profitable market for both manufactured goods and capital. Moreover war between the United States and Mexico would follow, with the inevitable Mexican defeat damaging the cause of Catholicism and the prestige of France's ally, Spain. These were the motives that led the government, in February, 1844, to instruct its minister in Washington to oppose annexation in every way. Even though he was cautioned to work behind the scenes, rumors of the French attitude were soon circulating, arousing Americans to new heights of indignation at this meddling in their affairs.

Concerns About California

Seeming designs of both France and England on California also fanned the flames of expansionism. Here the danger was more imagined than real, for neither had any serious intentions toward that distant land. Both, however, had allowed their nationals to loan money freely to the Mexican government, and, when repayments bogged down, both began thinking of compensation in the form of California land. As early as June, 1839, the Mexican Congress and British creditors agreed on a plan through which half the debt would be wiped out by grants of 125,000,000 acres there. In the end this speculation collapsed, but not before it had planted the seed of fear in the United States.

This was nurtured over the next years as the plan was revived over and over again. In 1839, Alexander Forbes, the British vice-consul at the Mexican port of Tepic, published his widely circulated *California: A History of Upper and Lower California*, which not only described the region in glowing terms but pleaded with his countrymen to take lands there in compensation for their debts. "I know of no place," he declared, ". . . better calculated for receiving and cherishing the superfluous population of Great Britain." In 1841 the English minister in Mexico City, Sir Richard Pakenham, was infected by the California fever and began urging his home government to plant a colony there. Over the next years two private colonization schemes stirred American fears. One, engineered by Robert C. Wyllie, urged English bondholders to accept payment in California lands; the other, planned by a young Irish priest named Eugene McNamara, would have planted a colony of two thousand Irishmen in the lower San Joaquin Valley.

News of each of these plans, sweeping the United States in distorted form, aroused a flurry of interest that soon swelled to immense proportions. Americans could not know that the British government steadfastly opposed expansion into California, partly because it feared war with the United States, partly because its "Little England" policy of that period discouraged further extension of the empire. Instead they quaked at each new rumor, and with each grew more insistent that California be annexed at once. By the end of 1845 such a staid journal as the *American Whig Review* believed that Britain's designs must be frustrated by any means, while less restrained writers were asking: "Why not extend the 'area of freedom' by the annexation of California? Why not plant the banner of liberty there?" Even the American minister to Mexico believed that "it will be worth a war of twenty years" to prevent England from taking California.

France also showed an alarming concern with that Mexican province. Its government, dreaming of reviving the empire lost in 1763, muscled into the scene in 1840 when a few French nationals were rumored killed during one of the periodic revolutions. From that time on a diplomatic agent, Duflot de Mofrás, was stationed there to keep his home government informed and to besiege it with demands to acquire "this magnificent heritage." This meddling bore fruit in 1844 when a French vessel, the *Angelina*, was attacked by insurgents during another revolution. For a time war threatened before ruffled feelings were calmed, but Americans never forgot that California was nearly lost to them forever. Why risk such a disaster when they could annex that golden land at once?

To Expand Democracy

This blusteringly aggressive attitude was made possible by still another force that contributed to the expansion of the 1840's. During the early years of that decade the American people suddenly awakened to their God-given destiny in world affairs. Since the inception of the Republic they had known that their democratic institutions were too perfect to be confined within narrow boundaries, and that the "Americanization" of first North America and eventually all the world was inevitable. In this calm belief there was no hint of aggression; Thomas Jefferson summed up his countrymen's opinion when he spoke of the United States as a "standing monument and example" to freedom-loving people everywhere. "We can," the *North American Review* agreed, "wait the peaceful progress of our own principles." By the beginning of the 1840's, however, this passive policy appeared insufficient. Not only were American institutions failing to alter Europe's monarchistic systems, but those backward nations were threatening to muddy the pure waters of democracy in America itself. Positive steps were needed to extend the "area of freedom" (in Andrew Jackson's happy phrase), and prevent the spread of an "area of absolutism." As one congressman put it, the nation must repel "the contaminating proximity of monarchies upon the soil that we have consecrated to the rights of man."

Once made, this decision was easy to rationalize. Expansion into contiguous lands would allow the United States to fulfill its role as the mother of liberty. It would elevate and enlighten the millions kept in chains by the archaic governments of Mexico or England, endowing them with a new spirit of enterprise. Wrote one enthusiast of the Mexican Californians: "They are only a grade above the aborigines, and like them will be compelled by the very nature of things, to yield to the swelling tide of Anglo-Saxon adventure." Expansion would not only bring freedom to the downtrodden abroad, but would solidify the liberties of the American people by creating new states to challenge the centralized authority of the federal government and by luring men westward where the democratic forces of the frontier could radiate over all the land. Surely a benevolent Deity wanted nothing less than this for His chosen people.

A Catchy Phrase

One thing more was needed before this exuberant belief could be translated into action: a catchy phrase that would sum up the Americans' faith in themselves. This was provided by the editor of the New York *Morning News*, John L. O'Sullivan, who in December, 1845, wrote of "our manifest destiny to overspread and to possess the whole of the continent which Providence has given us for the development of the great experiment of liberty and federated self-government entrusted to us." Manifest destiny! There was a pulse-tingling phrase indeed. Overnight the magic words swept the nation. Congressmen fastened upon them. "The right of our manifest destiny," declared one. "There is a right for a new chapter in the law of nations." Editors seized upon them as they urged on the nation its God-given duty to extend American blessings to the less fortunate. "Prophecy," one wrote, "looks forward to the time when the valley of the Mississippi shall overflow with a restless population, and Europe be subjected to a new migration." This was America's destiny. This was the will of God. All who opposed expansion were traitors to their country and their Creator.

War with Mexico

Don Nardo

While the goals of Manifest Destiny were grand in scope, the phrase was actually coined in an article supporting a very specific course of action: that the United States annex Texas, even if it meant war with Mexico. In the following excerpt from his book *The Mexican-American War*, Don Nardo gives a brief account of the outbreak of the conflict. After a clash between troops on the Texan-Mexican border, President James Polk asked for a declaration of war so that American troops could solidify their hold over the areas of Texas and New Mexico. After less than two years of fighting Mexico ceded Texas, New Mexico, and California to the United States, almost doubling American territory. At the war's end in February 1848 ardent supporters of Manifest Destiny were even arguing that the United States should annex all of Mexico.

As the U.S. presidential election of 1844 neared, tensions rose in Mexico City. To Mexican leaders, who watched nervously as Texan statehood once again became a central campaign issue, the election seemed like a dangerous repeat of the one in 1840. During the intervening four years, they had warned the United States again and again that annexing Texas would cause a war. And this was no idle threat. The unpleasant reality was that if an annexationist won the 1844 election and Texas joined the Union, they would feel compelled to preserve Mexico's integrity by declaring war on the United States.

Yet this does not mean that all Mexican leaders wanted a war. To be sure, several still clamored for a fight and arrogantly assumed they could not lose. But in fact, a number of them desired to avoid such a conflict with the United States

From *The Mexican-American War*, by Don Nardo (San Diego: Lucent Books, 1999). Reprinted with permission.

because they believed they had only a marginal chance of winning. Leading the Mexican antiwar faction was the new Mexican president, José Joaquín Herrera (1792–1854), who felt that his country was ill-prepared to wage a full-scale war. In the first place, he pointed out, the morale of the nation's soldiers was at an all-time low because there was not enough money in the treasury to pay them. He also took into account the U.S. population advantage. Although the United States had a much smaller standing army than Mexico had, its population was more than twice that of Mexico, so it could easily raise additional troops if necessary.

Herrera also considered another critical factor—firepower. He knew that the United States was a heavily industrialized country with many cannon factories. By contrast, Mexico had almost no heavy industry and few cannon factories. In addition, the United States had a powerful navy, while Mexico had no navy at all. In the view of Herrera and other thoughtful, cautious Mexican statesmen, a war between the two countries would be like the legendary contest between David and Goliath, only this time David would have no sling.

For all these reasons the Mexicans anxiously waited for the news of the U.S. election results in November 1844. They hoped that the Whig Party candidate, Henry Clay, would win, because Clay openly opposed both annexation and war. However, the nominee of the Democratic Party, James K. Polk, was a staunch expansionist who favored annexing Texas. In President Herrera's mind, Mexico's fate appeared to hang in an awful balance between these two Americans, their goals, their rhetoric, and their chances of winning the election. The vast majority of American voters probably did not realize that when they cast their ballots they were deciding two national futures, that of the United States and that of its southern neighbor.

The State of the American Military

To Herrera's great disappointment, Polk won the election, which immediately put Mexico's more moderate leaders in a difficult position. They had to uphold their country's honor and stop the Americans from taking Texas. But they needed to do it without getting involved in a potentially disastrous war. There was obviously little chance of changing Polk's mind about annexation, so negotiation would not be easy; therefore, there seemed little choice but for Mexico to continue its hard-line stance and hope to contain American expansionist ambitions. To that end, after the U.S. election Mexican authorities once more warned that annexing Texas would be construed as an act of war.

But American leaders were not scared off by these warnings. They knew they would have a clear military advantage over Mexico if war did break out. . . .

Polk and his generals knew that the United States had a significant advantage in its heavy industry, which could turn out many more cannons and munitions than the Mexicans could hope to match. American leaders could also rely on their powerful navy to blockade Mexican harbors, cutting off the country's vital supplies of trade goods, and to ferry American soldiers to strategic jumping-off points for attacking Mexico's interior.

But most of all, American leaders counted on the large population of the United States and the patriotic attitudes of the vast majority of its citizens. If the country's borders and way of life were threatened, they reasoned, surely Americans of all walks of life would, as Polk had phrased it, "rush with alacrity to her defense." And they were right. In fact, patriotism "played an important role in forming popular American perceptions of the Mexican War," says Johannsen. "The symbols of American nationalism [the flag, the American eagle, and so on] assumed virtually an objective [real, tangible] existence as they touched the springs of sentiment and belief." When the call for troops actually went out (in May 1846), the various states competed with one another to see which could provide the most recruits. In Illinois, three times as many young men volunteered as the military could accommodate; and the situation was similar across the land.

Texas Joins the Union

It was, therefore, with unbounded confidence that his country's human and material resources could and would support

A War for Texas

The outbreak of the Mexican War had a long and complex background in years of uneasy relations between the two countries. To many Americans, the frequency of revolutions in Mexico rendered that country's republican government more a sham than a reality. The United States had lodged claims against Mexico for losses incurred by American citizens during the revolutions, but even though the claims were arbitrated in 1842 at Mexico's request, they remained unpaid.

Yet for all the moments of irritation and tension, the cause of the Mexican War might be simply stated in a single word—Texas. The United States wanted Texas, and Mexico did not mean for the Americans to have it. From the moment Texas gained its independence from Mexico in 1836, Mexico blamed the United States for its loss and nurtured hopes for its recapture. The boundary with the United States, as far as Mexico was concerned, continued to be the Sabine River, which separated Louisiana and Texas. For the United States, it was the Rio Grande, the "traditional" line claimed in the 1803 treaty with France, which suggested that Texas was a part of the Louisiana Purchase, and confirmed by John Quincy Adams in his 1819 negotiations with Spain. The land between the two rivers—the Sabine and the Rio Grande—was the disputed territory.

Sentiment in support of the annexation of Texas to the United States gained strength as it was linked with questions of western settlement and territorial expansion. John L. O'Sullivan, outspoken New York journalist and editor of the *Democratic Review*, reflecting the romantic idealism of the time, placed the issue in broader perspective (and unwittingly coined a phrase that soon became a popular American idiom) when he asserted that America's claim to Texas was "by right of our manifest destiny to over spread and possess the whole of the continent which Providence has given us for the development of the great experiment of liberty and federated self government."

Robert W. Johannsen, *Wilson Quarterly*, Spring 1996.

his expansionist policy that Polk approached the presidency. And he wasted no time in implementing that policy. Guided by the combined efforts of the outgoing Tyler and incoming Polk, Congress passed the proposal for Texan annexation on March 1, 1845, three days before Polk delivered his inaugural address. "Be it resolved," the bill stated,

> that a state, to be formed out of the present Republic of Texas, with suitable extent and boundaries, and with two representatives in Congress . . . shall be admitted into the Union, by virtue of this act, on an equal footing with the existing states, as soon as the terms and conditions of such admission . . . shall be agreed upon by the governments of Texas and the United States.

Texas was now officially part of the United States, at least from the American point of view. The Mexicans had a completely different way of seeing the situation, of course. According to the Mexican ambassador in Washington, D.C., the United States had illegally taken control of Mexican territory. He immediately requested his passport and returned to Mexico City, breaking off diplomatic relations with the United States. Meanwhile, in his inaugural address, Polk defended the annexation of Texas as the right, expedient, and safe thing to do. "The Republic of Texas has made known her desire to come into our Union," he said,

> to form a part of our confederacy and enjoy with us the blessings of liberty secured and guaranteed by our Constitution. Texas . . . possesses an undoubted right to dispose of a part or the whole of her territory and to merge her sovereignty as a separate and independent state in ours. I congratulate my country that by an act of the late Congress . . . the assent of this government has been given to the reunion. . . . None can fail to see the danger to our safety and future peace if Texas remains an independent state or becomes an ally or dependency of some foreign nation more powerful than herself.

One particular section of Polk's speech no doubt infuriated Mexican leaders: "The world has nothing to fear from military ambition in our government," he declared. "Foreign powers should therefore look on the annexation of Texas to the United States not as the conquest of a nation seeking to extend her dominions by arms and violence, but as the peaceful acquisition of a territory once her own." To the contrary, in Mexican eyes there was much to fear from Polk's government, for it had been through arms and violence that the Texans had fomented their "rebellion" against Mexico; now the Americans had placed their own stamp of approval on that rebellion! Insulted, Herrera and his ministers were tempted to lash out and send troops into Texas. But they wisely refrained. By breaking off relations with the United States, they had sent Polk a clear message of their displeasure, and it was up to him to make the next move. . . .

Polk began searching for some excuse to force the Mexicans into war. He felt sure that he could acquire the needed public backing for the engagement. True, the issues of expansionism and war with Mexico were controversial, and he could expect some Americans strongly to oppose and protest such a conflict. Yet he had his finger squarely on the country's pulse, correctly perceiving that a majority were eager for U.S. expansion all the way to the Pacific, even if it meant war.

Many of the nation's major newspapers, for example, had already come out in favor of the expansionist viewpoint. Early in 1845, the *Washington Union* had suggested that that westward expansion into Mexican territories was inevitable. An editorial asked: "Who can arrest the torrent that will pour onward to the West? The road to California will be open to us. Who will stay [hold back] the march of our western people?" Openly approving of the idea of war, the *Union* added: "A corps of properly organized volunteers . . . would invade, overrun, and occupy Mexico. They would enable us not only to take California, but to keep it."

The Destiny of the "Superior" Race

Shortly after the *Washington Union* issued these remarks, the editor of the popular *Democratic Review*, John O'Sullivan, suggested that God had created the vast lands of the American frontier specifically for the use of the citizens of the

United States. "Our manifest destiny," he exclaimed, is "to overspread the continent allotted by Providence [God's will] for the free development of our expanding millions." The term O'Sullivan had coined, "manifest destiny," immediately caught on. Most of those who embraced its central theme assumed that, since God intended the United States to control the continent, there must be something special about Americans and their nation. This notion was summarized in 1846 in another popular publication, the *New Englander*, which asserted that the United States

> sprang from the noblest stock on earth's face, either of past or present times—a stock the most intellectual, as well as moral, and a stock which in physical qualities had at the time the nation was founded, and yet has, no equal. The very best of the nation of this best stock, founded the United States. . . . From the earliest period of the country to this day, the noble stock that first came to these shores has been widening and strengthening in its principles, and though modified by the thousand other causes that must be at work in so large a people and one so situated, it is destined to perpetuate . . . its wisdom and worth to the latest generation. . . . The government of these United States is believed by the far-judging of the whole world to be the model government in the earth; and to be thought therefore worthy at least of being held up before other nations . . . as a sort of guide, by which they may direct their own steps in the cause of general progression of the human race.

Though this tract seemed on its face to be mainly a political glorification of the American system, the frequent use of the term "stock" (physical, moral, and so on) betrayed its underlying racist content. And it and other pieces like it tended to reinforce a belief, then widely held in the United States, that white, Protestant Americans were superior to other peoples. Such misguided notions provided a convenient justification for pushing aside the millions of Native Americans and Mexicans who stood in the way of white expansion. According to this view, it was only right that such "inferior" peoples give way to their white "betters.". . .

Old Zach Goes to Texas

Although there were certainly some Americans who despised and rejected such views as ignorant and racist, a majority more or less acepted them. And this played right into President Polk's hands; otherwise, he could not have so successfully pursued his expansionist policies, nor gotten away with deliberately provoking war with Mexico.

The question was how to push the Mexicans into fighting while making it look like they, and not the Americans, were the aggressors. A border incident seemed the best approach. To carry out such an important and potentially dangerous assignment would require a military commander of special abilities; in this regard Polk remembered a conversation he had had with old Andrew Jackson a few months before. In the event of a war with the British over Canada, Jackson had told him, he should entrust the field army to Brig. Gen. Zachary Taylor, affectionately called "Old Zach" by his men. Taylor was "unlikely material for building a national hero," comments John Eisenhower:

> He was an old soldier by the standards of the day, nearly sixty-one years of age, deliberate and unpolished in manner. Long service in every American war since 1812 had dulled whatever appetite he had ever had for fighting, and somehow he had been able through the years to combine soldiering with his lifelong love of farming. . . . But these characteristics were only one side of Taylor's makeup. In battle he had always been a tower of strength. . . . In the Seminole [Indian] War [in 1835], he had been awarded for leading 1,100 men through swamp water up to the waist, achieving a surprise victory.

At Polk's orders, in mid-1845 Taylor moved into southern Texas, in command of some four thousand troops, more than half the country's standing army at the time. Taylor camped at Corpus Christi, near the Nueces River, about two hundred miles north of the Rio Grande. He and Polk knew well that the Mexicans recognized the Nueces as the southern border of their Texas province, while the Americans considered the Rio Grande itself as the border marker. Since the United States had already annexed Texas, in Polk's and Taylor's logic all lands north of the Rio Grande were American soil.

On learning that Taylor's troops had entered Texas, Mexican leaders, including Herrera and the other moderates, were outraged. But they still wanted to avoid a fight if at all possible, so they decided not to react unless Taylor was so audacious as to cross the Nueces. The standoff continued for a few months until Polk, who had hoped that the Mexicans would cross the Nueces and attack Taylor, grew frustrated with his opponents' restraint. In January 1846, he ordered Taylor to cross the river himself. One of Taylor's officers, Col. Ethan Allen Hitchcock, who was disturbed by the hostile tactics of his superiors, recorded in his diary:

> He [Taylor] is immediately to proceed with his whole command to the extreme western border of Texas and take up a position on the banks of . . . the Rio Grande, and he is to expel any armed force of Mexicans who may cross the river. . . . I have scarcely slept a wink, thinking of the needful preparations. I am now . . . waiting [for] the signal to muster. Violence leads to violence, and if this movement of ours does not lead to others and to bloodshed, I am much mistaken.

Gunfire on the Nueces

Once across the Nueces, Taylor camped his army near the Mexican town of Matamoros. A few days later, on April 11, a Mexican general, Pedro de Ampudía, entered the town with two thousand of his own troops. Knowing that even more Mexican soldiers were on their way to reinforce him, Ampudía confidently sent Taylor a message that stated in part:

> I require you in all form, and at the latest in . . . twenty-four hours, to break up your camp and return to the east bank of the Nueces River while our governments are regulating [negotiating] the pending question in relation to Texas. If you insist upon remaining upon [Mexican soil], it will certainly result that arms, and arms alone, must decide the question; and in that case I advise you that we accept the war to which, with so much injustice on your part, you provoke us.

Taylor arrogantly responded to Ampudía's earnest warning

by building a fort. "He seems to have lost all respect for Mexican rights," Hitchcock wrote,

> and is willing to be an instrument of Mr. Polk for pushing our boundary as far west as possible. When I told him that . . . Mr. Polk would seize upon it and throw the responsibility on him [i.e., blame Taylor for any trouble that ensued], he at once said he would take it, and added that if the President instructed him to use his discretion, he would ask no orders, but go upon the Rio Grande as soon as he could.

A few days later, the Mexicans made good on their threat to take action if Taylor did not withdraw. Gen. Mariano Arista arrived with reinforcements and took charge of the Matamoros garrison. Seeing that the Americans had still not retreated, he ordered sixteen hundred of his cavalrymen to take up positions a few miles from the American fort. Apparently he hoped that this show of force would persuade Taylor to back down.

Arista did not suspect, of course, that this was precisely the kind of offensive move that Taylor and Polk had been hoping for. Preparing for battle, Taylor dispatched a sixty-three-man patrol to scout the enemy's location and strength. On April 26 the members of the patrol stopped to rest at a ranch house and there, soon after a large force of Mexicans surprised and surrounded them, shots rang out. It remains uncertain who fired first and the gunfight lasted only a few minutes. But the outcome proved momentous. Eleven Americans were killed, most of the others were wounded or captured, and only four managed to escape and make it back to the American camp. Taylor quickly sent a message to Polk, telling him "Hostilities may now be considered as commenced."

"American Blood upon American Soil"

President Polk received Taylor's letter on May 10, 1846. By that time, most of the country had heard about the events on the Nueces River. As Polk began drafting his war declaration, a number of prominent Americans immediately expressed their displeasure with the idea of armed conflict with

Mexico. Leading the nation's minority against expansionism, manifest destiny, and the annexation of Texas, Representatives John Quincy Adams and Joshua Giddings called Polk's and Taylor's actions immoral and dangerous. Their feelings and those of other concerned Americans were reflected by a perceptive and moving entry in Colonel Hitchcock's diary:

> I have said from the first that the United States are the aggressors. We have outraged the Mexican government and people by an arrogance and presumption that deserve to be punished. . . . We have not one particle of right to be here. . . . It looks as if the government sent a small force on purpose to bring on a war, so as to have a pretext for taking California and as much of this country [Mexico] as it chooses. . . . My heart is not in this business . . . but, as a military man, I am bound to execute orders.

Undeterred by such sentiments, Polk finished his war declaration on May 11 and sent it to Congress. His words were dramatic and blunt:

> The cup of forbearance had been exhausted even before the recent information from the frontier. . . . But now, after reiterated [repeated] menaces, Mexico has passed the boundary of the United States, has invaded our territory and shed American blood upon American soil. She has proclaimed that hostilities have commenced, and that the two nations are now at war. As war exists, notwithstanding all our efforts to avoid it, exists by the act of Mexico herself, we are called upon by every consideration of duty and patriotism to vindicate with decision the honor, the rights, and the interests of our country.

Congress reacted posthaste to Polk's martial words. The House of Representatives passed the war measure that same afternoon by a vote of 173 to 14; the next day the Senate approved it too; and on May 13, Polk signed it. Whatever the potential consequences, there was no going back now. The United States of America and the Republic of Mexico had joined themselves irrevocably in a mighty struggle for control of the continent.

Manifest Destiny as a Turning Point in U.S.–Indian Policy

Reginald Horsman

Reginald Horsman, a history professor at the University of Wisconsin, is the author of several books on American history, including *Race and Manifest Destiny: Origins of American Racial Anglo-Saxonism*. In the following essay he argues that the doctrine of Manifest Destiny, which first appeared in the 1840s, marked an important shift in the way that the U.S. government had viewed American Indians since the 1780s. U.S. leaders had always believed that their nation would expand into Indian lands, he explains, but they hoped that this could be accomplished by "civilizing," or assimilating, the Indians, rather than exterminating them. By the 1840s, however, the goals of expanding the frontier largely overshadowed concerns about Indian welfare. The doctrine of Manifest Destiny, which held that the white race was divinely ordained to spread across North America, marked both the shift in attitude and the start of a more aggressive U.S.-Indian policy.

In the late 1780's, and particularly after the formation of the new government in 1789, American leaders began to show a great desire to justify their expansion westwards over the Indians. Their solution to the dilemma of advocating an enlarged area of liberty and the blessings of a free government, while at the same time exterminating the aboriginal inhabitants, was conditioned by the eighteenth-century view of natural man and his improvability. Whatever the attitudes of the frontiersmen, those who formulated American opinion and a national policy in the late eighteenth and the first

From "American Indian Policy and the Origins of Manifest Destiny," by Reginald Horsman, *University of Birmingham Historical Journal*, vol. 10, no. 2 (1968). Reprinted with permission from the author. Footnotes in the original have been omitted in this reprint.

quarter of the nineteenth century saw the solution to their dilemma in the bringing of civilization to the Indian inhabitants of North America. This attitude was essentially one of great optimism. It did not preach any innate Indian inferiority, but rather viewed the Indian as existing at a lower stage in the evolution of society and civilization. These aboriginal inhabitants were to give up their state of nature, but in exchange were to be given the inestimable blessing of American civilization; the highest and happiest state that man had yet attained. . . .

"This March of Civilization"

The full expression of this philosophy of expansion over the Indians came with the Presidency of Thomas Jefferson, who combined a sense of mission to the Indians with a clear vision of the expansionist destiny of the United States. Jefferson was too imbued with eighteenth-century ideas of the natural man to doubt the improvability of the Indian. 'I believe the Indian then,' he wrote in the 1780's, 'to be in body and mind equal to the whiteman.'. . . Jefferson ignored the agricultural aspects of Indian society, and preached the adoption of agriculture and private property as the route to the blessings of civilization. 'Let me entreat you therefore,' he told a delegation of Indians in December 1808, 'on the lands now given you to begin every man a farm, let him enclose it, cultivate it, build a warm house on it, and when he dies let it belong to his wife and children after him.' . . .

Whatever Jefferson thought of the natural man, however, he was not giving the Indians a choice between their existing state of society and American civilization. Jefferson had no doubt that the United States was offering the Indians the chance of participating in the greatest state of society the world had ever known; a chance to leap over the intervening steps to the high plateau of American civilization. As late as 1824 Jefferson wrote that a traveller coming eastwards from the Rockies to the seaport towns would see the equivalent of a survey in time 'of the progress of man from the infancy of creation to the present day'. He wrote that living in the first range of mountains in the interior of the country, 'I have observed this march of civilization advancing from the sea-coast, passing over us like a cloud of light, increasing our knowledge and improving our condition, insomuch as that we are at this time more advanced in civilization here than the seaports were when I was a boy. And where this progress will stop no one can say. Barbarism has, in the meantime, been receding before the steady step of amelioration; and will in time, I trust, disappear from the earth.' With this confidence in the ultimate good of what the United States was accomplishing, the Indians could not be allowed to stand in the way. If they did not accept the inestimable benefits of American civilization then they were doomed. . . .

American Indians and the Ideology of Expansion

In the years between 1815 and 1830 American Indian policy was confronted with a major dilemma, a dilemma which inevitably affected the ideology of expansion. On the one hand confidence in the American mission and progress reached new heights. In the early days of independence there had always been a lingering fear that the experiment of a free, republican government would prove a failure, that those Europeans who prophesied chaos for the American 'mobocracy' would prove correct. Yet, in the years after 1815, it was quite clear that the United States was advancing dramatically in total strength. Immigrants were entering American ports in increasing numbers, settlers were pouring west, new states were entering the Union; from one end of the country to the other the story was one of growth and prosperity. Confidence in America as the bastion of freedom and progress reached new heights. In August 1825, American soldier Edmund Pendleton Gaines wrote of the United States as 'one great political family, whose fair fame has already attracted the admiration of every civilized country, and whose example has led to the establishment of liberty in South America, and promises to aid in its final extension and permanent establishment throughout every portion of the world'. In December 1828 one member of Congress supported the bill for an American establishment on the Columbia River on the grounds that 'It proposes an extension of the blessings of civilization, of freedom, and happiness, to the human race.'

The basic question for many was that posed by Jackson in his second annual message in December 1830: 'What good man would prefer a country covered with forests and ranged by a few thousand savages to our extensive Republic, studded with cities, towns, and prosperous farms, embellished with all the improvements which art can devise or industry execute, occupied by more than 12,000,000 happy people, and filled with all the blessings of liberty, civilization, and religion?' A member of Congress who supported removal asked 'What is history but the obituary of nations?' He wanted to know 'are we to check the course of human happiness—obstruct the march of science—stay the works of art, and stop the arm of industry, because they will efface in their progress the wigwam of the red hunter, and put out forever the council fire of his tribe?' There were, of course, still those who believed in the improvability of the Indian, and argued for eventual assimilation, but the prevailing mood and policy of the government had changed. Removal in reality acknowledged the failure of the post-Revolutionary policy of assimilation, and was known to be only a temporary expedient. By 1830 it was quite clear to many Americans that the American population was going to sweep forward to the Pacific.

Calling on Providence

In the 1830's and 1840's the American view of the Indian merged into a more elaborate ideology which built a basis of justification for American expansion over any lands. The Americans had no need to develop a whole new set of attitudes for they had already been deeply involved in the problem of rationalizing an advance which ruined and dispossessed those with whom they came into contact. More and more the talk was of superior or inferior race rather than of different stages of human society. The idea of the Anglo-Saxons or related races as divinely appointed to civilize the world assumed an increasingly important share of the argument. The confidence in American institutions also reached new heights. 'Foreign powers do not seem to appreciate the true character of our Government,' Polk announced in his inaugural in 1845. 'Our Union is a confederation of independent States, whose policy is peace with each other and all the world. To enlarge its limits is to extend the dominions of peace over additional territories and increasing millions.'

Having convinced themselves in the 1820's and 1830's that the failure of the Indians to benefit from the American advance had stemmed from their inherent inferiority, and that Providence had ordained that the Americans would bring peace, freedom, and a better civilization to the world on a stepping-stone of less able races, the proponents of expansionism had no difficulty in extending their arguments to cover the Mexicans. One newspaper made a simple and direct connection: 'The Mexicans are *aboriginal Indians*,' it was maintained, 'and they must share the destiny of their race.' Most expansionists were merely content to use analogy. 'The Mexican race now see, in the fate of the aborigines of the north, their own inevitable destiny,' argued the *Democratic Review*. 'They must amalgamate and be lost, in the superior vigor of the Anglo-Saxon race, or they must utterly perish.'

Manifest Destiny and Racism

The full elaboration of the new notions of race came, however, from [lawyer and statesman] Thomas Hart Benton. 'I know of no human event, past or present, which promises a greater, and more beneficent change upon earth,' argued Benton, 'than the arrival of the van of the Caucasian race (the Celtic-Anglo-Saxon division) upon the border of the sea which washes the shore of the eastern Asia. The Mongolian, or Yellow race, is there, four hundred millions in number, spreading almost to Europe; a race once the foremost of the human family in the arts of civilization, but torpid and stationary for thousands of years. It is a race far above the Ethiopian or Black—above the Malay, or Brown, (if we must admit five races)—and above the American Indian, or Red: it is a race far above all these, but still, far below the White; and, like all the rest, must receive an impression from the superior race whenever they come into contact. It would seem that the White race alone received the divine command, to subdue and replenish the earth! For it is the only race that has obeyed it—the only one that hunts out new and distant lands, and even a New World, to subdue and replenish.' With the death of the eighteenth-century Americans the Old Testament was once again gaining ground over the natural law.

In this speech on the future of the American race, Benton talked more specifically of what had happened to the American Indian: 'The Red Race has disappeared from the Atlantic coast: the tribes that resisted civilization, met extinction. This is a cause of lamentation with many. For my part, I cannot murmur at what seems to be the effect of divine law. . . . Civilization, or extinction, has been the fate of all people who have found themselves in the track of the advancing Whites, and civilization, always the preference of the Whites, has been pressed as an object, while extinction has followed as a consequence of its resistance.' This argument that Benton had carried on since the 1820's that was maintained by [statesman Henry] Clay, and endorsed by John Quincy Adams and Jackson, formed a consistent thread in the ideology of American expansion. It was still being maintained at the end of the nineteenth century; it was argued with passion that the benefits that American rule conferred, the enlargement of the area of freedom, justified the transformation or dispossession of peoples who might stand in the way. Ultimately, of course, this philosophy depended upon a supreme confidence in the way of life that was being offered, and this confidence was present in abundance. Indians, Mexicans, or Filipinos became merely obstacles in the path to a better world.

Rationalizing Imperialism

In the years from the Revolution to the Mexican War the United States had begun with the presumption that the destruction of the Indians would be a major blot on the national character; a blot for which the United States would have to answer to other nations throughout the world, to future historians, and to God. It can easily be maintained that even in the early years the United States never translated this concern into a practical programme, and that indeed, like Maria Theresa, the more she cried the more she took. Yet, at least in the 1790's and the first decade of the nineteenth century, there was an optimism that all would be well, a belief, however misinformed, that the Indians would assume American civilization, and thus American expansion would directly benefit not only those expanding but also those who stood as a barrier. By the 1820's this concept of Indian improvability was under major attack, and in the 1830's and 1840's a more common assumption was that the Indians had succumbed because they were doomed by Providence, and that the sufferings of whoever stood in the way of expansion was nothing beside the benefit to humanity of extending the area of American civilization and freedom. This doctrine was so convenient that it could be used to extend a slave system over a Mexican area that had abandoned slavery.

To treat American Indian policy as a purely domestic concern is to ignore what it tells us of the American attitude towards alien peoples. It would seem fruitful to regard American Indian policy as part of the expansion of Western Europe, particularly the so-called Anglo-Saxons, over peoples throughout the world; an expansion which reached its height at the close of the nineteenth century. In this way American Indian policy can help explain not only the assumptions of what for convenience is called 'Manifest Destiny' but also the underlying assumptions of imperialism.

Manifest Destiny—or Genocide?

W. Eugene Hollon

The doctrine of Manifest Destiny not only called on Americans to spread their civilization throughout the North American continent, it also declared that they were justified in doing so. In the 1840s Manifest Destiny was used to justify war with Mexico for control of Texas; in the years that followed it was used to justify war with American Indians for lands in the Southwest and the Great Plains. In the following selection, historian W. Eugene Hollon describes the many battles fought between American Indians and the U.S. government between 1860 and 1890. In these decades U.S. soldiers decimated the major tribes. Hollon suggests that the broken treaties and widespread slaughter of the North American Indian wars are the most regrettable legacies of Manifest Destiny. Professor Hollon is the author of several books, including *Frontier Violence: Another Look*, from which the essay below is excerpted.

Few people were as good at fighting against professional soldiers or won as many battles as the American Indians, yet they won no wars. The late Fred Allen once observed, with as much bitter truth as humor, that "all books and movies about the Indians are the same—the redskins invariably get it in the end." Estimates of the number of Indians massacred in the United States since 1789 vary from 4000 to 10,000. Thousands more have been killed by alcohol, smallpox, chickenpox, measles, and other diseases against which the victims had little or no immunity. In addition, the whites have suppressed or practically destroyed their culture and religion. And not one of the 370 treaties made with the Indians since 1789 has been kept by the federal government (at least, not one that I have discovered).

The allegations made by some modern observers that there never was an organized campaign of genocide against the Indians may be correct, but it is difficult to describe the slaughter of the peaceful Diggers in California in any other terms. This tragic example may not represent a microcosm of 100 years of Indian-white relationships, but it is a fact that whenever the Indian got in the white man's way, the consequences were violent. A special commission reported to President Grant as early as 1869 that "The history of the border white man's connection with the Indian is a sickening record of murder, outrage, robbing, and wrongs committed by the former, as the rule, and occasional savage outbreaks and unspeakable barbarous deeds of retaliation by the latter, as the exception.". . .

The period that witnessed the largest number of conflicts occurred between 1860 and 1890. The theater was a vast one; it extended from Minnesota to the Pacific Coast, and from the Canadian border to Mexico. During these three decades the once great Cheyenne were brought to ruin—along with the Ute, Sioux, Apache, Comanche, Kiowa, Nez Percé, and all of the other tribes that stood in the way of what Senator Beveridge called "The March of Empire." The fundamental cause of the trouble was the overrunning of Indian lands by white settlers. With the outbreak of the Civil War and the withdrawal or reduction of regular troops at the far-flung frontier garrisons, Indians throughout the Great Plains and Southwest took to the warpath to pillage wagon trains and raid isolated settlements, in efforts to reclaim their hunting grounds.

The Navajo and the Cheyenne

The Navajo were the first to declare full-scale war, and United States troops and New Mexico militia finally subdued them after three years of almost constant fighting. By mid-July 1864 some 2000 men, women, and children had died of starvation or had been killed by soldiers. Another 8000 had been rounded up and placed on the small Bosque

Redondo reservation in eastern New Mexico. Meanwhile, the Navajos' hogans had been destroyed, their livestock stolen or killed, and their food supplies depleted.

Life was not easy for the captives. The soil at Bosque Redondo was too poor to grow crops, the water unbearable, and wood extremely scarce. By 1868 the federal government finally realized that the only way the Navajo could be held in that God-forsaken region was through force, and that the wisest thing to do was to let them return to their canyons and mesas of northeastern Arizona. Some 7000 men, women, and children eventually survived the "long walk" back to their beloved homeland. Since their return the Navajo tribal council has kept the promise to remain at peace. Even though the struggle has been far from easy, their ordeal was brief and less severe than that of any other Western tribe.

The turn for the Cheyenne, Arapaho, Sioux, Crow, and other natives of the Great Plains came next. In 1851 these tribes allowed the federal government to build military roads and a chain of forts across their hunting grounds. Soon stagecoach lines, wagon trains, soldiers, and miners were driving wedges through the tribal land, and they were followed by settlers staking out ranches and farms. Up to that time, the Cheyenne especially had always remained friendly toward the whites, but as they witnessed their buffalo herds decimated, treaties ignored, and land expropriated, their attitude changed drastically. For the next two and a half decades they remained almost constantly at war with militia or federal troops. By 1880, "the fighting Cheyenne" were too weak to resist any longer, having suffered perhaps more casualties in actual combat than any other Plains tribe. . . .

Destruction of the Buffalo

The second half of the decade of the 1860's also witnessed the negotiation of numerous treaties between the United States and most of the Western tribes. At Medicine Lodge, at Fort Laramie, at the mouth of the Little Arkansas, and elsewhere, chiefs of the Cheyenne, Arapaho, Comanche, Kiowa, Sioux, Modoc, Nez Percé, and Bannock "touched the pen" or "put their mark" on treaties that they either did not understand or had no alternative but to accept. In every case they agreed to cede portions of their lands and to restrict their hunting and farming activities to the small reservation allotted to them. And without exception they were to find it difficult if not impossible to make a living by traditional means. Commanders at army posts throughout the West were charged with keeping them in line, a task made easier by a cruel and effective ally—starvation.

For centuries the Plains Indians' existence and much of their culture had depended upon the buffalo. But at about the time their hunting grounds were reduced and their movements restricted, white buffalo hunters moved onto the Plains and indulged in a systematic slaughter of the gregarious beasts. Unfortunately for the animal's future existence, his bones, hide, and meat all possessed commercial value. His ultimate extinction would leave the Indians with a choice between complete surrender to military control over their lives or outright starvation.

The army realized the vital role of the buffalo to the Plains Indians and actually encouraged its destruction. "Instead of stopping the hunters," General Philip Sheridan told a congressional committee, "you ought to give each hunter a medal of bronze with a dead buffalo on one side and a discouraged Indian on the other. . . . Send them powder and lead, if you will, but for the sake of peace, let them kill, skin, and sell until the buffalo are exterminated. Then your prairies can be covered with cattle and the cowboy, who follow the hunter as a second forerunner of an advanced civilization." Ironically, General Sheridan's philosophy has been memorialized more widely than he possibly could have imagined; hundreds of millions of United States coins long carried the imprint of a buffalo on one side and that of a Plains Indian on the other. . . .

Reservations and Poverty

In the mountains, on the Great Plains, and in the desert the Indians fought desperately to hold on to their hunting grounds. By 1874 most of the Kiowa chiefs, among them Big

Tree, Satanta, and Satank, had been captured or killed and their people rounded up by the army and confined to a small reservation in southwestern Oklahoma. There they have remained at peace ever since, but the price they have paid for "following the white man's road" has been wretched poverty. The same has been true of their neighbors, the Comanche. The last of the great Comanche chiefs, Quanah Parker, surrendered in 1876 when the so-called Red River War finally ended and he and his band returned to the reservation. Also by this time, all of the Apache except Geronimo's small band of Chiricahua had been settled on reservations in New Mexico and Arizona.

Not until 1886 were troops successful in taking Geronimo prisoner and bringing the last of the wars of the Southwest to a close. The overwhelming number of soldiers and settlers had made existence off the reservation, however temporary, too dangerous. By this time the Navajo and Pueblo had long since returned to their dreams and ceremonies, and the Southern Cheyenne, Arapaho, Kiowa, and Comanche were too reduced in number and too beaten in spirit to offer further resistance. As for the smaller desert tribes such as the Pima, Yuma, Papago, Havasupai, and Hopi, they had found that the job of taming the formidable environment left them little time or inclination for anything else. Besides, their reservations consisted of lands that had been their traditional homes for centuries and, fortunately, were too poor and isolated for the white man to bother with.

Red Cloud and Chief Joseph

Before the Indians in the Southern Plains and the desert Southwest had been killed or "civilized," the army had its problems with the tribes of the north. The Homestead Act of 1862 sent wave after wave of farmers, or "nesters," onto the Northern Plains. These pioneers, combined with the ranchers and miners, paved the way for a showdown over control of the last major frontier region of the West. Meanwhile, in the mid-1860's, whites tried to open the Bozeman Trail, which drove through the center of the Indian hunting grounds of Wyoming to the mining fields of western Montana. The great Sioux Chief Red Cloud made life so hazardous for the travelers on the road that the army built a chain of forts to protect them. But when small companies of troopers ventured beyond the garrisons, they frequently ran into ambushes and were lucky to escape annihilation. Because of the determined efforts of Red Cloud's people, the army eventually abandoned the trail—in one of the rare occasions of Indian victory over the whites. But not for long.

Further west, in Oregon, the federal government tried to deprive some of the tribes of their reservation, but General O.O. Howard found in the principal Chief of the Nez Percé an amazingly formidable opponent. Against overwhelming odds, Chief Joseph repeatedly defeated or thwarted the army before retreating over the Bitterroot Mountains into western Montana. General John Gibbon later swept down on the Nez Percé camp on the Big Hole River and shot and bayoneted every Indian in sight. Miraculously, the Chief rallied his forces, beat off the attackers, and escaped. He then continued in a general eastward direction through Yellowstone Park and eventually reached the Bear Paw Mountains, where the feeble remnants of the tribe were captured only thirty miles from its goal, the Canadian border. . . .

The Battle of the Little Big Horn

No tribes fought harder for their lands than the Hunkpapa, Miniconjou, Brule, and Oglala Sioux of the Northern Plains. In 1868 they forced the army to acknowledge that their sacred land in the Black Hills would forever belong to the Sioux. But when gold miners poured into the Dakota country after 1874 and the government tried to force the Indians to accept a new treaty, war broke out anew. In June 1876, the Crow and Shoshoni joined the soldiers under General George Crook to fight their ancient enemies, the Sioux, in the Battle of the Rosebud. Warriors under Crazy Horse and Sitting Bull then moved further west to the Little Big Horn [River], where they combined with other Sioux and Cheyenne warriors to constitute a force estimated by the army at approximately 15,000. (The Indians probably were more accurate in their estimate— 3000 warriors.) The so-called "Custer Massacre" that followed shocked the nation, which was then in the midst of celebrating the centennial of its independence.

The Sioux eventually lost the Black Hills for having disgraced the army. With the nation's honor at stake, it could be expected that thousands of soldiers would chase them all over the Plains until they were killed, driven into Canada, or rounded up on reservations. After years of intermittent fighting, the Plains and mountains were finally made safe for miners, cowboys, and farmers. Meanwhile, the Indians were never paid justly for the Black Hills. They saw the end long before it came, their ponies having been killed off or stolen, their supplies depleted, and their rifles no match for the Hotchkiss guns and other superior weapons of the white soldiers.

The Ghost Dance

For all practical purposes the reservations were prisons, and when individuals or groups tried to escape their miserable surroundings, the soldiers were quick to punish them. Their only hope was a messiah, and one appeared before the end of the century. He was a Paiute named Wovoka, and he preached that the ghosts of dead Indians would return to drive out the whites and that the vanished buffalo would reappear. Soon the Plains and mountains and deserts would belong to the original owners, and the old way of life would be restored. The army became alarmed as the Ghost Dance spread throughout the West. Suspicions that Sitting Bull planned an uprising by the Ghost Dancers resulted in his assassination. But the real climax came in late December 1890, in South Dakota, where a band of half-starved Miniconjou Sioux under their aged chief, Big Foot, appeared to have resisted arrest. After the smoke from the Hotchkiss guns had cleared, more than half the band of 350 men, women, and children lay dead in the snow. Some sixty soldiers, caught in their own crossfire, were killed or severely wounded.

For the army the event was hardly an honorable one, although it represented a significant victory in the dreary history of Plains warfare. The Indian's spirit by now was completely broken, and all hope that he could live out his life in his own way was gone. Warfare and disease already had reduced the red man's population to approximately 250,000—less than one-third of the number that had inhabited the continent three centuries earlier.

The Sioux who fell at Wounded Knee died in the same year that the census bureau announced that there no longer was an American frontier. By this time the Western tribes had lost three-fifths of the land that had been granted to them by treaty since 1851. What they have managed to keep to this date is largely sand and rock, but that is another story. By the mid–twentieth century the white man had developed a tremendous sense of guilt over the physical violence and cultural genocide practiced against the Indian. It is one reason that Dee Brown's *Bury My Heart at Wounded Knee*, published in 1970, remained on the best-seller list for more than fifty-two consecutive weeks.

In his emotion-packed book, Brown glorifies the Indian, but he stacks the cards heavily against the whites. Thus, his work could hardly be called an objective treatment of the subject of Indian-white relations between 1860 and 1890. Yet thousands of readers, conditioned as they are to generations of Indian hating, probably agree with the following comment, made by one of the reviewers: "Nothing I have ever read has saddened and shamed me as this book has. Because the experience of reading it has made me realize for once and all that we really don't know who we are or where we came from, or what we have done, or why."

Chapter 3

Gold Fever

The California Gold Rush and the American Dream

Malcolm J. Rohrbough

The California Gold Rush was a turning point in U.S. history in a variety of ways. In the following excerpt from his book *Days of Gold: The California Gold Rush and the American Nation*, Malcolm J. Rohrbough, a professor of history at the University of Iowa, describes how the Gold Rush was a turning point in the way Americans viewed their nation. For nineteenth-century Americans, the frontier represented opportunity: Because of the widespread availability of land, almost any family could make a living through farming. The Gold Rush dramatically reaffirmed this vision of the United States as a nation where anyone could achieve wealth through hard work. In 1849 and 1850 over 40,000 gold-seekers embraced this vision of the American dream, though only a small proportion of them found wealth in California.

The discovery of gold in John Sutter's millrace at about ten o'clock in the morning of January 24, 1848, set in motion the people and events that we know as the California Gold Rush. The discovery and the subsequent spread of the news across the continent launched hundreds of ships and hitched up a thousand prairie schooners. The three-masted vessels departed from the ports of Boston, New York, and Philadelphia, and farther to the south, from Wilmington, Charleston, and New Orleans. The overland schooners embarked from county-seat towns and villages across the breadth of the nation, from the subsistence farms of the Ohio River valley to the great plantations of the lower Mississippi River valley.

Those who joined the procession—in 1849 and annually thereafter for a dozen years—embraced every class, from the wealthy to those in straitened circumstances, from every state and territory, including slaves brought by their owners. In numbers, it represented the greatest mass migration in the history of the Republic, some eighty thousand in 1849 alone and probably three hundred thousand by 1854—an immigration largely male and generally young, but not exclusively either—by land across a continent and over thousands of miles of ocean to new and heretofore unimagined wealth.

A Shared National Experience

The consequences of the California Gold Rush were vast and far-reaching. Like a stone dropped into a deep pool, the impact of the discovery of gold spread outward in ever-widening circles to touch the lives of families and communities everywhere in the Republic. For those who went to California, the decision to go raised questions about marital obligations and family responsibilities in which the opportunity for wealth was measured against prolonged absences that imposed new duties, often with reduced resources. For those who remained on the farm or in the shop, its impact was no less profound, for the absences of tens of thousands of men over a period of years led to the reshaping of a thousand communities across the breadth of the American nation.

When the impact on families and communities is totaled up, the Gold Rush emerges as a shared national experience, not simply an incident in California's history. In its repercussions, it was the most significant event in the first half of the nineteenth century, from Thomas Jefferson's purchase of Louisiana in the autumn of 1803 to South Carolina's secession from the Union in the winter of 1860. No other series of events produced so much movement among peoples; called into question so many basic values—marriage, family, work, wealth, and leisure; led to so many varied consequences; and left such vivid memories among its participants.

The opportunities associated with the search for gold in 1848 and the next dozen years lay in the context of other work that Americans regularly performed at midcentury. It was a world in which editors, elected officials, ministers, and other public figures still praised the American experience for its economic democracy, as exemplified by the continuing, widespread availability of land as a basis of economic advantage and national equality. Whatever the opportunities associated with land ownership, the work was hard. Farm families, who had assured title to 80 or 160 acres or even more, labored long hours in the fields for the return of a few hundred dollars each year. Growing numbers of working people had left the countryside and small towns for jobs in small factories and shops in emerging urban centers, where they increasingly had lost control of their work conditions in a new economic system that had begun to impose itself on this predominantly rural landscape. The California Gold Rush offered to men and women accustomed to endless hard and repetitive labor over a lifetime in the fields, shops, or small factories in pursuit of a modest freehold estate the economic opportunity that the nation was supposed to represent.

The Gold Rush and the American Dream

At the same time that it promised wealth, the Gold Rush assumed a form that spoke to American values at midcentury: an image of instant success available through hard work; an affirmation of democratic beliefs under which the wealth would be available to all; the discovery of gold as a logical and inevitable closure to a war that established a continental nation. The discovery of gold in 1848 and its widespread availability to Americans everywhere thus seemed to represent a reincarnation of the American dream, the promise of advantages unknown to their predecessors and of success for themselves and their posterity. The search for gold in California became the ultimate example of economic democracy: anyone with a pick, pan, and shovel could participate, at least in the early years, regardless of wealth, social standing, education, or family name.

The Argonauts—for so they were called by a nation that still knew and valued classical references—went west for something real. Among the most astounding features of the California Gold Rush was that the most outrageous stories of wealth were true. The Golden State—it would join the Union in 1850—produced a seemingly endless flood of gold. While agricultural farm laborers earned a dollar a day for twelve hours of work in the fields, and skilled artisans and craftsmen perhaps a dollar and a half for the same hours, men who were recently farmers and mechanics made sixteen dollars a day washing gravel in the streambeds of California's Sierra foothills. In the six years from 1849 to 1855, the Argonauts harvested some three hundred million dollars in gold from California.

These are aggregate numbers. We might usefully here make reference to some individuals. In November 1847, Eddin Lewis, one of the most prominent farmers in Sangamon County, Illinois, with the help of hired laborers to whom he paid a dollar a day, butchered 255 hogs and shipped 6,000 pounds of barreled pork and lard south to the Mississippi River market early in 1848. From pork and lard, as well as from the sale of live hogs, several sides of beef, and 350 bushels of corn, Lewis recorded in his journal a cash income of over three hundred and fifty dollars for the year 1847.

In the fall of 1850, some two thousand miles to the west, C.C. Mobley noted in his diary that in the previous week he and the members of his company had averaged thirty-five dollars a day or two hundred and five dollars each for the week, and the week before, twenty-five dollars a day, or one hundred and fifty dollars each. Mobley and his companions had, in two weeks, with a pick, pan, and shovel, each made as much cash money as one of the wealthiest citizens of Sangamon County after building his farm for a generation. Mobley wrote that his fortnight's labor "was doing a fair business. I am perfectly satisfied with it at all events." He should have been. And it should not surprise us that so many attempted to emulate his example.

An Examination of National Standards and Values

During the dozen years from the discovery of gold to the secession of South Carolina and the firing on Fort Sumter, the social and economic effects of the California Gold Rush prompted an examination of national standards and values.

It posed issues of class and wealth in America's supposedly democratic and egalitarian society; it introduced questions about gender, with traditional roles and expectations for women juxtaposed against new and changing circumstances; and it quickly emphasized the presence of many different races and ethnic groups, for California, originally home to Native Americans and the Californios of Spanish and Mexican heritage, soon became the destination of peoples from across this hemisphere, Europe, and Asia.

Because the California Gold Rush was about wealth and its acquisition, it inevitably posed questions about the nature of wealth in America, how Americans acquired wealth, what they thought about wealth, and the relationship between wealth and family position. It delved into the deepest recesses of men's and women's expectations: their dreams for themselves and their families, their attitudes toward the present and past and visions of the future, and the relations of individuals to their families, their roles and responsibilities to siblings, parents, children, and spouses. This was a nation of outward democratic values that was already exhibiting signs of stratification. For many Americans, the discovery of gold in California offered the unheard-of opportunity to change their status and condition. The roster of Argonauts included men of wealth and position, who sought to buttress their status and realize advantage through investment, trade, and speculation; professional people, tradesmen, and merchants, many dogged by long-standing debts, who sought to clear their ledgers of failure and begin anew through the golden discoveries of a few months; as well as those from marginal economic backgrounds, who sought the economic advantage heretofore seemingly denied them, who with a few months' or years' work (and they were accustomed to hard work) might provide themselves and their children with the clothes, education, and privileges they never had enjoyed.

The Allure of California

The 49ers ostensibly left home to seek wealth, but behind this professed motive—scarcely anyone could object to an expedition to pick up gold nuggets—lay a wide variety of unspoken motives. For many participants, the voyage to California (whether by land or sea) was a declaration of independence. By their participation in this unique and distant adventure, they would establish their separate identities; the venture would distance them from the influence of their parents, especially in the case of younger sons, whose prospects at home were minimal and who perhaps could expect treatment in like proportion. At the same time, whatever their inner feelings or the circumstances of their partings, most 49ers displayed much concern for maintaining contact with their families and communities and for retaining the good opinion of both. One of the themes that runs through accounts of the Gold Rush is the anxiety among the 49ers over how their successes or failures would affect their reputations among their families, friends, and communities in the East.

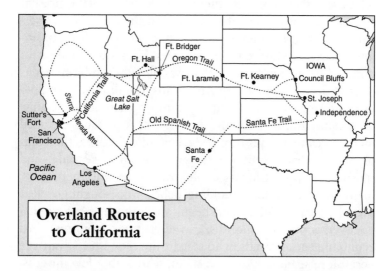

Overland Routes to California

The discovery of gold and the response to these accounts were closely linked to a place, in this case a range of foothills, with its canyons and streambeds, on the other side of the continent. The Gold Rush introduced the nation to California, a remote and exotic prize of the recent war against Mexico. Images of California now flowed with increasing frequency into the national consciousness as this distant place became the home (albeit temporarily) to members of the nation's families and communities. The news about California came initially from official sources, but over the next decade, spreading the word became the work of individual correspondents and small-town newspapers. Within a few years, Americans everywhere knew about California through the first-hand reports of their friends and neighbors.

From these many attempts to describe California emerged the shadowy outlines of a place that was at once familiar in its increasingly American institutions and presence and, at the same time, alien in terms of its physical landscape, its native peoples, its values, and its several varied societies. In these fleeting images, California emerged as a new world that simultaneously beckoned and threatened. The opportunities to make money, 49ers agreed, were beyond imagination. But the different values and the siren song of the life of the gentle climate mixed with the continuing search for riches also provoked fears. These same qualities might exert a powerful hold on the displaced Argonauts, and families and communities in the East found themselves forced to confront the increasing attractions of this remote place, even as the economic opportunities associated with it became gradually more uncertain.

After the Rush

Surrounded by opportunities to make fortunes—or so they were represented in the local press across the nation—it later became difficult for the 49ers to explain how they had squandered such golden chances. As the prospects for individuals to make substantial fortunes declined and all but disappeared with the passage of time, the search for dramatic economic advantage demanded increasing justification—to themselves, to their families, and to their communities. In the end, thousands of Argonauts soldiered on in remote gold fields in the face of repeated failures. Many returned empty-handed, others not at all. But for many, the decision to return to their families and communities became entwined with a sense of personal failure. The years that stretched out through the decade of the 1850s left the 49ers discouraged, disillusioned, embarrassed to have to admit their own shortcomings. The idea of failure and unfulfilled dreams became as much a part of the California Gold Rush as the large strikes reported in the local newspapers.

The California Gold Rush began with blazing headlines, sermons preached on the departure of companies of Argonauts, and parades to the waterfront with singing and shouting, the creak of a thousand wagons and the echoing stamp of teams of harnessed mules and oxen, all in response to a few golden flakes that emerged from the American River on a sunny and chilly January morning. It ended with a few men with long beards and brown complexions tramping down streets of towns they once knew well, with occasional accountings of money borrowed and interest paid, and finally with a deep and prolonged silence. Many never returned. They simply vanished into a California landscape once golden and now simply remote. Or the rush for gold ended with aging brothers and uncles writing from distant addresses in California, or Oregon, or Washington, sometimes with a family known only through daguerreotypes and letters, sending an annual letter to their cousins and distant kin in the East. The Gold Rush sometimes led to permanent separation and hard feelings, and almost always to a sense of loss. The older generation lamented the permanent absence of a husband or brother; the younger generation no longer recognized the names mentioned around the dining table or in the parlor on Sunday afternoons after church.

"Nothing Was Ever the Same Again"

The Gold Rush survived in the varied memories of the participants. Men and women carried vivid recollections of the California Gold Rush for the next half century. For some men, it was the most significant adventure of their lives, a moment of camaraderie and companionship, of adventure and independence, before they returned to the family, marriage, farm, trade, or commerce that dominated the rest of their lives. For some families, the memories remained bittersweet. The departure of the 49ers marked the disappearance of a beloved relative or friend, or perhaps of a whole branch of the family that went West to join a 49er. It was the symbol of permanent separation, which marked the family and community with the divisions that emerged from the Gold Rush. For many, it lingered in anniversaries of departure and return, anniversaries repeated on a larger scale within communities. A final manifestation of such nostalgia was the departure in 1890 of a chartered passenger train of some twenty cars, bound from Boston to California. There, at camp after camp, the aging 49ers revisited the scenes of their youth, when they had ranged across the Sierra in a hunt for gold, and attempted to explain to their grandchildren the experiences that bound them together with memories that only had strengthened in the intervening forty years. Matching such grand occasions were the occasional notices in papers seeking word of family and friends who long since had vanished into the haze of the golden West. Whatever the memories, the search for gold in California cast a long shadow for its participants, one that mixed vivid memories of youth with the search for fabulous wealth. Whether returned, moved permanently to California, or vanished, the 49ers, along with their families, and their communities, were not the same again. Nothing was ever the same again.

A Veritable Revolution: The Economic Significance of the California Gold Rush

Gerald D. Nash

The California Gold Rush was a turning point in the economic development of not only California, but the entire United States and even the world. In the article that follows Gerald D. Nash describes the industries in California that grew to support gold mining, as well as the demand that the gold rush created for better means of cross-country transportation, such as the transcontinental railroad. Nash notes that the outpouring of gold from California affected monetary systems worldwide, and even suggests that it stimulated Karl Marx to formulate his revolutionary theories on capitalism and communism. Nash, who died in November 2000, was a professor at the University of New Mexico and a leading scholar in the history of the American West. He wrote a dozen books in the field, the last of which is *A Brief History of the American West Since 1945*.

To many Californians the mention of January 24, 1848, conveys no special meaning, nor is that date widely commemorated in the state. Yet it has a special significance in the history of California, for on that day James Marshall, a moody carpenter from Missouri, discovered the first golden nuggets that resulted in the stampede known as the California Gold Rush. In the remoteness of Sutter's Mill, Marshall could scarcely imagine that his find would set off a succession of events that would have a far-ranging importance for California, the United States, and the world. The timing of the

From "A Veritable Revolution: The Global Economic Significance of the California Gold Rush," by Gerald D. Nash, *California History*, Winter 1998–1999. Reprinted by permission of the California Historical Society. Endnotes in the original have been omitted in this reprint.

event was crucial also because it happened when the nation was just about to feel the growing impact of the Industrial Revolution—a revolution that in the next half-century would transform the United States from an agrarian society into an industrial giant. Within this broad context the Gold Rush helped to trigger momentous economic changes. In the language of economists, it served as a multiplier—an event that accelerated a chain of interrelated consequences, all of which accelerated economic growth. In both state and nation it spurred the creation of thousands of new businesses, banks, and financial institutions. It stimulated rapid agricultural expansion, quickened the volume of trade and commerce, and created demands for new forms of transportation. Since 1848, the Gold Rush has always had a romantic aura, of course. But it should not be forgotten that it was also a major chapter in California's economic development. As one historian [Howard R. Lamar] has noted, "The American emphasis on the gold and silver rushes as adventures rather than economic industrialization stood in embarrassing contrast to the more realistic accounts of Mexican, South African, and Australian mining."

The Development of California

The Gold Rush spawned a wide range of entrepreneurial activities and led thousands of individuals in California and elsewhere to embark on new business ventures, in manufacturing as well as in service industries. Food, clothing, hardware, mining supplies, all kinds of luxuries, and steamboats for river traffic—these were only a few of the items in great demand, and ambitious men and women scurried to provide them. When mining machinery came to be in short supply, newcomers in less than a decade created an iron industry in northern California. There they manufactured stamp mills, steam engines, and nozzles for hydraulic operations. Already by 1861 more than a thousand workers in San Francisco toiled in the manufacture of mining equipment. The city boasted thirteen iron foundries and thirty machine shops. Twenty-three other foundries operated in other parts of the state. Mining also required many auxiliary operations in need of explosives, and as early as 1855 newcomers to California had built two powder works, reducing the need for imports from the East.

Gold mining stimulated other industries as well. It created an enormous demand for lumber, not only for housing, but for mine shafts and tunnels. Within a decade Mendocino and Humboldt counties were producing thirty-five million board-feet annually. California also quickly established itself as one of the most important flour-milling states in the Union. In 1848, California had no commercial flour mills to speak of; but by 1860 two hundred flour mills were operating, supplying not only local demand, but exporting large quantities to the entire Rocky Mountain region, and also to China, Japan, Great Britain, and parts of Europe.

The decade after the Gold Rush was an opportune time for wagon and carriage makers. Among the ablest was a young newcomer from the Middle West who made a name for himself very quickly in Placerville. After making his fortune in pioneer California, John Studebaker eventually returned to Indiana. At the turn of the century he became one of the most important automobile manufacturers in the nation—with capital he had amassed during California's pioneer era.

The state's rapid population increase generated a seemingly unlimited demand for clothing, which local enterprisers quickly filled. Within a decade the Mission Woolen Mills became one of the largest in the West. Levi Strauss, one of the most imaginative clothing manufacturers in San Francisco, had great success when he developed blue jeans, a garment particularly well suited for miners and workmen in the 1850s—and generations of other people in succeeding years. Since there was a large number of cattle in California, development of a leather industry in a very short time was eminently feasible. By 1860 the fabrication of boots, harnesses, saddles, and belts for machines was well established.

Retail trade flourished under the conditions stimulated by the Gold Rush. Creation of instant markets with tens of thousands of eager consumers fostered a wide range of wholesale and retail establishments catering to miners. John Bidwell, Alonzo Delano, and Charles M. Weber were some of the merchants who quickly became highly respected citizens and powerful political leaders in the California of the 1850s. Collis P. Huntington, later a railroad tycoon, laid the basis for his fortune in the wholesale trade in Sacramento. He and his partner, Mark Hopkins, began by building the largest wholesale and retail hardware store there and one of the biggest in the entire West. In later years these men branched out to organize the Central Pacific Railroad, which they justly viewed as a key to further expansion of the economy.

A Major Stimulant to Agricultural Development

Without a doubt, the Gold Rush was the major stimulant of California agriculture in the 1850s. Certainly farming was hardly less significant than gold mining in laying the foundations of California's new economy. Often, when individuals did not succeed in mining they turned to agriculture. Thousands became small farmers, viticulturists, fruit growers, and dairy farmers. Others became sheep and cattle raisers who found lucrative markers not only in California, but up and down the Pacific Coast. The Gold Rush was not merely a local economic event. California's products found their way to the Pacific Rim as well. The Gold Rush coincided with the opening of Japan to trade by Commodore Matthew Perry in 1853, and California benefited more from these contacts than any other American state. Commercial relations with China expanded also as a result of aggressive efforts by San Francisco merchants. They found that California farm products enjoyed considerable success in Asia, as did beef and mutton. By 1860, Henry Miller, a German immigrant, had become the largest rancher in the state, with more than three million head of cattle. And the one million sheep reported in that year outnumbered the state's inhabitants.

In just a few years after the first gold discoveries California became one of the most productive grain producers in the nation. Stimulated by the population surge prompted by the Gold Rush, thousands of newcomers became wheat farmers, especially in the San Joaquin and Sacramento valleys, where the soil was well suited for grain culture. The Gold Rush occurred at a most propitious moment for Cali-

fornia wheat culture. The ships that brought the gold seekers to the Pacific Coast often sailed back to Atlantic ports
without substantial cargo. With the development of wheat
farming, these empty vessels were able to take on bulky grain
shipments, giving Californians access to East Coast, British,
and continental European markets. Moreover, the Gold
Rush had a dynamic impact on the state's agriculture because
it coincided with revolutionary technological advances in the
1850s. Cyrus McCormick had just developed his reaper, a
machine that greatly reduced the need for hand labor and did
much to increase productivity. Since California during the
Gold Rush had a chronic labor shortage, such a labor-saving
device was particularly important in boosting production.
Moreover, the vast open stretches of virgin land in the San
Joaquin Valley were extremely well suited to the development of mechanized farming. In some ways, McCormick can
be considered as one of the fathers of mechanized agriculture
in California during the gold-rush era and even in succeeding years. In 1850, relying on crude, labor-intensive methods, California farmers produced just seventeen thousand
bushels of wheat; ten years later their total was sixteen million bushels. Technology and commercial conditions combined to make wheat no less profitable than gold.

The population drawn by the Gold Rush created exciting
new markets for California farmers. Climate and soil aided
them in quickly developing a wide range of crops. In the
1850s Californians grew apples and oranges, peaches and
plums, cherries and figs, among a wide range of new varieties.
In only a few years California was well on the way to becoming the fruit basket of the nation. At the same time, new
farmers were producing impressive quantities of vegetables,
from corn to carrots, squash, and potatoes. Since the growing season was much longer than in the East, the output of
California's farmers was prodigious, and very profitable. . . .

Obstacles to Growth

The growth of mining, business, and agriculture stimulated
the establishment of banks and financial institutions. Such
expansion was slow in the 1850s only because the California

Constitution of 1849 prohibited the creation of commercial banks. The prohibition received widespread support because members of the constitutional convention clearly remembered the Panic of 1837, which, rightly or wrongly, they attributed to the lax issuance of unbacked paper money by banks. Before 1849 California had had no banks, but the Gold Rush created new needs. Miners required places of safekeeping for their gold, and individuals desired banks to

---

The Economic Cost of the Gold Rush

From the vantage of the sesquicentennial of the California gold rush, historians now realize that, although people at the time could hardly have grasped the idea, the nation had entered a new era. With the California gold rush Americans began for the first time large-scale exploitation of finite non-renewable resources. . . .

Since Europeans founded colonies in the Americas, they believed that the New World continents constituted a vast and inexhaustible commons, endless like their image of the sea.

Gold, however, taught a new lesson. The mineral wealth of the United States was not infinite. Minerals and carbons once taken from the ground do not replenish themselves. They are not renewable resources.

In fact, the very soil itself could be so degraded by the mining process that it could be moribund for centuries to come. The industrial era and the discovery of gold came almost simultaneously. Both produced a lasting legacy. In celebrating and taking stock of the impact of the rush for mineral wealth that began in 1848, neither historians nor the general public should lose sight of the economic, environmental, and social cost of extracting nonrenewable resources. The California gold rush cast a long shadow. What once seemed merely another example of America's limitless good luck in finding wealth proved, in the long run, to be just the opposite. It was the first signal of a future when one kind of luck would run out.

Martin Ridge, *Montana*, Autumn 1999.

transfer money. Furthermore, the increasing number of business establishments involved in trade and commerce looked for banks to execute their transactions. Initially, eastern banks established branches to provide such services, Wells Fargo among the most prominent. By the late 1850s Californians were also providing capital to develop mining throughout the West, including Oregon, Idaho, Arizona, and Colorado, but most importantly for the rich silver mines on the Comstock Lode in Nevada. Californians organized hundreds of stock companies to finance such ventures. The lure of greater profits led one of the most powerful financiers, Sam Brannan, to lobby the California legislature for the removal of the constitutional prohibitions on commercial banking. Finally, in 1862, the lawmakers authorized the establishment of state-chartered savings banks; two years later they allowed commercial banking. As the Civil War further fueled an economic boom, scores of new bankers appeared. One of the most important was William Ralston, who in 1864 organized the Bank of California. Along with William Sharon, his manager in Nevada, Ralston became the dominant presence on the Comstock Lode. The bank financed not only the major mining ventures there, but provided capital for new railroads, steamship lines, water companies, hotels, and a wide range of service industries, even including cemeteries. Few examples better illustrated the multiplier effect of the Gold Rush than the California banks that spawned a large number of new enterprises that built an intricate economic structure in the state.

In that structure, transportation played a dominant role, and the Gold Rush did much to underscore its importance. No other event so dramatized California's geographical isolation. From the beginning, the Argonauts scrambling to reach the gold fields encountered arduous difficulties. Whether they came by ship around the Horn, or sailed to Central America and then made their way across the disease-ridden Isthmus of Panama, or whether they came by land across the prairies in covered wagons, the journey was an ordeal. Those who survived the trek were especially eager to link California more closely to the rest of the nation, as were business people in the East. In the minds of most Californians, and many Americans, transportation held the key to a blossoming of the state's economy.

The Transcontinental Railroad and the Panama Canal

Between 1848 and 1862 Californians experimented with various ways to end their isolation. They tried wagon trains over the Sierra and coastal steamers along the Pacific Coast, and petitioned Congress to appropriate moneys for a transcontinental highway from Missouri to the West Coast. Seventy-five thousand people signed this petition, fully one-half of the state's population. Yielding to such pressure, Congress in 1856 appropriated $500,000 for a road to stretch from Missouri to Carson City, Nevada. Work was completed in September 1858 and almost immediately John Butterfield secured a federal contract for carrying the mails. He also promised passengers that he would deliver them to western destinations in twenty-five days or less. But neither the stage line, nor the Pony Express, nor the transcontinental telegraph lessened the desire for a railroad in the minds of most Americans.

Support for the building of a transcontinental railroad gathered additional momentum with the outbreak of the Civil War, which underscored California's isolation. In California the project was most ardently promoted by Theodore Judah, a young engineer who had come from Connecticut in 1854 to work on the Sacramento Valley Railroad. Unable to raise the capital needed for the enterprise in San Francisco, he made the rounds of wealthy individuals in Sacramento. In 1860 he approached Collis P. Huntington and his hardware store partner Mark Hopkins, as well as other successful merchants such as Leland Stanford and Charles Crocker. Each agreed to provide about $20,000 for experimental surveys of routes across the Sierra. In June of 1861 the five men incorporated the Central Pacific Railroad. Such a vast undertaking could not be accomplished solely by private enterprise, however, and a few months later Judah and Huntington journeyed to Washington, D.C., to lobby for federal aid.

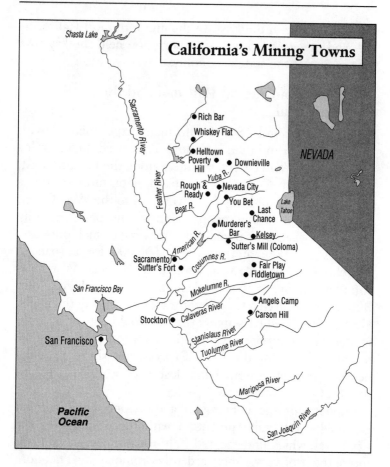

California's Mining Towns

Shasta Lake

Sacramento River

Feather River

Yuba R.

Bear R.

American R.

Cosumnes R.

Mokelumne R.

Calaveras River

Stanislaus River

Tuolumne River

Mariposa River

San Joaquin River

NEVADA

Lake Tahoe

Rich Bar

Whiskey Flat

Helltown

Poverty Hill

Downieville

Rough & Ready

Nevada City

You Bet

Last Chance

Murderer's Bar

Kelsey

Sutter's Mill (Coloma)

Sacramento

Sutter's Fort

Fair Play

Fiddletown

Angels Camp

Carson Hill

Stockton

San Francisco Bay

San Francisco

Pacific Ocean

Within a year, the wartime Congress, in part responding to Judah and Huntington's political pressure, enacted the Pacific Railroad Act of 1862, which granted lands and loans to the company and the Union Pacific Railroad so that the work could begin. Although the transcontinental railway was not completed until 1869, after 1862 the end of California's geographical isolation was in sight. The Gold Rush had hastened removal of yet another obstacle to California's dramatic economic growth.

The population surge prompted by the gold discoveries also stimulated the building of a canal across the Isthmus of Panama. Between 1848 and 1869 tens of thousands of people headed for California across that once-remote area.

The sudden influx brought new economic opportunities for some of the region's inhabitants. It also fostered a considerable increase in prices for many goods, benefiting some and injuring others. This influx of tourists prompted a group of American investors to build the Panama Railroad across the isthmus. Although it was only 47.5 miles long, the difficult terrain slowed construction, and it was not until 1855 that the line became operational. But the influence of the Gold Rush on transportation development did not end with the Panama Railroad. The project fixed the dream of a transisthmian canal firmly in the minds of many Americans of that generation. The dream persisted so vigorously that the building of the Panama Canal between 1880 and 1914 was in a very real sense a consequence of the California Gold Rush of 1849. . . .

Worldwide Ramifications

The Gold Rush and the resulting increase of gold in circulation contributed to higher price levels throughout the world. In the decade before 1848, prices had declined in developed nations. The tight money policies of the Bank of England and also the Bank of France had contributed to this decline and led to a shortage of specie. California's gold production changed that situation and precipitated the rise in wholesale and commodity prices. The effects in the United States were also notable. No longer did the nation have to depend mainly on capital brought by immigrants, or produced by imports. Instead, the coinage of gold increased the amount of money in circulation and produced a favorable trade balance for the United States. . . .

In many ways, the California Gold Rush precipitated a veritable economic revolution in the state, the nation, and the world. Production of precious metals affected price levels, labor, wages, capital investment, the expansion of business, finance, agriculture, service industries, and transportation. True, the California experience was not entirely unique. Precious metals had influenced the course of civilizations for thousands of years before 1848. When Emile Le Vasseur, the great French economist, in 1858 traced the historical relationship between the value of gold and the value of commodities, he identified fourteen major revolutions in world history, of which the California Gold Rush was the last in his lifetime. Many of his views were shared by his contemporary, Karl Marx, who just one year later declared that his observations on capitalism were made in direct response to the gold discoveries in California. As Marx wrote in 1859, "The enormous material on the history of political economy which is accumulated in the British Museum; the favourable view which London offers for the observation of bourgeois society; finally, the new stage of development upon which the latter seems to have entered with the discovery of gold in California and Australia led me to the decision to resume my studies from the very beginning and work up critically the new material." Those studies were soon to culminate in *Das Kapital*, a revolutionary book stimulated by the gold discoveries of the 1850s. . . .

In the final analysis, it might be said that the economic significance of the Gold Rush can also be understood in a psychological and philosophical context. As the French philosopher Michel Foucault once wrote, "the signs of exchange, because they satisfy desire, are sustained by the dark, dangerous and accursed glitter of metal. An unequivocal glitter, for it reproduces in the depths of the earth that other glitter that sings at the far end of the night; it resides there like an inverted promise of happiness, and because metal resembles the stars, the knowledge of all these perilous treasures is at the same time knowledge of the world." Thus, the economic impact of the Gold Rush is rooted as much in emotions as in rational behavior. It touched a deep-seated nerve in the human psyche. Consequently, it had a profound influence not only on contemporaries, but on later generations, and is bound to exercise a continuing fascination in the future.

The Gold Rush as Melting Pot

Walter Nugent

In the span of just a few years, the Gold Rush transformed California frontier society. Immigrants from around the globe were drawn to California's booming economy, and the ethnic and racial diversity that resulted remains a part of California culture today. Walter Nugent, a former professor of history who has taught at the University of Notre Dame and Indiana University, describes the many groups that came to California after 1849 and one that was forced out: the California Indians, who were driven out of their native lands to make way for white settlers. The following essay is excerpted from Nugent's book *Into the West: The Story of Its People*.

California's ethnic and racial diversity was already high in 1849 and has remained so ever since. Its 38.5 percent foreign-born in 1860 came from several dozen countries, with China (34,935) and Ireland (33,147) followed by Germany (20,919), England-Wales-Scotland (17,262), and Mexico (9,150). Among them also lived 8,000 French, 5,000 Canadians, 5,000 African-Americans, 3,000 Italians, and others. Irish and Chinese remained the two largest foreign-born groups forty years later, ahead of Germans, British, Canadians, and Mexicans. The proportion of foreign-born in California in 1860 was three times the United States' 13 percent. The gap narrowed a little but always remained wide; in 1910, when the national foreign-born population reached its all-time peak at 14.7 percent, California's was still 24.6 percent.

Being early on the ground helped many groups get along. Although California has always had its nativists, it also has included enough Irish, Jews, and Italians since Gold Rush

From *Into the West: The Story of Its People*, by Walter Nugent. Copyright © 1999 by Walter T.K. Nugent. Used by permission of Alfred A. Knopf, a division of Random House, Inc.

days to integrate these Europeans much better into main-stream economic and cultural life than east of the Mississippi, where they arrived relatively late. Contrast, for example, the early success of the Irish in northern California with the "No Irish need apply" nativism of New England in those same 1850s.

The Chinese in California

Nonwhites, however, were ghettoized early. The several thousand blacks in California in 1852 were all free, some operating businesses, churches, and a newspaper. But they were excluded from juries, voting, homesteading, and inter-marrying. The large Chinese population also found that early settlement in no way helped them. Migration to California, the *Gum Saan* or Gold Mountain, was a small part of a much larger relocation from southeastern China in the mid– and late–nineteenth century to Southeast Asia, the western Pacific, and beyond. Those who went to California came from a few districts around the Pearl River delta in Guangdong and Fujian provinces in the south, not from a broad cross section of China. Most sailed with the Pacific Mail Steamship Company from Hong Kong to San Francisco (clipper ships to the late 1860s, then steamships), paying a hefty fifty dollars for the four- to five-week voyage. By 1850 a few Chinese merchants had appeared. Large-scale migration—20,000—began in 1852. The number fluctuated greatly over the next thirty years, until the Chinese Exclusion Act of 1882 cut off most of the traffic. By that time around 136,000 Chinese (the most until well into the twentieth century) lived in the United States: 90 percent in the West, 68 percent in California.

The Chinese usually arrived as contract laborers. They worked first in the mining counties of the Sierras, more often in service trades than as miners, then in railroad building, in construction work, and by the 1870s and 1880s in all sorts of occupations and at every level from owner-operators to tenant farmers to wage laborers. The 1882 Exclusion Act and its successors, together with male skewedness, gradually reduced their bachelor society to a low of 29,000 Chinese-born Californians by 1920, less than 1 percent of the state population compared with over 9 percent in 1860. . . .

Irish Catholics

The Irish migrants to California included more men than women, but in much closer balance than the Chinese. The very poorest Irish could not go anywhere, and more than a million starved at home in the Great Famine of the late 1840s. Those with a little land to sell, or a trade to practice, were able to buy passage and sail to some port between Quebec and Baltimore and then drift west. Others came by way of Australia. . . .

By 1859 San Francisco and the northern California Gold Rush region included a hundred thousand Catholics, most of them Irish, served by fifty-seven churches and sixty priests. Irish nuns of the Presentation order and Sisters of Mercy began operating hospitals and schools in San Francisco in 1854, and in 1863 the Mercy Sisters arrived in Grass Valley to teach school and "to establish an orphanage for the children of the miners who were killed in the accidents which occurred so frequently." In 1860 Eugene O'Connell, head of All Hallows College in Dublin, became vicar apostolic of the territory, which included the Sacramento Valley and western Nevada. He found plenty of work. One-third of the population, O'Connell reported to Rome in 1866 and 1871, was Catholic: seven thousand in Virginia City and an equal number in the Sacramento Valley. Though population stabilized in the Gold Rush area, it exploded on the other side of the Sierras when the Comstock Lode opened in 1859. O'Connell's priests, parishes, and people expanded fourfold during the 1860s, and by 1871 five congregations of nuns were teaching school and caring for the sick and orphaned.

Jews in Northern California

Jews appeared in northern California from 1849 on, enough to establish themselves in Sacramento, San Francisco, the mother lode towns in the Sierras, and Humboldt, Shasta, and Siskiyou counties close by Oregon. In 1849 and 1850 the Edinburgh-born Gabriel McCohen helped organize the

Hebrew Benevolent Society and raised funds for a Jewish cemetery in San Francisco. Moses Hyman's home in Sacramento hosted High Holy Day services by 1850, and the first

The Removal of the California Indians: A Record of Brutality

Adding greatly to native suffering was the "Act for the Government and Protection of Indians," passed by the legislature in 1850, which, as historian Albert Hurtado puts it, "protected them very little and governed them quite a lot." The pretense was that the law provided a way of disciplining dangerous Indian vagrants and caring for dependent Indian orphans, but in fact, under its cover of legality, thousands of Indian men, women, and children were kidnapped and sold to Anglo and Mexican employers. . . .

The conclusion of anthropologists Robert Heizer and Alan Almquist is admirably candid: "This was a legalized form of slavery of California Indians. No other possible construction can be made of the facts."

As a result of the genocidal violence, the forced labor, and the inevitable epidemics of disease, the Indian population of California, estimated at 150,000 in 1848, had fallen to only 30,000 by 1860: 120,000 lives lost in just twelve years, a record of brutality without parallel in the history of the United States. A minority of the remaining natives lived in isolated rancheritas, but most clustered in dingy shanties on the outskirts of towns like San Jose or Los Angeles, eking out a livelihood as cheap day laborers. It wasn't until the mid–twentieth century that California Indians used the courts to obtain compensation for the lands stolen from them during the gold rush, but the final awards totaled less than a thousand dollars per person. This settlement brings to mind the comment of Bartolomé de Las Casas when he learned of the official Spanish policy of offering Indians conversion before attacking their villages: one doesn't know whether to laugh or to weep.

Robert V. Hine and John Mack Faragher, *The American West: A New Interpretive History*, 2000.

synagogue in the Far West was dedicated there in 1852. In Mokelumne Hill, Jewish women had formed a Hebrew Ladies Benevolent Society in 1860, by which time scores of Jews were carrying on community life in many places and were already numerous enough to splinter into Polish or German, Orthodox or Reform, or Sephardi congregations. Cauffman Mayer wrote from San Francisco in 1853 that fifty families observed Pesach (Passover) that spring. McCohen's society in 1854 sponsored a Purim ball that "about 200" ladies attended, and so many people observed Pesach the next month that "one man has sold $160 worth of horserad-ish" for the seder. . . .

Jewish charities and commerce also flourished in San Francisco by the end of the 1850s. Some Jews joined the Gold Rush as miners, but more typically they served San Francisco, Sacramento, and the mining towns as clothing and dry goods merchants, jewelers and watch repairers, and manufacturers. The most famously successful Jewish entre-preneur in the Gold Rush, Levi Strauss, had arrived from Bavaria in 1850, aged twenty, with "a considerable stock of merchandise," including duck and denim cloth. By 1853 he and his two brothers in New York had formed Levi Strauss Work Clothes. It prospered even before he began copper riveting the pockets of blue denim work pants in the late 1860s; from that point Levi's achieved worldwide success and many imitators.

A Mix of Europeans

The ethnic mix of San Francisco and the Gold Rush region was as rich as a tub of cioppino, the local bouillabaisse. "Syd-ney Ducks" from Australia transferred the skills they learned in the Victoria goldfields to the mother lode. The French government ran a lottery to pay for emigration to California, and it may have sent as many as three thousand people. More than six thousand Germans had populated San Fran-cisco by 1860, many after paying the Hamburg-America line's one-way fare of eighty-two dollars. In 1851 the local Germans organized the Pacific Ocean Singers (*die Sänger an Stillen Meer*), and in 1852 they formed the San Francisco

Turnverein. Newspapers and a German-language hospital followed, as did other accoutrements of German-American life similar to those in places like Cincinnati or Chicago: breweries, restaurants, saloons, churches, musical groups, and benevolent societies.

Italians had cut a *bella figura* in northern California ever since a few Genoese settled in San Francisco's North Beach, then "the Latin Quarter." Northern Italians continued to arrive, to become commercial fishermen at nearby Fisherman's Wharf. Some came to prospect for gold, but others brought enough capital to start small businesses, thus becoming part of the establishment, such as it was, in the city's first American decade. Spectacular successes in the twentieth century, such as Amadeo Pietro Giannini's Bank of America and the great wineries like Gallo and food concerns like Del Monte, should not distort the fact that most Italian migrants were fishermen, farmers, small tradesmen, or laborers. . . .

The Gold Rush and California Indians

Conspicuously missing from the ethnic and racial groups that participated in the Gold Rush were Hispanics and Indians. The Spanish presence was never strong north of Monterey and increased little. As for the California Indians, the Gold Rush has been accurately called a disaster for them. They virtually disappeared from the Bay Area and the mother lode country. What happened to them? At first (1848) several thousand were recruited or forced into mining, while others (especially in the mountains north of the Sacramento Valley) managed to trade with whites and continue tribal life for a time. But white numbers and aggressiveness defeated them. By late 1849, writes [historian Malcolm J.] Rohrbough, "they largely had disappeared from the gold camps, and the influx of gold seekers (many of them also hunters) had devastated their fragile economic base. In the [hard] winter of 1849–50 . . . their isolated raids in search of subsistence aroused the fury of the Americans [who] organized a series of raids against [them] in the mountains." After California became a state in 1850, Anglo-American ranchers and settlers pressured the U.S. Army and formed volunteer militias to attack and kill Indians or press them into indentured servitude, as state law permitted. Miners [writes historian Albert Hurtado] "vehemently and brutally objected to competition from cheap Indian labor," state government responded to white citizens, and through the 1850s Indians went unprotected. The belief that Indians should be removed so that the land could be put to better use justified an ethnic cleansing in California no less complete than in the valleys of the Ohio and the Mississippi a generation or two earlier. The Indians of California, as a result of Gold Rush demographic change, experienced disease, economic deprivation, enslavement, and outright massacre, retail or wholesale.

The Colorado Gold Rush and the Reimagining of America

Elliot West

Elliot West is a history professor at the University of Arkansas and the author of *The Contested Plains: Indians, Goldseekers, and the Rush to Colorado*. He describes in the article below how the California gold rush transformed the Pacific Coast in the minds of Easterners. Before 1849, the region had been viewed as a far-off, exotic frontier. Two years after the discovery of gold at Sutter's Mill in 1848, California was seen as the land of plenty, and it was made a U.S. state in the process. A similar process, writes West, transformed the popular perception of the Midwest in the 1850s and 1860s. The Great Plains and the Rocky Mountains had been viewed as barren, inhospitable regions before the 1858 discovery of gold just west of what is now Denver. As with California, the Colorado gold rush attracted farmers and merchants as well as miners, and very soon the region became much more than just a gap between the Atlantic and Pacific coasts.

In the eve of the Civil War, America had a hole right in the middle of it. Not an actual pit, of course; no one riding west from Kansas City would have tripped and fallen into an abyss. The hole was in America as it existed in millions of minds. People in the eastern and far western United States pictured the country between them as detached, physically and historically. Plains and mountains seemed to have no part in what America was and would be.

That hole began suddenly to fill on July 6, 1858, the day a party of thirteen prospectors found gold dust in a small

Reprinted by permission of the Montana Historical Society from "Golden Dreams: Colorado, California, and the Reimagining of America," by Elliot West, *Montana: The Magazine of Western History*, Autumn 1999. Copyright © 1999 by the Montana Historical Society. Footnotes in the original have been omitted in this reprint.

creek flowing from the Front Range of the Rocky Mountains. The next spring a stampede to the diggings had an economic and environmental impact that was enormous and obvious.

Another change was easier to miss. The Colorado gold rush was a key moment in American mental geography. With its sister episode, the discovery of California gold, it reshaped the nation's perception of itself. During the middle years of the nineteenth century, the republic changed in size, purpose, and values. The two gold rushes helped knit its parts into a newly imagined union—sure in its blessings, imperial in vision, blindly arrogant, naively confident of a future of untarnishable luster.

The Great American Desert

The momentous shift in America's self-image began during the tumultuous 1840s. The decade opened with the nation two-thirds the present size of the lower forty-eight states. Its western border lay against Texas and along the crest of the Rocky Mountains, on the far western edges of the Great Plains. The image of that borderland was vague and unpromising. Occasionally it was called the "Great American Desert" but most often the "prairies" and the "plains." The public understood those terms to mean great grasslands, windswept and rolling. It was well known that this country hosted lots of wild game, but the image was of open and exposed landscape, mostly treeless and covered with short, wispy vegetation. It was interesting, but in a Mongolian sort of way.

In any case, it was obvious what this country was *not*. It had no place in the nation's ideas of future greatness. By the 1840s the early republican dream of agrarian abundance had merged with two others: hopes for a modest but vibrant industry; and a vigorous commerce sending the fruits of garden and factory out to the world. In those terms the plains and the mountain fringe were next to useless. At best this country was a possible pasture, but as a future domain of full harvests, bustling market towns, and the occasional metropolis, it seemed a bum bet.

But in 1840 that was no problem. The plains were out there on the farthest edge of things. In fact, some thought the border's unpromising strangeness would serve us well. Zebulon Pike, the first agent of the United States to describe the region as desert and steppes, thought that overly restless Americans, "so prone to rambling and extending themselves on frontiers," would finally stop their wasteful ways and live by proper husbandry once they faced this vast expanse fit only for herds of game and tribes of "wandering and uncivilized aborigines." The plains and mountain front, then, were the republic's outer edge in a double sense. Geographically, this was our western boundary; mentally, it was the place where the vision of abundance and purpose weakened and faded toward nothing.

Then suddenly the national map was dramatically redrawn. In three great gulps—the annexation of Texas, the granting of the far Northwest from England, and the seizure of California and the Southwest in the Mexican War—more land was acquired than in any other previous act, including the Louisiana Purchase. Almost overnight America became a transcontinental, dual-oceanic nation. In 1844 our size was impressive. In 1848 it was imperial.

The California Gold Rush

Next came arguably the most stunning coincidence in American history. At exactly the moment of the last act of expansion, just nine days before the treaty was initialed ending the Mexican War, James Marshall found those famous glittering flecks in the American River in northern California. "Boys, I believe I have found a gold mine," he announced. He was right, and within a few years tens of thousands more came looking for theirs, first from other parts of the Pacific Coast, then from South America, the Sandwich Islands, Canton, and Australia, then from Europe and elsewhere in the United States. It was history on fast-forward: dozens of towns within a few months, a port rivaling most in the mercantile world, an explosive economy rapidly diversifying.

These two developments—expansion to the Pacific and the discovery of gold—reshaped fundamentally the nation's image of itself and its future. The ballyhoo and chest-puffing that followed was as much about what would be done with these western possessions as about their size and expanse. This new territory, many said, brimmed with the raw stuff of our old agricultural vision. "Shall this garden of beauty . . . lie dormant in its wild and useless luxuriance?" asked an Illinois editor. The question was rhetorical, but many answered anyway that California's broad valleys and the wide embrace of Texas held fabulous fresh potential for America as a prolific garden, "not [only] for our own use," New York Democrats assured their supporters, "but for the use of man."

The coincidence of gold, however, brought out and amplified the newer motifs of the national vision. Gold summoned images of bustling, productive cities and far-reaching commerce. The spirit of gold seeking—its plunging optimism and mix of labor and luck—fit the values of an urban speculative culture far better than the earlier rural faith in thrift, steady sweat, and plod. Gold was "the motive power which will put in operation the already-prepared vast machinery of American enterprise," a memorial of California citizens declared early in 1849. It was "but a means of accelerating the march to national supremacy." Congressman John McClernand (D-Illinois) predicted that the new country's resources, "trophies of a just and brilliant war," would soon birth a great city beside San Francisco Bay, bind Europe to Asia with thriving commerce, and inspire a railroad linking the Atlantic and Pacific. The *American Review* added soon afterwards that gold "contains the elements, the principles, the forces" to establish "a great American epoch in the history of the world. . . . The acquisition of these territories on the Pacific, seems destined to make our country the world's historical center."

Coast would be bound to coast, trade to mines and factories. Cities and farms, east and west, would be woven into a grand continental enterprise. A strong racist undertone ran through this vision. Current residents of the western empire, Native American primitives and Hispanics sunk in "voluptuous pride" and "inglorious ease," had neither the eyes to see the land's promise nor the will to fulfill it, according to the new prophets. An Illinois editor wrote that these lesser peoples were "reptiles [who must] either crawl [away] or be crushed." First conquest, then the earth's sudden gift of its most precious resource: the way was open for the full flower of national destiny. America would be the golden land in truth as well as metaphor.

"A Great Disconnecting Wilderness"

But there was a problem. The grand vision of farms, manufacturing, and trade had been applied to the country east of the Missouri, and now it was projected westward to the Pacific Coast. But what about the country in between? It remained apparently useless. The plains and mountains were no longer our western fringe, however. They were the American center. The vision of national destiny reached out *over* the continent, but it did not yet *cover* the continent. To the contrary. The heart of the expanded nation seemed to have nothing much to do with anything. As the former mountain man and . . . Indian agent Thomas Fitzpatrick put it, there was "a great disconnecting wilderness" at the nation's center. America, that is, had a hole right in the middle of it.

Travelers crossing from the imagined land of plenty in the east to the other on the Pacific called the plains "a dreary waste as far as the eye can reach," a "barren, trackless waste . . . an expanse of hot, bare sand," a bleak landscape that "equals any other scene on our continent for desolation." An overlander in the late 1850s thought the plains had only one useful function—erosion: "It looks as if the great Creator has made this vast desert as a sort of storehouse of materials from which he is day by day transporting them to other regions, where they can be made more available for the use and to the benefit of man."

True, there were occasional wild and exotic sights—bison and antelope, spectacular storms, mirages, and the Plains Indians, who, travelers believed, always threatened to attack or rob them. But mostly travelers were oppressed by what one called "so much sameness." The rolling, unbroken openness reminded many immigrants of the high seas. The plains were "an ocean of land, the same day in and day out," Tom Sanders remembered. An army unit traveled four days through a tree-less stretch of eastern Colorado. When a line of streamside cottonwoods finally appeared on the horizon, an Irish private called out: "Be Jesus! We're in sight of land again!"

The comparison went beyond appearance. On the plains, as at sea, people might find high adventure, or see schools of playful bison frolicking in the grassy waves, or meet those col-

---

Mining Strikes Throughout the West

California is counted as the first of the great mining rushes of the nineteenth century, but the little-known Georgia gold rush of 1829 actually prefigured it. Thousands of miners clamored into the foothills of the southern Appalachians, extracting as much as ten million dollars in gold and pushing the Cherokees off their homeland. Shockingly disorderly mining towns appeared overnight. One miner wrote home of "gambling houses, dancing houses, drinking saloons, houses of ill fame, billiard saloons, and tenpin alleys that were open day and night." Yet within a couple of years, mining companies had consolidated most individual claims, and the men who remained working in the diggings were toiling for wages. What happened in Georgia was a preview in miniature of what would happen in the Golden State, as well as dozens of other mining strikes throughout the West. . . .

From California, prospectors spread out across the mountains and deserts, making a series of strikes that spawned a seemingly endless round of rushes: to the Fraser River in British Columbia in 1858; the Colorado Rockies west of the emerging city of Denver and the Washoe country of Nevada in 1859; Idaho and Montana in 1860 and 1862; the Black Hills of the Dakotas in 1876; Leadville, Colorado, and Tombstone, Arizona, in 1877; the Coeur d'Alene region of Idaho in 1883; and, closing out the era, the northern Yukon country of Canada in 1896–97, which quickly spread to Nome and Fairbanks, Alaska.

Robert V. Hine and John Mack Faragher, *The American West: A New Interpretive History*, 2000.

orful but threatening land pirates, the Pawnees and Sioux. But for anyone hoping to move west, the Great Plains and Rockies comprised an alien place with no more promise than the middle of an ocean as somewhere to stop, start a farm, or plant a town. Like the sea, this country was something to get across.

Once again, however, mental geography was about to change. Only a generation into the future the American center would be pictured as the heartland of national hope, a region of bursting fields and prospering communities offering all we needed to confirm our destiny as a great and powerful people. The shift, one of the most sweeping in our history, was a startling reprise of the recent transformation of the Pacific Coast. As in California, the central moment came as a flash of light in a mountain stream.

The Agrarian Dream

The change began, however, in that straggling line of Missouri River towns along the eastern edge of the plains—Kansas City and Westport, Leavenworth, Atchison, St. Joseph, and a few others. In 1850 these communities considered themselves ports o'call where overland travelers could outfit themselves for the long voyages across the inland sea of land to the Pacific settlements. But as farmers moved into eastern Kansas the towns also became market centers for those lovely prairies in the first thirty or so miles beyond the Missouri. In a classic promotional impulse, civic leaders soon pushed outward the imagined zone of cultivation. If corn was harvested thirty miles west of Leavenworth, why not fifty? If the land had been cropped around Lawrence, why not around Topeka, and fifty, eighty, a hundred miles farther on?

By 1855 this creeping boosterism had pushed the agrarian dream well past the middle of present-day Kansas. Flattering military reports of the far eastern plains were projected onto a much wider region, so land considerably west of the ninety-eighth meridian was pictured as well watered and nicely timbered. Everyone understood that living well on the plains depended on rivers, the larger and more reliable the better. Now one booster wrote that the Arkansas rose in Utah, cut all the way through the Rockies, and flowed vigorously across the plains, "watering and fertilizing the valleys through which it meanders." The Smoky Hill and Republican rivers, which in fact rose on the plains near the present Kansas-Colorado border, more than a hundred miles east of the Front Range, also were said to begin "far up among the Rocky Mountains" and tumble to the Missouri through banks thick with timber: oaks six feet through the trunk, elms, sycamores, walnut, cherry, and beech.

Farmers tilling the "rich, black vegetable mould" would send their bounty to market via steamboats that would ascend these rivers for hundreds of miles, according to promoters. One provided a map predicting regular steamboat traffic from the Atlantic coast to the base of the Rockies, near what is today Denver. Railroad companies joined the chorus. As they built toward the Missouri Valley they looked ahead hungrily to an inland empire full of farmers shipping their crops back east. A pamphlet for the Hannibal and St. Joseph Railroad, first to reach the Missouri, crowed about the grand possibilities of western Kansas: "As the whale remarked to Jonah, 'I deem it a good opening for a young man.'"

By the late 1850s dream-chasers could stand in the Missouri Valley and imagine the great American garden reaching out to some indefinite point to the west. Nonetheless, the process was almost all puff and blow. Or, as one writer admitted, no "foot-prints" of civilization were yet imprinted on most of the plains.

The Colorado Gold Rush

Then came the moment that sent this change rocketing forward. In summer 1858 William Green Russell, a Georgian with experience in the California diggings, led a party to pursue long-standing rumors of gold in the eastern Rockies. Word of their modest find on July 6 filtered out to Kansas City and arrived on the East Coast ten years almost to the day of the first astounding reports from California in September 1848. The United States was mired in one of the worst depressions of the century, and over the winter a shabby army of men, shaken loose by the hard times, gravitated to the Missouri Valley. "Hoosiers, Suckers, Corn crackers, Buckeyes, Red-horses, Arabs and Egyptians," said the *Missouri Republican,*

> some with ox wagons, some with mules, but the greatest number on foot, with their knapsacks and old-fashioned rifles and shotguns. . . . Many have sold out all their homes, all their valuables, to furnish themselves with an outfit for Pike's Peak mines. . . . [They] blindly rush headlong into the wild delusion of glittering sands full of golden eggs.

In spring 1859, more than a hundred thousand persons, twice the number that crossed to California ten years earlier, flooded across the central plains to the Front Range. They walked, pushed wheelbarrows, pulled handcarts, and rode in farm wagons, ambulances, carriages, and phaetons drawn by oxen, mules, horses, milch cows, and, in one case, four hunting dogs. There was a "wind wagon" fitted with sails—a comic failure, but testimony of the gold seekers' imagination and naive hopes. One group afoot planned to sleep in the barns they thought Indians had built for their buffaloes.

The diggings that had sparked the rush soon played out, but in early summer genuine strikes were confirmed in the mountains, and as miners flocked to Central City, Idaho Springs, and other camps, a cluster of supply towns blossomed along the base of the Front Range, Denver the most prominent. Within another year a rough political structure was in place. A critical core of Anglo-American society had appeared in what had been pictured as the republic's empty center.

In reshaping the mental map, the Colorado gold rush obviously had its most immediate impact on the Rocky Mountains. The Front Range was now seen as a place of vibrant towns populated by hard-muscled young Americans pulling wealth from the ground, the newest evidence of God's blessing on His chosen people.

The mental force of the gold strikes was felt just as powerfully on the plains that stretched out six hundred miles to the east. Until now the push for reimagining this country had come from its eastern border. Now a new vision was projected from its western edge, from the Rockies. Correspondents wrote that area valleys were already being planted:

"That the Platte and Arkansas bottoms will yield abundantly to the industrious farmer, there can be no doubt, [and] neither can they be excelled for cattle." Others added that High Plains winters were so mild that domestic herds could graze all winter with hardly a shiver as gardeners tilled happy rows of vegetables virtually year-round.

Back on the eastern side of the plains, Missouri Valley boosters also moved into high gear. Leaders in each town worked to portray their jumping-off place as the true gateway to the gold mines. The trick lay in convincing the crowds that the overland route closest to a particular town was the easiest and fastest way west. There were three such routes—the northern road up the main valley of the Platte River, the southern path up the Arkansas River, and the central route up the Kansas River. Local boosters tried to raise one road over the others with glowing descriptions of its lovely terrain, its rich grasses and stands of timber, its sure sources of water. Thus urban promotion translated directly into a remaking of the image of the plains. As one critic wrote, town boosters "have changed the course of rivers, removed mountains, lengthened streams and made bleak hills and barren sand wastes smooth and even highways."

More than fifty guidebooks appeared in 1859, most of them linked to one town and one route. Champions of the northern and southern roads reported lush pastures, plenty of water, and easy travel all the way to the mines. The central route ascended the Kansas and Republican rivers through country known to only a few non-Indians. Advocates of this route, undeterred by mere ignorance, described the region in the sunniest terms. Repeating earlier booster fictions, they said the two rivers flowed all the way from the Rockies (rather than rising far out on the plains). One book's map showed a large Kansas Lake on what was in fact the arid high plains. Another, answering immigrants' concern for protection, simply moved two forts northward from the Arkansas River to the central route it described as lush and flat—and now safe as well.

To pump traffic westward through their stores, hotels, and liveries, Missouri Valley promoters also puffed up the land awaiting travelers at the far end of the trails. The Rockies were littered with fifty-dollar nuggets and dusted with "the purest gold that has ever been discovered." But that was only the start. Farmland of the high plains, according to one guidebook, "recalls the luxuriance of the tropics, or the magnificence of the ideal world of old navigators." Rumors of drought were dismissed, and in any case, wrote a promoter, there was "a peculiarity in the soil that enables it to withstand the absence of rain." Ranchers too would find magnificent pasturelands of natural grasses that could sustain "millions of cattle" year-round.

The Fuel of Greatness

Precisely ten years after the reimagining of the Pacific Coast, the same process was transforming the continental center. Gold again worked its magic. Once the precious metal was found, all else was assumed to follow: the original dream of flowering gardens, the newer vision of instant cities, budding industry, and speculative fever, and with those, a robust trade. The new Eldorado, an editor stated, would be "the evangel of a new commerce." The sleeping possibilities of mountain and plain would awaken, and "the buffalo path will turn into highways for hurrying merchandise."

Wish fed reality. Within months mercantile outposts were popping up beside the Platte road. Freight cattle wintering along the Front Range became the seed herds for ranchers; farmers planted crops beside every likely tributary of the South Platte and upper Arkansas; Denver and other piedmont towns funneled goods in and out of mountain settlements. Over the next decade the Missouri Valley was bound by trade and interest to the western plains and Rockies, and both regions were woven into the rest of America by the rhetoric of national ascendance. The gold that poured from the mountains was called the fuel of greatness. It would build eastern factories, which in turn would heft us to our proper place. Growing cities would be fed by the generous soil of the heartland. The great pasture of the center, "boundless, endless, gateless," would fatten the cattle that every great nation must have, "vegetable food alone degenerating people to the condition of the Macaroni Eaters of Italy."

Carnivore dreams are a good reminder of how mass imagination helps determine what we do with the places we inhabit, and thus shapes the history we make. Imagined America changed more between 1845 and 1876 than at any time in our history. The vital events are well known—with two conspicuous exceptions. Gold rushes, one on the far western edge of the expanded nation and the other in the middle, redrew the mental contours of the nation far more than we have recognized.

Events of 1845–1848 left America thinking continentally, but by deepening the strains between North and South they came close to fatally fracturing the expanded nation. The Civil War insured that the Union would remain; it allowed the survival of a vague image of an ocean-to-ocean nation. But what exactly would that nation be? The redrawing of America, begun fifteen years before the war, continued for a dozen years after it. This was our larger, more significant reconstruction. It involved far more than pulling the South back into the Union. The entire nation was being reperceived, with the role and image of each region rethought.

A New National Vision

Gold reconstructed the West and America, physically and mythically. The strikes in California and Colorado drew floods of new population and spawned centers of Anglo-American power where none had been before. They also gave a shape to the new territory's vague promise of instant cities, humming trade, bountiful fields. Unlike images of earlier Wests, fitting a slower, steadier rural life and virtues, those of the gold rushes caught a new intoxicating spirit of plunge and grab. Mining camps, chugging locomotives, and throbbing smelters—they were fitting symbols of the new national vision.

That vision was as flawed as ever. Anyone who got in the way, notably Indian peoples and Hispanics, at worst were assaulted as lower life-forms and at best patronized as anachronisms who were, as the commissioner of Indian Affairs told a delegation of Plains tribes in 1867, "by the law of God, and the great law of nature, passing away." In unstoppable numbers the newcomers rolled over everything before them, then paid their own price for the overblown rhetoric. Droughts and blizzards devastated plains settlers in 1860 and 1861, again later in the decade, then again in 1872. Thousands were driven back east. Mining camps busted by the dozen. Denver, Queen City of the Plains, often languished in depression.

But as usual with Americans, and almost always with the West, belief shouted down the facts. "An erroneous impression has gone forth that Kansas is subject to drought," the Kansas Board of Immigration wrote in 1861, astonished at the rumors. Boosters assured everyone that the mines were bottomless, cattle would have plenty to eat, and farmers had nothing to fear. Doubts dissolved. The lovely dream spread and colored nicely.

By 1876, as the republic marked its hundredth birthday and the formal reconstruction of the South drew to a close, the West was also in its final stages of re-vision. The theme of gold bound it to the Union and expressed its larger meaning. California "sits in the circle of sister States," as a Napa orator put it on the centennial day, "her veins throbbing with gold and silver and precious metals, her heart sending out its pulsations to all lands and climes, her lap full of all good things for the healing of the nations." The rhetorical starburst was at least as great in Colorado, born and confirmed in gold and admitted that year as the Centennial State.

The two coasts now were linked by the technology of a new age, the final connection marked appropriately with the hammering of a golden spike and the telegraphed word "Done." The hole in the center had been filled. This geographical alchemy transformed the popular image of other parts of the region as well—Montana and Idaho in the 1860s, parts of the Southwest in the 1870s and 1880s. In fact and fancy, the West was integrated into an America looking toward its second century, one that would show the terrible contradictions and self-deceptions, as well as the true possibilities, of dreams born from the rush for gold.

Chapter 4

The Transcontinental Railroad

Turning | Points
IN WORLD HISTORY

The Transcontinental Railroad and the Development of the West

Leonard J. Arrington

Leonard J. Arrington, who died in 1999, was a noted Mormon historian who taught at the University of Utah and Brigham Young University, directed the history division of the Church of Jesus Christ of Latter-day Saints, and wrote twenty-one books from 1972 to 1980 on American, Western, and Mormon history. In the essay below he describes the race to build the first transcontinental railroad after the Civil War. He also discusses the significance of the railroad in promoting development of the West. Railroads increased immigration to and settlement of the western frontier, stimulated the development of cattle, mining, and other industries, and led to the rise of western cities such as Los Angeles, Denver, and Omaha.

In his widely read book, *The Stages of Economic Growth*, W.W. Rostow declares that the construction and use of railroads has been historically the most powerful single initiator of economic growth. "It was decisive," he wrote, "in the United States, France, Germany, Canada, and Russia; it has played an extremely important part in the Swedish, Japanese and other cases." If this was true of the nation, it was even more true of the American West. Without dependable rivers or the possibility of constructing transportation canals, the West could hardly have been settled to any degree of completeness without the railroad. By lowering the costs of transporting agricultural products and mineral ores from the western interior to the manufacturing East, the railroad fur-

From "The Transcontinental Railroad and the Development of the West," by Leonard J. Arrington, *Utah Historical Quarterly*, vol. 42, no. 1 (1969). Reprinted by permission of the Utah State Historical Society. Footnotes in the original have been omitted in this reprint.

nished food for the burgeoning urban population, supplied raw materials for an expanding industry, and generated much of the capital which financed America's industrialization. By opening the West for settlement, the railroad also widened the market for eastern industry and brought a rich resource base into productivity. More than any other single agency the railroad converted a nation of diverse sections into "one nation, indivisible."

Concept of the Pacific Railroad

By the commencement of the Civil War in 1861, a substantial network of railroads had spread throughout the region east of the Mississippi. During the thirty years after the pioneering "Baltimore and Ohio" was placed in operation in 1830, the nation had constructed some 31,000 miles of railroads. These reached out to Wisconsin, Iowa, Missouri, and Texas. To the west lay an enormous land mass, largely uncharted, consisting of the Great Plains, Rocky Mountains, Great Basin, and California. Some, like Horace Greeley who crossed it in 1859, thought the region so uninviting—so short of water, timber, and game—that a hundred years would be required to settle it. Others recognized that the initial requisite was the laying of a band of steel which would tie the region militarily, politically, culturally, and economically to the expanding Republic. The prime obstacle to the realization of this goal was the division between the North and South. Powerful southern leaders argued for a road which ran across the southern portion of the nation, to connect St. Louis, Memphis, and New Orleans with Los Angeles or San Diego. Northerners and midwesterners contended for a road which began at Chicago or St. Louis and spanned the northern or central portion of the continent. The secession of the South in 1861 and the strong desire to assure a connecting link with California led to the passage of the Pacific Railroad Act.

Signed by Abraham Lincoln on July 5, 1862, the Pacific Railroad Act provided a bold two-pronged effort. The Union Pacific Railroad Company was organized to construct a railroad westward from the Missouri River port of

Council Bluffs, Iowa; the Central Pacific Railroad Company was authorized to construct a road east from Sacramento, which subsequently connected with San Francisco in late 1869. Each company was granted ten alternate sections of public lands (increased to twenty sections in 1864) for each mile of track laid. In addition the two corporations were to receive a thirty-year government loan, the amount of which varied with the terrain. The government agreed to lend each company $16,000 for each mile of track across the Plains, $48,000 for each mile in high mountain areas, and $32,000 for each mile in the Great Basin. Each company was authorized to issue first-mortgage bonds up to the amount of the government loan.

The Civil War, however, precluded extensive railroad construction. Labor was scarce, materials had a higher priority in other uses, and financial resources were slow in forthcoming. Of the two thousand shares of stock which the Union Pacific Railroad Company was authorized to sell, only thirty-one were subscribed during the first year of the canvass, and five of these were purchased by Brigham Young on behalf of the Mormon church. (Brigham Young was made a director of the company in 1865). With the end of the war, both companies mobilized to accomplish the gigantic task.

The Race to Complete the Road

Leader of the Union Pacific forces was Dr. Thomas C. Durant, a railroad promoter who employed General Grenville M. Dodge as chief engineer. Their construction army, directed by General Jack Casement and his brother Daniel, consisted of a motley crew of ex-soldiers from both the Union and the Confederate armies, ex-convicts, youthful Irish and German immigrants, and a scattering of settlers along the route. As many as ten thousand workers came to be involved in the labor of grading, bridge-building, and laying track, with an equivalent number of horses and mules. Their pay ranged from $2.50 to $4.00 per day, and they lived on "buffler" meat, bacon, beans, hard-tack, and coffee. The term "construction army" is not an exaggeration, for the chief of each unit was usually a former Union officer, and the men worked near stacks of carbines held in readiness to cope with surprise attacks by Indians who objected to this symbol

---

The Need for a Transcontinental Railroad

On July 2, 1862 . . . a much harried President Lincoln signed the Pacific Railroad Act, mandating the greatest engineering feat ever attempted, a feat that would fundamentally change Mr. Lincoln's nation.

Signing that act, which obligated private interests to risk more than $100 million, was the culmination of some thirty years of growing pressure. If Manifest Destiny had earlier impelled American expansion to the Pacific Ocean, it also demanded the bridging of the Great American Desert, whose emptiness bifurcated the nation into Atlantic and Pacific coastal communities. . . .

The United States had perhaps grown too swiftly during the first half of the nineteenth century. The slender coastal republic of 1800 with its 5 million or so inhabitants had exploded west and south, signing treaties with a congeries of Indian tribes, and negotiating such brilliant and timely agreements as the Louisiana and Gadsden purchases. The immense geographical booty of the Mexican War, together with Anglo-American settlement of the vexing and complicated Oregon Territory boundary question, rounded out the continental United States.

One of the largest nations on earth by 1853, when the ink dried on the Gadsden Purchase Treaty, the United States had a population of some 24 million, burgeoning through tremendous natural increase and massive drafts of European and African immigration. An impressive 400,000 European immigrants were added to the American genetic pool in 1850 alone. This growing population—energetic, brawling, and often visionary—was still, however, closely tied to the coastal plains, seemingly forever halted by the ice-tipped crags of the Sierra Nevadas in the West and the turgid Mississippi River in the East: a nation severed by topography.

John Hoyt Williams, *A Great and Shining Road*, 1988.

of permanent trespass upon their hunting ground.

Writers made much of the "hell on wheels" construction base camps with their crude shacks for offices and supplies, and hundreds of tents for workmen augmented by those of saloonkeepers, gamblers, and prostitutes. But the work accomplished belies the impression of generalized dissipation. Following the route of the Mormon Trail, the U.P. track, by the end of 1866, had been laid almost as far as North Platte, Nebraska, 300 miles west of Omaha. By the end of 1868, track had been laid through Wyoming and into Utah, as the company hurried to build as much subsidized road as possible.

Meanwhile, the Central Pacific was building eastward from Sacramento. This enterprise was the brain-child of the young railroad engineer Theodore Judah. At great personal sacrifice Judah had surveyed a route, advanced a proposal to build a road over the Sierra, and lobbied for congressional approval. He had finally induced four Sacramento merchants to support the project. They were Leland Stanford (later the governor of California), Collis P. Huntington, Mark Hopkins, and Charles Crocker. When their Central Pacific was given the "go ahead" in the Pacific Railroad Act, Judah had expected to superintend the construction. He soon became convinced that the primary motive of his partners was to maximize construction profits, even at the cost of sound engineering, so he sold his interest.

Charles Crocker, who replaced Judah as construction boss, found it difficult to employ workmen until he thought of the Chinese. Hiring them by the hundreds, often directly in Canton, Crocker had 8,000 Orientals in his employ by the end of 1866, and perhaps 2,000 Caucasians. The work was perhaps the most challenging in the history of American enterprise. All of the steel and rolling stock had to be shipped 15,000 miles by sea to San Francisco and by riverboat or barge to Sacramento, a task which required 10 months. More than 200 miles of the Central Pacific roadbed was above 6,500 feet. Although paid only $25.00 to $35.00 per month, the hardy Chinese drilled away week after week at the numerous tunnels through the granite cliffs of the Sierra. Under the necessity of building some 37 miles of peaked snowsheds for protection against the threatening avalanches of snow, "Crocker's Celestials" laid only 39 miles of track in 1867. More than a year was required to cut the 1,650-foot tunnel at Donner Summit. Even this task was substantially shortened by the introduction (by the Scottish scientist James Howden) of the first nitroglycerine made in America. Blasting operations used up 400 kegs of powder a day.

When the difficult passage over the Sierra was completed in 1868, Huntington requisitioned every available ship on the Eastern Coast to carry supplies, and Crocker's men hurriedly laid track across the sun-blistered ridges and deserts of Nevada. They had less trouble with the Indians than their Union Pacific counterparts because Huntington insisted that the Indians be permitted to ride. "We gave the old chiefs a pass each, good on the passenger cars," he recalled, "and we told our men to let the common Indians ride on the freight cars whenever they saw fit."

The Meeting at Promontory

Observing the companies building parallel grades for track, Congress named Promontory Summit as the meeting place on April 9, 1869. (Central Pacific agreed to buy forty-eight miles of track which Union Pacific had built to that point from Ogden.)

By May 10, 1869, Union Pacific had laid 1,086 miles of track and the Central Pacific 690. On that day the two companies participated in a joining of the rails ceremony which marked the completion of one of the most colossal and daring enterprises in American history—an achievement comparable only with the construction of the Erie Canal and the laying of the Atlantic cable.

In the wake of the first transcontinental railroad there followed four other transcontinentals. The Northern Pacific was constructed westward from Minneapolis across central Minnesota, southern North Dakota and Montana, western Washington, and northern Oregon to Portland. It was completed in 1883. In the same year the Atchison, Topeka, and Santa Fe was completed from eastern Kansas through Colorado, New Mexico, Arizona, and southern California to Los

Angeles. Likewise in the same year the Southern Pacific was completed from New Orleans through southern Louisiana, Texas, New Mexico, Arizona, and California to San Francisco. Finally the Great Northern Railway was completed in 1893, and ran from St. Paul to Seattle, across Montana, Idaho, and Washington. Any one of these five systems was a major undertaking by any standards. That all should have been built within thirty years after the Civil War demonstrates American ingenuity in solving many complex problems of engineering and finance. All told, more than seventy thousand miles of railroad were built in the trans-Mississippi West during the quarter century after the Civil War. . . .

Impact of the Railroad

The transcontinental railroads and their many local "feeders" promoted the development of the West in four major ways: (1) The construction of the railroads brought income to western residents which made possible developmental investments such as the purchase of machinery, the construction of homes, and the financing of immigration; (2) the completion of the railroad network facilitated western colonization and settlement; (3) the completion of the railroad and its feeders stimulated the development of cattle grazing, mining, and other industries which required transportation services for their profitability; and (4) the extension of the railroads westward made it profitable to locate factories nearer to the sources of raw materials and encouraged the development of western manufacturing activity. The expansion of these industries in turn brought an industrial population close to western farming regions, providing large new markets close at hand for the produce of the farms.

An estimated $500 million was expended by the Union Pacific-Central Pacific during the four years the Pacific Railroad was under construction. Without being too precise one supposes that each of the other transcontinental lines and several of the "feeder" networks expended an equal amount, if not more. Much of this, of course, went in the form of contracts for iron, steel, and other products to firms in the East. But substantial sums also went into the pockets of western laborers, farmers, freighters, and businessmen. Draft animals, meat products, grain and flour, fruit and vegetables, water, timber, and ballast were among the provisions and supplies which came almost inevitably from western territories, as did much of the labor involved in grading the roadbed. Coal mines were opened to supply locomotives with fuel, and hundreds of local supply houses were established to meet the special demands of the railroads. The construction of the roads provided the training and discipline to prepare local labor power for various kinds of industrial endeavor. The needs of the roads also led to the strengthening and development of financial institutions which could handle and manipulate large sums of capital. Once the technique of raising and handling large sums of capital was learned, the same technique was applied to manufacturing and other forms of endeavor. Businessmen learned the advantages of the corporate form of business organization, local stock exchanges arose, and new business enterprises multiplied in the wake of the railroad.

Perhaps most important of all, by outrunning the course of settlement the railroad changed the nature of pioneering:

> It was now possible to travel with comparative ease into the midst of the government domain, to secure provisions and supplies while the land was put under cultivation, and to grow specialized products for markets in the United States or in Europe. Coupled with the inducements of the government land system, the railroads settled the West with the rapidity of a prairie fire.

Within twenty years after the completion of the transcontinental railroad, the population of Nebraska rose from slightly more than 100,000 to more than a million. Similarly, the population of the Dakotas rose from less than 15,000 in 1870 to more than 500,000 in 1890. Colonization was rendered more successful as the various railroads promoted new techniques of farming, introduced new crops and varieties of livestock, and transported new types of agricultural machinery. The geography of the nation's agriculture was revolutionized; the center of crop production moved from Indiana and Illinois to Iowa, Kansas, and Nebraska. New areas were opened up for dry farming and irrigation, and westerners used the railroad to market their farm products. That the number of farms in the nation increased from two million in 1860 to six million in 1900 is largely attributable to the construction of western railroads.

Expanding rail lines also played a major role in the development of the western cattle and mining industries. Millions of Texas-bred cattle were shipped over these lines, as were millions of tons of western silver, lead, and copper. Nor has the era of railroad promotion ended. To give the example of just one company, current programs of the Union Pacific Railroad Company include the production and distribution of educational films, the granting of scholarships and funds for research, the sponsorship of educational trains, the development and maintenance of recreational resorts and national parks, and an industrial development program in which plots of ground in various western cities are acquired and improved, serviced with trackage and utilities, and leased or sold to industrial interests for the construction of factories and warehouses and for other purposes.

America's New Frontier

The railroad was a catalyst, an exciter, a pump primer which speeded up the processes of settlement and escalated the West's income from agriculture, trade, and industry. Completion of the first transcontinental line set in motion a chain reaction of developments which culminated in the advanced economies of such great western cities as Los Angeles, San Francisco, Salt Lake City, Denver, Phoenix, and Omaha. But the railroad was more. It was a medium of cultural interchange and excitement. Trains brought visitors from Boston, New York, London, Berlin, and Tokyo to observe the "New America." They were impressed and they wrote books— tons of them. While the railroad helped to build the western economy, it also helped to create the "myth" of the West— a myth which has been preserved in thousands of novels, movies, and television serials. The West of imagination and the West of reality were both products of the joining of the rails at Promontory, Utah, on May 10, 1869.

The Destruction of the Buffalo and the Opening of the Cattle Driving Frontier

Richard White

In this excerpt from his book *"It's Your Misfortune and None of My Own": A History of the American West*, Stanford University history professor Richard White describes what he calls "the transformation of the Great Plains" that occurred in the decades following the Civil War. This transformation began with the destruction of the vast buffalo herds that roamed the plains. White hunters killed buffalo for sport or profit, and the U.S. army slaughtered the herds in an effort to starve out the Indian tribes that hunted them. The final blow to the herds, writes White, was the expansion of the railroads into the plains, which created a more profitable means of shipping hides to market.

Longhorn cattle replaced the buffalo as the herd animal of the Great Plains. Ranchers preferred the animal in part because they were hardy enough to withstand the long drive from the open range to shipping centers along the railroads. The era of cattlemen and cowboys was born as the railroads advanced and gave rise to cattle towns such as Abilene, Kansas, and later Wichita and Dodge City.

The western prairies and the Great Plains often appeared forbidding to migrants, but they are not necessarily an inhospitable place for human beings. Plains nomads and horticulturists knew this land in loving detail and lived on it successfully. German Russians, fresh from the steppes of the Ukraine, found the grasslands a familiar and comfortable place. Migrants used to the forests of eastern North Amer-

From *"It's Your Misfortune and None of My Own": A History of the American West*, by Richard White. Copyright © 1991 by the University of Oklahoma Press, Norman, Publishing Division of the University. Reprinted by permission of the publisher.

ica or of northern Europe, however, found it terrifying. Beret, a character in O.E. Rölvaag's novel *Giants in the Earth*, called it "the great stillness where there was nothing to hide behind." Finding the plains forbidding, the ambition of many settlers was to transform it.

The Decline of the Buffalo

The transformation of the Great Plains began with the near extinction of the bison. The decline of the species began before the arrival of white settlers. The range of the buffalo, or bison, as it should properly be called, once extended well east of the Mississippi and west of the Rockies, but the huge herds of historical times grazed the short-grass plains. How many buffalo grazed the plains will never be known. Bison numbers probably peaked at about 25 million animals. Current estimates put the southern herd (that is, the herd south of the Platte River) at from 6 million to 7 million animals in the mid–nineteenth century, and as late as 1870 the southern herd still numbered well over 3 million animals. The herd north of the Platte was probably somewhat smaller.

Hunters had eliminated those bison east of the Mississippi by the end of the eighteenth century, and bison largely had disappeared from the prairies west of the river in the early nineteenth century, but even in the West the bison may have begun to decline even before the advent of widespread hide hunting for the fur trade. The plains bison herds always existed in tenuous equilibrium with disease, wolves, hunters, weather, and accidents. By the 1840s bison were in trouble, not so much from overhunting, although that was increasingly a factor, as from a combination of drought, habitat destruction, competition from exotic species, and introduced diseases. During periods of drought, such as the one that struck the Great Plains in the late 1840s, bison had to compete with Indian horse herds and wild mustangs for food and water in critical riverine habitats. Drought seems to have contributed to the "big die-up" of 1867, when millions of bison supposedly starved between the Concho and Brazos rivers. At the same time, livestock taken by Indian raiders and cattle driven across the plains by white migrants spread tuberculosis and brucellosis to the buffalo herds. The creation of the overland trails and the spread of white settlement to the edges of the Great Plains drove the bison from critical riverine habitat and denied them the peripheral tallgrass habitat on which they depended as a refuge from drought and hunting. The result was a buffalo population already unable to maintain its numbers when the white hunters struck.

The first commercial pressure on the western herds came with the development of a significant market for their robes and for pemmican—a mixture of pounded dried buffalo meat, fat, and berries that kept for years. Pemmican became a staple high-energy food on the plains, and the fur companies purchased large quantities of it to feed their trappers and *engagés* in the subarctic. Indians increased their kills of buffalo to supply pemmican and robes. Also in the 1830s and 1840s new hunters appeared to prey on the herds. The removal of eastern Indians to lands west of the Missouri brought an influx of people who soon became skilled buffalo hunters, making seasonal forays onto the plains.

Coupled with this commercial hunting was a second kind of hunting. The opening of the overland trails started an onslaught on the buffalo by migrants, soldiers, and various eastern and European sportsmen. These people killed bison in numbers far beyond what they could ever use. They hunted largely for sport and left the carcasses to rot on the plains. The consequences of this hunting disturbed both the plains nomads and horticulturists. By mid-century various Indian groups, particularly those along the Missouri River, the Platte River, and the Santa Fe Trail, began to complain of dwindling numbers of buffalo.

The Coming of the Railroads

The coming of the railroads sounded the death knell for the herds. The railroads provided a new means of getting the bulky skins to market at the same time that a new tanning process made it possible for eastern tanneries to turn the hides into a cheap leather for straps and machine belts. Previously the market for hides had been confined to buffalo robes. Hunters had to kill the animals during the winter when their fleece was thick, and they could profitably kill no more than Indian women were willing to process into robes. Turning the hides into leather, however, removed these bottlenecks; hunters could kill as many animals as they could skin, and they could kill them at any time of the year.

With a new market, a new means of transportation, and a new hunting season that stretched throughout the year, professional buffalo hunters moved onto the southern plains in the early 1870s. Killing bison to feed the railroad crews expanded to hunting for hides and for tongues, which were salted and shipped to market. The southern hunt peaked between 1872 and 1874. In all, the hide hunters took an estimated 4,374,000 buffalo during these years. To that number has to be added the Indian kill of approximately 1,215,000 on the southern plains during this same period, as well as the smaller number of bison killed by settlers and sportsmen. In the 1870s Congress passed a bill protecting the bison, but President Grant vetoed it.

The scale and procedures of this slaughter made it a kind of industrial hunting unlike anything seen in the West before. Hide hunters worked on foot. Their preferred method was to get downwind of the buffalo, a species with very poor eyesight. Once positioned, the hunter killed the animals at long range with high-powered rifles. A herd often went peacefully and serenely to its death. As long as the animals did not smell the hunter or were not startled, they kept grazing, oblivious to the other bison dying around them. A lone hunter might kill a hundred animals at a single stand before the herd stampeded. The most skilled hunters took 2,500 to 3,000 buffalo in a single year. One party of 16 hunters is supposed to have killed 28,000 buffalo during a few months in 1873. . . .

The Consequences for Indian Peoples

The elimination of the buffalo by white hide hunters cut the heart from the Plains Indian economy. Various military commanders encouraged the slaughter of bison for precisely this reason. Without the buffalo, Plains Indians could not effectively resist American expansion. But the disappearance of the buffalo had a meaning for Indian peoples that was more than economic. The buffalo were not just a source of tepees and robes, of meat and tools. The animals were crucial to the cosmology of both the plains nomads and the horticulturists. In 1871, for example, with the buffalo already growing scarce on the central plains, Quaker agents tried to persuade the Pawnees not to hunt the buffalo that season. The hunt was certain to be unrewarding, and it would just as certainly be dangerous, because the Sioux were determined to drive the Pawnees from the remaining buffalo grounds. The Quakers urged the Pawnees to concentrate on farming; with the buffalo gone, they would in the future have to depend solely on their agriculture for support.

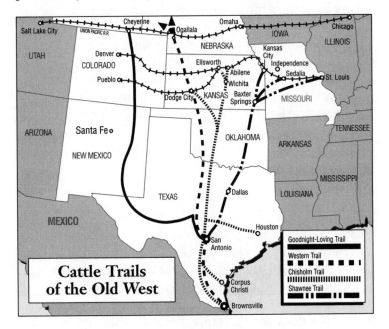

The Pawnee chief Peta-la-sharo tried to explain why, given the Pawnee understanding of the world, the Quaker position made no sense. The hunt had to continue. Without the buffalo, he told the Quakers, there could be no agriculture. Offerings of buffalo meat were central to the Pawnee ceremonies, and it was only these ceremonies that ensured the continuance of the natural cycles that allowed humans to live on the planet. Without buffalo there would be no annual renewal, and the corn could not grow.

Indians like the Pawnees would hunt buffalo until the very end, both because they had to and because they did not believe that their hunting had anything to do with the animals' disappearance. The Sioux, for example, recognized that the buffalo were growing less numerous, but they believed that the buffalo were withdrawing underground because they had been mistreated. They would return and allow themselves to be hunted only when all hunters accorded them the ritual respect that was their due. Whites were unlikely to give them such respect, but in 1890 when the Ghost Dance religion spread to the Sioux, it promised a world where the dead would live and whites would disappear. Then the buffalo would return. Such a return was perfectly logical, given Sioux beliefs. A world purged of the whites would be a world that was hospitable to buffalo. But whites would not vanish. The buffalo would not return. And the disappearance of the buffalo marked the final blow to the old life. In the words of the Crow warrior Two Leggings: "Nothing happened after that. We just lived. There were no more war parties, no capturing horses from the Piegan and the Sioux, no buffalo to hunt. There is nothing more to tell."

Cattle on the Great Plains

The elimination of the great free-roaming herds of bison created an ecological vacuum on the Great Plains. Cattle moved in to fill that vacuum. The first cattle appeared even before the buffalo had vanished. During the overland migrations, traders, who bought exhausted or injured cattle and oxen from overland migrants, and teamsters, who used oxen to haul supplies for the army, both discovered that cattle could winter on the plains. These traders and teamsters created the first cattle herds on the plains, but the real stocking of the Great Plains came after the Civil War, when Texans began the long cattle drives that would spread the famous Texas longhorns throughout the West.

The expansion of cattle onto the Great Plains was no more a purely ecological phenomenon than was the elimination of bison. Both were intimately connected with the growth of the American economy and the expansion of the railroads to the west. Economy, culture, and ecology all combined to create conditions that led to an explosion in the numbers of cattle.

The Texas longhorns were a new breed descended from a cross between the criollo cattle introduced by the Spanish and Anglo American introductions such as the English longhorn. Ambitious Texas ranchers had begun efforts to market these cattle in the 1850s, but the Civil War cut the state off from its markets. The longhorns increased until they probably numbered about 5 million head. As commercial beef cattle, the longhorns were a butcher's nightmare—"eight pounds of hamburger on 800 pounds of bone and horn." These long-legged animals, whose horns often spread five feet from tip to tip, put on weight slowly and did not reach full weight until they were eight to ten years old. Even when fully mature, the animals remained lean, weighing only about 1,000 pounds, and their meat was stringy and tough. But cattle raisers tolerated such commercial deficiencies because of the animals' hardiness. Longhorns could travel far on little water. They could defend themselves against predators, and as long as the herders tolerated winter death rates that ranged as high as 20 percent, they required no winter feeding. They were in this respect ideal animals for driving north and west to stock the range.

The Rise of Cattle Towns

The longhorns had, however, an additional liability which would have a significant influence in shaping the cattle industry in the West. Texas longhorns carried with them a small tick that transmitted splenic fever, commonly called Texas or Spanish fever. Longhorns endured the tick and the fever with equanimity, for they, from long exposure, were largely resistant to the disease. The tick died during northern winters, and cattle buyers could safely ship their cattle east for fattening after the frost. But spring, summer, and fall cattle drives from Texas exposed domestic stock to the tick, and the passage of Texas cattle through a farming region meant devastation to dairy herds, oxen, and breeding stock. As early as 1851, Missouri had banned Texas cattle, and the state instituted a more effective ban in 1861. Following the Civil War in 1867, Kansas established a special quarantine line east of which the cowboys could not drive their herds. Cattle towns thus had to lie somewhere west of thickly settled farming regions, and when farmers appeared around them, the town merchants who depended on the drives usually undertook measures to compensate farmers for any stock they lost to Texas fever.

Abilene, Kansas, was the first of the cattle towns created by the convergence of the longhorns, the railroads, and ticks. In 1867 an Illinois entrepreneur named Joseph McCoy, beating out rivals who had much the same idea, established a shipping point for cattle at the small town of Abilene, located where the Kansas Pacific Railroad crossed Mud Creek. Connected to Texas by the Chisholm Trail through Indian

Cattle Towns and Cowboys

Undoubtedly the cowboy would have flourished at some time in the late nineteenth century, but the Kansas Pacific Railroad brought him upon the scene early with the establishment of cattle shipping points in towns west of the settled areas—Abilene, Ellsworth, and finally Hays City. The first of the Kansas Pacific's cattle towns was Abilene. . . .

Legions of audacious Texans rode up the Chisholm Trail to that garish trail oasis, where they celebrated the end of their overland journeys with whiskey, dance-hall girls, and gambling. At first the riders were called "drovers" or simply "Texans" (McCoy named his hotel the Drover's Cottage) but soon they were "cowboys" and they made songs about themselves—"I'm Bound to Follow the Longhorn Cows," "The Dying Cowboy," "Get Along Little Dogies," "The Old Chisholm Trail," and of course "The Railroad Corral," in which they sang about rousting steers from the long chaparral and driving them far to the railroad corral, using the tune of "The Irish Washerwoman.". . .

Territory, Abilene became the first of the cattle towns. The heyday of the long drives, and with it the heyday of the cattle towns, had begun. Every summer for nearly twenty years the herds moved north. Cattle towns such as Wichita, Caldwell, and Dodge City succeeded Abilene and competed to attract the herds and the cowboys who drove them. The towns could make money from both.

Even as Kansas cowtowns and Texas cattle raisers began their profitable partnership, cattle raising was expanding onto huge expanses of grassland beckoning to the north. Many of the cattle driven from the prolific bovine womb of Texas were bound for pastures on the Great Plains. The nearly legendary Colonel Charles Goodnight blazed trails to stock the ranges of Colorado and New Mexico. John Iliff, a Colorado cattleman who became known as the "cattle king of the plains," had begun as one of the traders buying out footsore and exhausted oxen and cattle from emigrants, fat-

Without the railroad and the trail town, the image of the cowboy never would have become fully formed. He would have been only a stock handler on horseback, a man wearing a big hat, a bandanna, boots and spurs. Without the trail town he would have had no destination, no relationship with the Calico Queens and Painted Cats, the dance-hall girls of a dozen Bull's Head Taverns & Gambling Saloons, Long Branches, Alamos, and Lady Gays. He would have had no town marshals to challenge to the death in thousands of legendary walkdowns and shoot-outs on the Texas Streets that fronted the railroad tracks. He might have lived and died without ever seeing the steaming, smoking Iron Horse that hauled away the bawling Longhorns he drove up from Texas. Without the Iron Horse, the trail town, and the cowboy, a larger part of the myth of the American West would have faded into history, never to be perpetuated in multitudes of yellow-backed dime novels and millions of feet of film flicking shadows on motion-picture and television screens.

Dee Brown, *Hear That Lonesome Whistle Blow*, 1977.

tening them on bunch grass, and selling them to miners.
Goodnight himself eventually pushed cattle into the heart of
the Comanche country by establishing the first ranch in the
Texas Panhandle. His outfit at Palo Duro Canyon was 250
miles from the nearest railroad or supply base.

Others pushed cattle farther north. Of the 630,000 cattle
driven across the Red River in 1871, western Nebraska and
southern Wyoming got about 100,000. The government
provided a market for other cattle by purchasing nearly
50,000 head annually by 1880 to feed western Indians, but
the trail herds consisted largely of young cattle going north
to fatten on the western ranges. As railroads advanced, they
created new shipping centers and thus opened more and
more land for cattle raising. The Missouri, Kansas and Texas
Railroad reached northern Texas in 1873, giving Texas cattle
ranches there a direct link with Kansas City. Meanwhile, the
Texas Pacific ran west across the state to El Paso. The Santa
Fe and the Denver and Rio Grande opened up New Mexico
and much of the southern plains. The Union Pacific reached
Cheyenne, Wyoming, in 1867, and by the end of the 1870s,
Sydney in Nebraska and Pine Bluffs, Cheyenne, and Rock
River in Wyoming had become the leading shipping points
for cattle on the Union Pacific. By 1880 there were, exclud-
ing milk cows, approximately 4 million cattle in Kansas, Nebraska, Colorado, Wyoming, Montana, and the Dakotas,
and the boom was accelerating.

The Rise and Fall of the Cattle Kingdoms

T. Harry Williams, Richard N. Current, and
Frank Freidel

The cattle-driving frontier lasted only about twenty years, from 1865 to 1885, but remains one of the most memorable aspects of the American frontier. Mexicans in Texas had originally developed the techniques of cattle ranching, but only with the advance of the railroads across the plains in the 1860s and 1870s did the practice of driving cattle across long distances become profitable. The "cattle kings"—wealthy ranchers and stockmen—employed cowboys who drove the herds from Texas up along the Chisholm or the Goodnight-Loving Trail to cattle towns along the railroads of the Great Plains. The railroads made the profitable cattle drives possible, but in the 1880s they also helped bring an end to open range as they encouraged thousands of farmers to settle the plains. T. Harry Williams, Richard N. Current, and Frank Freidel were history professors at Louisiana State University, the University of North Carolina, and Harvard University, respectively, when they wrote their 1959 text *A History of the United States (Since 1865)*, from which the following essay is excerpted.

Shortly after the gold and silver seekers surged into the mineral empire, another great economic province began to take shape in the last frontier. The cattle kingdom was born on the Great Plains, its imperial boundaries stretching from the ninety-eighth meridian to the Rockies, from Texas to Canada. Like the mining domain, it had a brief and brilliant

From *A History of the United States (Since 1865)*, by T. Harry Williams, Richard N. Current, and Frank Freidel (New York: Knopf, 1959).

existence, from approximately 1865 to 1885, but during that period it influenced materially the course of national development and added another colorful chapter to the record of the last West.

A Kingdom Built on Railroads

The rise of the cattle kingdom was directly related to the expanding industrial society of urban America. The multitudes of the metropolitan centers created a new, huge market for meat and other foods, and . . . the meat-packing industry arose in Chicago and other cities to satisfy that market. At the same time devices for preserving fresh meats for long periods, notably the refrigerator car, were developed. The last element in the productive link was an adequate and available source of animals, and this was supplied by the vast herds of cattle that appeared on the grassy plains after 1865. Various factors enabled the cattle industry to spread over the West— the suppression of the Indians, the elimination of the buffalo, the laxity of the land laws—but the most important were the open range and the railroads. The open range, that is, the unclaimed grasslands of the public domain, provided a huge area where cattlemen could graze their herds free of charge and unrestricted by the boundaries which would have existed in a farming economy. The railroads gave the cattle kingdom access to markets and thus brought it into being; then they destroyed it by bringing the farmers' frontier to the plains.

In ancestry the cattle industry was Mexican and Texan. Long before the Americans invaded the Southwest, Mexican ranchers and vaqueros had developed the techniques and tools employed later by the cattlemen and cowboys of the Great Plains: branding (a device known in all frontier areas where stock was common), roundups, roping, and the equipment of the herder—his lariat, saddle, leather chaps, and spurs. All these things and others were taken over by the Americans in Texas and by them transmitted to the northernmost ranges of the cattle kingdom. Also in Texas were found the largest herds of cattle in the country, the animals descended from imported Spanish stock and allowed to run wild or semi-wild, the famous wiry, hardy longhorns; here too were the horses that enabled the caretakers of the herds to control them, the small, muscular broncos or mustangs, sprung from blooded progenitors brought in by the Spanish and ideally adapted to the requirements of the cow country.

The practice of driving cattle herds to market centers or from old to new ranges had been known before the Civil War and had been attempted on a limited scale in many parts of the country. But the concept of moving huge numbers of animals over long distances on a regular schedule was born in the postwar period, and its origin was directly related to the advance of the railroads across the plains. At the end of the war an estimated 5,000,000 cattle roamed the Texas ranges, and Northern markets were offering fat prices for steers in any condition. Early in 1866 some Texas cattlemen started their combined herds, some 260,000 head, north for Sedalia, Missouri, on the Missouri Pacific Railroad. Traveling over rough country and beset by outlaws, Indians, and property-conscious farmers, the caravan suffered heavy losses, and only a fraction of the animals were delivered to the railroad. But a great experiment had been successfully tested—cattle could be driven to distant markets and pastured along the trail and would gain weight during the journey. The first of the "long drives" prepared the way for the cattle kingdom.

The Long Drive

With the precedent established, the next step was to find an easier route leading through more accessible country. Through the efforts of Joseph G. McCoy, an Illinois stockman, special market facilities were provided at Abilene, Kansas, on the Kansas Pacific Railroad, and for years this town reigned as the railhead of the cattle kingdom. Between 1867 and 1871, 1,460,000 cattle were moved up the Chisholm Trail to Abilene, a town that, filled with rampaging cowboys at the end of a drive, rivaled the mining towns in robust wickedness. But as the farming frontier pushed farther west in Kansas and as the supply of animals increased, the cattlemen had to develop other market outlets and trails. Railroad towns that flourished after Abilene were Dodge City and Wichita in Kansas, Ogallala and Sidney in Nebraska, Cheyenne and Laramie in Wyoming, and Miles City and Glendive in Montana. Most used of the routes to the new sites were the Western Trail from central Texas to Ogallala and the Pecos or Goodnight-Loving Trail from middle Texas to New Mexico and up into Colorado and Wyoming. Over these and other approaches nearly 10,000,000 cattle were driven to the buying markets between 1866 and 1888. At first the animals were shipped east to the packing centers or to feeding centers in the Middle West, but soon it was discovered that they could be wintered and fattened on the northern plains. Northern feeders met southern breeders at the railhead towns, bought their steers, and started them north on another long drive.

From first to last, a long drive was a spectacular episode. It began with the spring, or calf, roundup. The ranchers of a district collected with their cowboys at a specified place to round up the stock of the owners from the open range. As the cattle were driven in, the calves were branded with the marks of their mothers. Stray calves with no identifying symbols, "mavericks," were divided on a pro-rata basis. Then the cows and calves were turned loose to pasture, while the yearling steers were readied for the drive to the north. The combined herds, usually numbering from 2,000 to 5,000 head, moved out, attended by the cowboys of each outfit. In addition to the individual brand of its owner, each animal bore a "road brand" to indicate it belonged to this particular assemblage. By all odds, the most important person on a drive was the cowboy or "cowpuncher," replete with forty-pound saddle, twenty-foot lariat, "six-shooter" revolver, chaps, and sombrero. Whether riding the range with his charges, stopping a stampede, or singing to himself or the steers under the stars, he seemed an incredibly romantic figure. Actually, he was a highly skilled technician engaged in work that was mostly dull and dangerous, and he could have had no comprehension of the stature he would later assume in American folklore. A drive culminated when the cattle were delivered to a railhead for shipment east or were turned over to northern buyers. In the latter case, another group of cowboys took over the animals and moved them to northern ranges. On the plains it was this second movement that was considered as the real "long drive." When ranchers planned to sell their cattle for rail shipment, the roundup and following drive were usually conducted in the fall, thus allowing the stock to fatten on the summer grass.

From Open Range to Private Ranch

For a period the cattle kingdom boomed with prosperity—and with swollen profits for the cattlemen. These magnates moved their stock over the open range, and the range was free. They asserted, nevertheless, claims to land, claims that were peculiar to the cow country, where large units were essential, and that could be characterized as occupancy rather than ownership. The big operators or companies leased acres by the millions from the Indians, appropriated huge areas along waterways, and obtained other blocks by manipulating loopholes in the land laws. Sometimes they threw barbed wire fences around their domains, but mostly they merely proclaimed grazing rights on a particular section and maintained their position by consent or physical power. Some cattle kings claimed rights to ranges 100 or 150 miles long and 50 miles wide. All cattlemen, however, had to have a permanent base from which to operate, and so the ranch emerged. The Texans had always moved from fixed abodes, and as the northern ranges filled up with cattle the cowmen there found it desirable to develop ranches. A ranch consisted of a dwelling, quarters for employees, and a tract of grazing land. It might be fenced in or open, owned or leased or held by some quasi-legal claim, but it was definite and durable. Possession of a ranch meant solid benefits to the owner. He could secure unquestioned access to precious water, and, perhaps most important, he had a place where he could hold his herd until the market price was satisfactory. As farmers and sheepmen encroached on the open plains, the ranch came to replace the range.

Like the mineral empire, the cattle kingdom was at first without government and laws, and its residents had to provide their own order and to frame regulations that met the peculiar requirements of their economy and culture. They formed organizations known as associations, some of them functioning on a county or some other form of local basis and some on a state level. Most powerful of these groups was the Wyoming Stock Growers' Association, which overshadowed the territorial government and actually governed the territory. As was true of the earlier miner agencies, the associations were legislative and executive agencies. They laid down rules defining land and water rights, the conduct of roundups, and the disposition of mavericks; they registered brands and inspected markings suspected of alterations; they blacklisted cowboys with shady pasts, refused membership to people they wanted to keep out, and punished immediately and drastically rustlers or anyone else bold enough to defy their edicts. They were often arrogant and sometimes unjust, but they were trying to bring a measure of order to an economy that might otherwise have succumbed to anarchy. For the usual individualism of the frontier they substituted disciplined communal life.

There was always an element of risk and speculation in the cattle business. At any time the "Texas fever," transmitted by a parasite carried by ticks, might decimate a herd. Rustlers and Indians frequently drove off large numbers of animals. Sheepmen from California and Oregon brought their flocks onto the range to compete for grass and force cattle out (cattle will not graze after sheep); bitter "wars" followed between ranchers and sheepers in which men and stock were killed and equipment destroyed. Farmers, "nesters," threw fences around their claims, blocking trails and breaking up the open range, and more wars, bringing losses to both sides, were fought. Cattlemen, seeking to improve meat quality, crossed longhorns with imported bulls; the result was a heavier animal but one less able to withstand the rigors of the range.

The End of the Long Drives

Despite hazards and uncertainties, the cattle kingdom prospered. In the early eighties, as the country entered on another period of expansion after the depression of 1873, Eastern and European demands for meat boomed the price of steers to as high as $50 a head. Producers hastened to increase the supply, even importing animals from the Middle West and East. Accounts of the lofty profits to be made in the cattle business—it was said that an investment of $5,000 would return $45,000 in four years—tempted Eastern, English, and Scottish capital to the plains. Increasingly the structure of the cattle economy, repeating the experience of industry, became corporate in form; in one year twenty corporations with a combined capital of $12 million were chartered in Wyoming. The inevitable result of this frenzied extension was that the ranges, already severed and shrunk by the railroads the farmers, were overstocked. There was not enough grass to support the crowding herds or sustain the long drives. Overstocking tumbled prices downward, and then nature intervened with a destructive finishing blow. Two severe winters, in 1885–1886 and 1886–1887, with a searing summer between them, stung and scorched the plains. Hundreds of thousands of cattle died, streams and grass dried up, princely ranches and costly investments disappeared in a season. The cattle kingdom never recovered. Ranchers turned to more modest endeavors, fencing in their tracts, raising hay for winter feed, becoming, in effect, farmers. Another phase of the frontier had receded forever into the American past.

The Closing of the American Frontier

John F. Stover

John F. Stover, a professor at Purdue University, is a leading authority on the history of North American railroads. In the following selection he discusses the transcontinental railroad's role in closing the American frontier. Railroads ended the cattle driving frontier when they extended down from the Great Plains into Texas and made the long drive unnecessary. Railroads opened access to western mining towns, transforming them from frontier outposts to centers of industry. The most significant turning point, however, was the railroad's transformation of Great Plains agriculture. The access to coastal markets and ports that railroads provided led to a boom in commercial agriculture on the prairies. In the last decades of the nineteenth century the railroads tied the Great Plains and the Rocky Mountains to the rest of the nation, thus closing the American frontier.

In the nineteenth century Americans experienced a succession of frontiers as the explorer, trapper, cowboy, miner, and finally the farmer conquered the West. Between the Civil War and World War I western railroads participated fully in the last three of these western developments. Perhaps the first was the role played by the expanding rail lines in the frontier cattle industry between 1867 and the eighties. The Kansas Pacific was building west across Kansas in 1866, the same year that Texas cattle drivers met the triple frustrations of hostile farmers, timbered terrain, and bandit rustlers in their drive toward Sedalia, Missouri.

Railroads and the End of the Open Range

Joseph G. McCoy (1837–1915), a livestock shipper from Illinois, believed that there should be some intersecting point of cattle trail and railroad in Kansas where northern and eastern buyers could meet Texas cattlemen with mutual profit. Shortly after the president of the Missouri Pacific had rudely ordered him out of his office, McCoy signed a favorable contract with the Hannibal and St. Joe Railroad to ship cattle from Missouri to Chicago. In searching for a trail head in central Kansas, McCoy found that neither Salina nor Solomon City would tolerate the idea of stockyards. He turned to Abilene on the Kansas Pacific, a town so small that only one of the dozen log huts could claim a shingle roof and a place so poor that the saloon keeper supplemented his income by raising prairie dogs. McCoy built his stockyards and shipped out the first train of twenty cars of longhorn cattle on September 5, 1867. By the end of the year a thousand carloads had been sent to market in Chicago. In 1868 some 75,000 Texas cattle were sold in Abilene, 300,000 head came north in 1870, and the peak was reached with 700,000 in 1871. None of the 75 bartenders (three eight-hour shifts of 25 men each working seven days a week) at the Alamo Saloon in Abilene now had any time for prairie dogs.

As the railroads pushed farther south and west and as the hordes of settlers and farmers followed them, the cattle trails and the cowtowns were pushed ever westward. Newton and Dodge City on the Santa Fe, Ellis farther west on the Kansas Pacific, and Ogallala on the Union Pacific in Nebraska all increasingly shared in the cattle business. Ellis and Dodge City together shipped out more than a million cattle between 1876 and 1879, with the latter place, being farther south, getting the bulk of the traffic. Between four and five million cattle had been driven to northern markets by 1880, but the decline in the traffic was well established by the latter year. Farmers were planting wheat on the old buffalo ranges, barbed wire was creeping ever farther to the west, and both Kansas and Colorado were soon to have effective quarantine laws against Texas cattle.

New railroad construction from the North into Texas was also making the long drive unnecessary. The Missouri-Kansas-Texas Railroad reached the Red River and northern Texas in 1873, and the St. Louis, Iron Mountain, and Southern Railroad diagonally crossed Arkansas to Texarkana shortly thereafter. Texas had more than quadrupled her own rail mileage in the seventies, increasing it from 711 miles in 1870 to 3,244 miles in 1880. Clearly, the days of the open range and the long trail drive were about over.

Railroads and the Mining Frontier

Also during the decade of the seventies a second frontier, that of the Rocky Mountain miner and prospector, was helped by the western railroad. A mania for narrow-gauge railroads appeared in the United States, as in England, shortly after a paper, "The Gauge for the 'Railways of the Future,'" was read by Robert F. Fairlie (1831–85) in 1870 before the annual meeting of the British Railway Association. Fairlie and his adherents argued very plausibly that a road of 3-foot 6-inch gauge would be much cheaper to build, equip, and maintain than standard-gauge line. It was also pointed out that a narrow-gauge line, with sharper curves and lighter equipment, was well adapted to mountainous regions or could be used in areas where the expected business was light. . . .

After silver was discovered in vast amounts at Leadville in the late seventies, [William Jackson] Palmer turned his [Colorado] line in that direction. John Evans (1814–96), early Colorado territorial governor, co-founder of two Methodist colleges, and former president of the Denver Pacific (Denver to Cheyenne), also wanted his narrow-gauge Denver, South Park, and Pacific to serve Leadville. Palmer's Denver and Rio Grande reached the booming silver town first. Former President Grant, just returning from his world tour, was aboard Palmer's private car "Nomad" as the first train entered the city to be welcomed by twelve brass bands and Horace A.W. ("Haw") Tabor (1830–99), bonanza king and lieutenant governor of the state. The rails of the Denver, South Park, and Pacific later reached the city, but with a grade so steep that on one occasion when a circus train was headed for Leadville, the elephants were unloaded to help push the train into the station. Soon, branches of the Denver and Rio Grande were snaking their way into Aspen, Durango, Silverton, and Farmington across the New Mexican border. There was economy in building the narrow-gauge lines, but the prosperous patrons of the little roads demanded, and received, service of the finest sort in the small-scale mahogany and red plush parlor, dining, and Pullman cars.

A comparable story of gold and silver strikes, of boom towns and the narrow-gauge lines that served them, could be found in both California and Nevada. In central Nevada in the middle seventies the Eureka and Palisade Railroad pushed its three-foot track 90 miles south of the main line of the Central Pacific to the bonanza claims of both silver and lead waiting in Eureka. A few miles west and three years later, in 1879, a parallel line, the Nevada Central Railway, was headed for the silver mines of Austin. General James H. Ledlie (1832–82), who had been the contractor for all the bridges, trestles, and snowsheds on the Union Pacific, completed the 93-mile Nevada Central just before midnight on February 9, 1880, the last day that the road was eligible for a Lander County subsidy of $200,000. Even then the deadline had been met only because the Austin Common Council had extended the limits of their town half a mile toward the narrow-gauge line.

Railroads and the Rise of Commercial Agriculture in the Midwest

In the years just after the Civil War western railroads played a major role in the frontier of the cowboy and the cattle industry of the Great Plains. In the same period an equally important contribution had been made by the narrow-gauge line in the expansion of the mountain mining frontier. The first full post-war generation (1865–1900) saw a vastly more important contribution to prairie agriculture by the railroad.

As prairie farming expanded in the generation after the war, American agriculture experienced a revolution composed of three factors: (1) an expansion and westward shift of the farming domain; (2) the use of new farming techniques (dry farming, irrigation, and increased mechanization) to meet the needs of prairie farming; and (3) the increased use of the railroad to distribute and market the western farm product. The expansion of the agricultural area can be seen in the nearly threefold increase (2,044,000 to 5,737,000) in the number of farms between 1860 and 1900 and in the fact that more new farm land was brought under cultivation in the generation after the Civil War than in the entire previous history of the nation.

In the same years the center of crop production shifted westward. Whereas Illinois and Indiana were first and second in wheat production in 1859, this honor had shifted to Minnesota and North Dakota by 1899. Illinois did retain its first-place rank in corn production in the same forty years, but second, third, and fourth places shifted, respectively, from Ohio, Missouri, and Indiana to Iowa, Kansas, and Nebraska. Mississippi had been first in the production of cotton in 1860, but by the turn of the century Texas had become the center of the Cotton Kingdom. The availability of transportation was an obvious necessity as this shift in the centers of agrarian production occurred. In the six leading prairie farm states mentioned above (Minnesota, North Dakota, Iowa, Kansas, Nebraska, and Texas) total railroad mileage increased from less than 1,000 miles in 1860 to over 42,000 miles in 1900. The availability of transportation in the western farming region helped create a shift from subsistence to commercial farming and made agriculture an intimate though subordinate factor in the post–Civil War industrial system.

Prairie farming was specifically tied into the industrial system in its nourishment of and dependence upon a whole series of cities on the eastern edges of the prairie. Chicago had its wheat pit, stockyards, and packing plants. Kansas City, Omaha, East St. Louis, and Milwaukee also had expanding facilities to serve the livestock farmers of the West. A trio of cities on the upper middle Mississippi, Rock Island, Moline, and Davenport, held a position in the production of farm implements surpassed only by the production of Chicago. The flour mills of Minneapolis served the western farming states and the nation. This entire agricultural-industrial complex was served by the growing rail network basically radiating out of Chicago through such rival but subordinate focal points as St. Louis, Kansas City, Omaha, and the Twin Cities. Admittedly, these prairie railroads were often guilty—as were most railroads in the late nineteenth century—of many abuses. Rate wars, pooling arrangements, rebating, discriminations of the long- and-short-haul, railroad-owned elevators that downgraded the farmer's grain—all these things plagued and irritated the farmer of the prairie. . . .

The Settling of America's Last Frontier

In spite of high freight rates, the long haul to market, and other transportation discriminations, farmers and settlers poured into the prairie states after the Civil War. Veterans headed for western homesteads via the new railroads of Iowa and Missouri. Second-class cars for immigrants and land-seekers were crowded in most of the prairie states in the seventies and eighties. The land agents of the Burlington, the Northern Pacific, and the Santa Fe all competed with each other and with the rival attractions of the steel mills and mines of Ohio and Pennsylvania as they met the immigrants and steerage passengers at eastern seaports. The extensive colonization literature of the Santa Fe paid off in 1874 when company agents convinced 1,900 Russian Mennonites, complete with $2,000,000 in gold drafts, that their future lay in fertile plains of Kansas. The Northern Pacific gained as settlers tried to emulate the reported success of Oliver Dalrymple's bonanza wheat farm in the Red River Valley of the Dakota Territory. The Burlington promoted extensive programs in agricultural research and new dry-farming methods in western Nebraska and eastern Colorado, even though it had no land to sell in those areas.

Settlers came in increasing numbers. The annual average of perfected homestead entries rose to more than 2,500,000 acres in the eighties and to more than 3,000,000 acres in the next decade. The first tier of trans-Mississippi states (Minnesota to Louisiana) more than doubled in population, from 4,500,000 to nearly 10,000,000, between 1870 and 1900. In the second tier of states (North Dakota to Texas) the increase during the three decades was more than fivefold: from 1,300,000 to over 7,000,000. The population of Nebraska in-

creased nearly nine times between 1870 and 1890, and that of
the Dakotas shot up from 14,000 to more than 500,000 in the
same years. As the frontier receded, the western railroad network grew more rapidly than the population. Between 1870
and 1900 the rail mileage of the eleven trans-Mississippi
prairie states had increased nearly eightfold, while the population had only tripled. This trend toward a relatively greater
rail service was a national one, since the miles of line per million inhabitants in the country had increased from 985 in
1860 to 1,858 miles in 1880 and to 2,544 miles in 1900.

The settling of America's last frontier, the trans-
Mississippi and mountain West, and the rapid growth of the
nation's railroads were in many ways simultaneous developments. As the early settlers pushed into the Great Plains just
after the Civil War, they were immediately helped in their
westward movement by a rail network that had already
reached the fringes of the frontier. A long generation later,
the frontier was fully closed as statehood came to the last of
the forty-eight continental states (Oklahoma in 1907, Arizona and New Mexico in 1912). In the same years, the railroad was nearing the close of its golden age as new, compet-
itive, and aggressive transportation facilities began to appear.
But in the short half-century between Appomatox and World
War I the railroads had helped the pioneer as he faced a
prairie frontier that was unique in its lack of wood and water.
They had built, with generous aid from the government, not
one but many lines across the mountains to the Pacific. The
railroad had speeded Texas-raised cattle from the Kansas
cowtown to the Chicago stockyards, had made more accessible the riches of the silver and gold mines of Colorado and
Nevada, and had taken to market the crops of the western
settler, who was now a commercial farmer. True, the railroad
corporations and the hard-headed, hard-hearted men who
ran them were often guilty of charging ruinous freight rates
and making other discriminations which seemed inexcusable
to farmers beset by falling farm prices, high interest rates,
and the necessity of competing in a world market. But it must
be said that the western railroads had done much to hasten
the settling and closing of America's last frontier.

The Frontier Thesis in Modern American History

Turning|Points
IN WORLD HISTORY

America's Frontier Heritage

Ray Allen Billington

Ray Allen Billington, who died in 1981, was a leading historian in the field of western expansion. His book *Westward Expansion* remains a standard text in the field. Billington was a disciple of Frederick Jackson Turner, who advanced the "frontier thesis"—the theory that the frontier played a crucial role in the development of the United States until 1890, when the frontier closed.

Billington and other historians have extended the frontier thesis to explain twentieth-century history. In the following essay, Billington maintains that America's image as the "land of opportunity" arose in the 1800s largely because of the cheap land and seemingly infinite resources that the frontier offered. The federal government's domestic policies of the twentieth century, he maintains, can be interpreted as attempts to solve the problems that the closing of the frontier created. He also argues that many aspects of American behavior, including inventiveness, optimism, and a strong work ethic, are part of the nation's frontier heritage.

To the American people, the rushes that symbolized the impending exhaustion of the public lands came as a shock. For generations they had been told that the supply was inexhaustible, and that westward expansion would go on for another five hundred years. Hence they were unprepared when the Superintendent of the Census announced in 1890 that the country's "unsettled area has been so broken into by isolated bodies of settlement that there can hardly be said to be a frontier line." His message, buried in an obscure public document, attracted little attention, but gradually the realization dawned that the frontier—the land of opportunity that had lured men and women westward for three centuries—would lure no more.

The Final Years of the Frontier

Actually these forebodings were decidedly premature. The West was but thinly occupied in 1890; only twice as many acres were under cultivation in the Far West as in the single state of Ohio, and even the tiny state of Delaware (which, according to its citizens, had three counties at low tide and two at high) contained more farms than Idaho or Montana, three times as many as Wyoming, and seven times as many as Arizona. There still was room along the frontiers for newcomers; there still was opportunity for the dispossessed to "grow up with the country."

So the migration continued, as the "westward tilt" of the continent spilled the adventuresome and the ambitious toward the setting sun. Four times as many acres were homesteaded in the West after 1890 as before, and twice as many have been since 1910 as in the prior fifty years. The persistence of the movement was also revealed by the regular shift westward of the center of population, from central Indiana in 1890 to the village of Mascoutah in Illinois' St. Clair County in 1970. During those years, too, those unable to find land in the American West turned northward toward Canada's open spaces; between 1900 and 1920 some three hundred thousand left the United States for farms in Manitoba, Alberta and Saskatchewan. The "last, best West" was still attracting, and the westward movement still helping shape the nation's economy and culture.

This migration softened the impact of the exhaustion of the public domain, but it could not hide the fact that the frontier movement was passing into history. As this realization slowly dawned, thinking Americans faced a series of troublesome questions. Could farmers long accustomed to land-exploitation adjust themselves to European habits of conservation? Could workers who (most economists believed) had maintained the world's highest living standard by dumping excess laborers on the frontier during crisis periods, accept increasing competition and lower wages? Would "radicals" demand destructive social reforms now that the discontented could no longer escape through the "safety valve" of the West? Could a people whose traditions and institutions had been formulated in an age of expansion adjust to a stable society? And, most important of all, could the democracy that had been nurtured by frontier opportunity survive in a closed-space nation?

A Broader Role for the Federal Government

The United States has been seeking answers to those questions for more than three-quarters of a century. Most of its leaders have recognized that the dog-eat-dog economy of the nineteenth century has been outmoded by the frontier's passing, and that cooperation rather than unrestricted competition must be the order of the future. They have also seen that only the federal government has sufficient power and resources to provide the people with the security and opportunity formerly provided by cheap land, and to serve as a watchdog over society in an era of increasing competition for dwindling natural resources. If this requires a more positive role on the part of the president and Congress, with a corresponding lessening of individual freedom, so be it. The passing of the frontier and the coming of the machine age have made the change imperative.

This is the reasoning that has shaped the political beliefs of progressive Americans since the dawn of the twentieth century. Theodore Roosevelt's "Square Deal" was rooted in the belief that the vanishing natural resources must be protected and equitably allotted; Woodrow Wilson's "New Freedom" sought to ensure individual opportunity by checking industrial monopoly; Franklin D. Roosevelt's "New Deal," John F. Kennedy's "New Frontier," and Lyndon B. Johnson's "Great Society" all were based on the realization that the state must care for a variety of needs formerly satisfied by the opportunity to flee westward. Implementing these beliefs has been the purpose of most of the important legislative programs of the twentieth century, from laws aimed at the conservation of natural resources, to those providing social security and medical aid.

Americans' Lingering Frontier Traits

Just as the frontier's closing has altered the nation's political climate, so has it affected American behavior. The aspects of the national character most closely linked with frontier opportunity—the migratory compulsion, inventive inclination, rose-tinted optimism, excessive wastefulness, strong work ethic, a unique social democracy—have during the last half-century gradually adjusted to the needs of a closed-space industrial-urban environment. Traits most closely linked to rural life have eroded most rapidly, others more slowly.

Thus the inventive urge remains strong and the patent office as busy as usual; technological improvement challenges the ingenuity of creative individuals just as the unique problems posed by expansion did. Similarly social democracy—a fundamental faith in equality—has persisted (save among minorities denied their proper place on the national escalator), even though the rags-to-riches fable on which it rested in the past is less widely believed. Today industrial opportunity opens the path to upward mobility for the industrious and talented, just as frontier opportunity did in the past. Hence class lines are less rigidly drawn in the United States than in European countries more steeped in tradition. The taxicab driver who calls his well-dressed customer "Mac" rather than "Sir" is responding to a frontier tradition that saw all men as potentially equal, and to be treated as such.

Americans also remain the most migratory of all western-world peoples, for transportation improvements give free vent to the wandering tendencies learned from our pioneer ancestors. We are eternally on the move—"permanently transitory" as one observer noted. We Americans live in automobiles, pausing in our eternal flight now and then at drive-in theaters, or drive-in restaurants, or drive-in banks, or "Park-and-Pray" churches. Some of us are forever on wheels, carrying our homes about with us like turtles; in the 1970s more than 750 thousand motor homes and trailers roamed the highways. We also shift about with alarming regularity; each year some thirty-six million of us move from one spot to another within the county where we live and another fifteen million shift from one county to another. So often do we move that bank statements, magazines and even dividend checks regularly include change-of-address slips. "If," wrote a Latin American visitor not long ago, "God were suddenly to call the world to judgment, He would surprise two-thirds of the Americans on the road, like ants."

The habit of wastefulness has proved equally hard to break. Conservationists have preached the necessity of preserving natural resources since the dawn of the twentieth century, bolstering their pleas with statistics to prove that the forests, fuel, minerals and soils of the United States would be exhausted within generations. These pleas have been met with bland indifference by most of the people, even after the energy crisis of the mid-1970s dramatically demonstrated that the United States lacks enough fossil fuels to satisfy its needs. Statisticians and politicians might urge saving, and a growing army of "environmentalists" might cry doom, but the majority refuses to listen. That 55 mph speed limit simply does not apply to anyone in a hurry (and what American is not, even when he has no place to go?). Besides, the old bus runs better at 65 than at 55. So we Americans have gone on squandering our birthright just as did our pioneer ancestors; the United States to Europeans is the land of the no-deposit-no-return bottle, the disposable tissue, the throw-away beer can, the bag-within-the-bag-within-the-bag at the supermarket. We still cling to a frontier-like faith that the future will provide, whatever the evidence to the contrary.

The work ethic that possessed pioneers has lost force, but its shadow remains. Today, with machines doing much of the drudgery formerly required of man, Americans still labor longer and harder than their cousins in older countries. We can find no time in our busy lives for the leisurely tea that is a treasured tradition in England, the restful siesta that soothes the Latin temperament, the unhurried lingering over a glass of wine in a sidewalk cafe that gladdens life in Paris or Rome. Only recently have the coffee-break, the two-martini lunch, and the interest in a shorter work week threatened the unending drive of middle-class America toward heart attacks and stomach ulcers. Even the one acceptable period of leisure—the cocktail hour—requires the consumption of liquids of such persuasive intensity that the maximum degree of rejuvenation is achieved in the minimum amount of time.

Finding Opportunity Beyond the Frontier

These are but symptoms of a changing national temperament that has manifested itself since the exhaustion of the government domain closed the door on frontier opportunity. The full shock of the frontier's closing has yet to be felt, and perhaps never will be if Yankee ingenuity and wise leadership develop substitutes for cheap lands. These could be in the form of sufficient energy to fuel continuing expansion of the economy, and wisely administered governmental programs to assure all people security and opportunity. If these things can be done, Americans may continue to enjoy the abundance, the freedom, and the opportunity for self-advancement that have been the frontier's principal contribution to the success of the Republic.

Appendix of Documents

Document 1: The Northwest Ordinance of 1787

In 1784, 1785, and 1787 the federal government enacted three ordinances that established the procedures by which the Northwest Territory (present-day Ohio, Indiana, Illinois, Michigan, and Wisconsin) should be settled and incorporated into the United States. The Northwest Ordinance of 1787 is considered the most important of the three because it established the procedures by which a territory could form its own legislature and eventually enter the Union. It also established the principle that new states would have equal rather than inferior status to older ones. Most of the states admitted to the Union after 1787 followed the plan of organization outlined in this ordinance.

THE ORDINANCE OF 1787

Ordinance for the Government of the Territory of the United States Northwest of the River Ohio

Be it ordained by the United States in Congress assembled, That the said territory, for the purposes of temporary government, be one district; subject, however, to be divided into two districts, as future circumstances may, in the opinion of Congress, make it expedient. . . .

Be it ordained by the authority aforesaid, That there shall be appointed, from time to time, by Congress, a governor, whose commission shall continue in force for the term of three years, unless sooner revoked by Congress; he shall reside in the district, and have a freehold estate therein, in one thousand acres of land, while in the exercise of his office. . . .

As soon as there shall be five thousand free male inhabitants, of full age, in the district, upon giving proof thereof to the governor, they shall receive authority, with time and place, to elect representatives from their counties or townships, to represent them in the general assembly; provided that for every five hundred free male inhabitants, there shall be one representative, and so on, progressively, with the number of free male inhabitants, shall the right of representation increase, until the number of representatives shall amount to twenty-five; after which the number and proportion of representatives shall be regulated by the legislature; provided, that no person shall be eligible or qualified to act as representative, unless he shall have been a citizen of one of the United States three years, and be a resident of the district, or unless he shall have resided in the district three years. . . .

. . . . As soon as a legislature shall be formed in the district, the council and house assembled, in one room, shall have authority, by joint ballot, to elect a delegate to Congress, with a right of debating, but not of voting during this temporary government.

And for extending the fundamental principles of civil and religious liberty, which form the basis whereon these republics, their laws, and constitutions are erected; to fix and establish those principles as the basis of all laws, constitutions, and governments, which forever hereafter shall be formed in the said territory; to provide, also, for the establishment of states and permanent government therein, and for their admission to a share in the federal councils on an equal footing with the original States, at as early periods as may be consistent with the general interest:

It is hereby ordained and declared, by the authority aforesaid, that the following articles shall be considered as articles of compact, between the original States and the people and States in the said territory, and forever remain unalterable, unless by common consent to wit:

ARTICLE 1. No person, demeaning himself in a peaceable and orderly manner, shall ever be molested on account of his mode of worship or religious sentiments, in the said territory.

ARTICLE 2. The Inhabitants of the said territory shall always be entitled to the benefits of the writ of *habeas corpus,* and of the trial by jury; of a proportionate representation of the people in the legislature, and of judicial proceedings according to the course of common law. . . .

ARTICLE 4. The said territory, and the States which may be formed therein, shall forever be a part of this confederacy of the United States of America, subject to the Articles of Confederation, and to such alterations therein as shall constitutionally be made; and to all acts and ordinances of the United States in Congress assembled, conformable thereto . . . The legislatures of those districts, or new States, shall never interfere with the primary disposal of the soil by the United States in Congress assembled, nor with any regulations Congress may find necessary, for securing the title in such soil, to bona-fide purchasers. No tax shall be imposed on lands the property of the United States; and in no case shall nonresident proprietors be taxed higher than residents. . . .

ARTICLE 5. There shall be formed in the said territory, not less than three, nor more than five states . . . whenever any of the said states shall have sixty-thousand free inhabitants therein, such State shall be admitted, by its delegates, into the Congress of the United

States, on an equal footing with the original States, in all respects whatever; and shall be at liberty to form a permanent constitution and State government: *Provided,* The constitution and government so to be formed, shall be republican, and in conformity with the principles contained in these articles; and so far as it can be consistent with the general interest of the confederacy, such admission shall be allowed at an earlier period, and when there may be a less number of free inhabitants in the State than sixty-thousand. . . .

Done by the United States in Congress assembled, the 13th day of July, in the year of our Lord 1787, and of the sovereignty and Independence the twelfth.

U.S. Congress, Ordinance for the Government of the Territory of the United States Northwest of the River Ohio, July 13, 1787.

Document 2: Thomas Jefferson's Instructions to Lewis and Clark

Thomas Jefferson and his private secretary Meriwether Lewis had been planning an expedition into the trans-Mississippi West since 1801, but only after the land became property of the United States under the Louisiana Purchase of May 2, 1803, could the president make his plans for the expedition public. In this June 20, 1803, letter to Lewis, Jefferson outlines the purpose and functions of the expedition.

The object of your mission is to explore the Missouri river, & such principal stream of it, as, by it's course & communication with the waters of the Pacific Ocean, may offer the most direct & practicable water communication across this continent, for the purposes of commerce.

Beginning at the mouth of the Missouri, you will take observations of latitude & longitude, at all remarkable points on the river, & especially at the mouths of rivers, at rapids, at islands & other places & objects distinguished by such natural marks & characters of a durable kind, as that they may with certainty be recognized hereafter. the courses of the river between these points of observation may be supplied by the compass, the log-line & by time, corrected by the observations themselves. the variations of the compass too, in different places, should be noticed.

The interesting points of portage between the heads of the Missouri & the water offering the best communication with the Pacific Ocean should also be fixed by observation, & the course of that water to the ocean, in the same manner as that of the Missouri.

Your observations are to be taken with great pains & accuracy, to be entered distinctly, & intelligibly for others as well as yourself, to comprehend all the elements necessary, with the aid of the usual tables, to fix the latitude and longitude of the places at which they were taken, & are to be rendered to the war office, for the purpose of having the calculations made concurrently by proper persons within the U.S. . . .

The commerce which may be carried on with the people inhabiting the line you will pursue, renders a knolege of these people important. you will therefore endeavor to make yourself acquainted, as far as a diligent pursuit of your journey shall admit,

> with the names of the nations & their numbers;
> the extent & limits of their possessions;
> their relations with other tribes or nations;
> their language, traditions, monuments;
> their ordinary occupations in agriculture, fishing, hunting, war, arts, & the implements for these;
> their food, clothing, & domestic accomodations;
> the diseases prevalent among them, & the remedies they use;
> moral & physical circumstances which distinguish them from the tribes we know;
> peculiarities in their laws, customs & dispositions;
> and articles of commerce they may need or furnish, & to what extent.

And considering the interest which every nation has in extending & strengthening the authority of reason & justice among the people around them, it will be useful to acquire what knolege you can of the state of morality, religion & information among them, as it may better enable those who endeavor to civilize & instruct them, to adapt their measures to the existing notions & practises of those on whom they are to operate.

Other object worthy of notice will be

> the soil & face of the country, it's growth & vegetable productions; especially those not of the U.S.
> the animals of the country generally, & especially those not known in the U.S.
> the remains and accounts of any which may deemed rare or extinct;
> the mineral productions of every kind; but more particularly metals, limestone,
> pit coal & salpetre; salines & mineral waters, noting the temperature of the last, & such circumstances as may indicate their character.
> Volcanic appearances.
> climate as characterized by the thermometer, by the proportion of rainy,

cloudy & clear days, by lightening, hail, snow, ice, by the access &
recess
of frost, by the winds prevailing at different seasons, the dates at
which particular
plants put forth or lose their flowers, or leaf, times of appearance
of particular birds, reptiles or insects.

. . . In all your intercourse with the natives treat them in the
most friendly & conciliatory manner which their own conduct will
admit; allay all jealousies as to the object of your journey, satisfy
them of it's innocence, make them acquainted with the position,
extent, character, peaceable & commercial dispositions of the U.S.
of our wish to be neighborly, friendly & useful to them, & of our
dispositions to a commercial intercourse with them; confer with
them on the points most convenient as mutual emporiums [trad-
ing houses], & the articles of most desireable interchange for them
& us. if a few of their influential chiefs, within practicable distance,
wish to visit us, arrange such a visit with them, and furnish them
with authority to call on our officers, on their entering the U.S. to
have them conveyed to this place at public expence. if any of them
should wish to have some of their young people brought up with
us, & taught such arts as may be useful to them, we will receive, instruct & take care of them. such a mission, whether of influential
chiefs, or of young people, would give some security to your own
party. carry with you some matter of the kine-pox [a serum used as
a vaccine against smallpox], inform those of them with whom you
may be of it's efficacy as a preservative from the small-pox; and instruct & incourage them in the use of it. this may be especially
done wherever you winter.

As it is impossible for us to foresee in what manner you will be
recieved by those people, whether with hospitality or hostility, so is
it impossible to prescribe the exact degree of perseverance with
which you are to pursue your journey. we value too much the lives
of citizens to offer them to probably destruction. your numbers will
be sufficient to secure you against the unauthorised opposition of
individuals, or of small parties: but if a superior force, authorised or
not authorised, by a nation, should be arrayed against your further
passage, & inflexibly determined to arrest it, you must decline it's
further pursuit, and return. in the loss of yourselves, we should lose
also the information you will have acquired. by returning safely
with that, you may enable us to renew the essay with better calculated means. to your own discretion therefore must be left the degree of danger you may risk, & the point at which you should de-

cline, only saying we wish you to err on the side of your safety, & bring back your party safe, even if it be with less information. . . .

Should you reach the Pacific ocean inform yourself of the circumstances which may decide whether the furs of those parts may not be collected as advantageously at the head of the Missouri (convenient as is supposed to the waters of the Colorado & Oregon or Columbia) as at Nootka sound or any other point of that coast; & that trade be consequently conducted through the Missouri & U.S. more beneficially than by the circumnavigation now practised. . . .

Given under my hand at the city of Washington, this 20th day of June 1803

Th. Jefferson
Pr. US. of America

Thomas Jefferson to Meriwether Lewis, Washington, DC, June 20, 1803.

Document 3: Excerpts from the Journals of Lewis and Clark

In accordance with Jefferson's instructions, Meriwether Lewis and William Clark each kept detailed records throughout their expedition. The complete journals were first published in 1904 and 1905. They filled eight volumes, and since then they have been reprinted many times in abridged form.

[Many of Lewis's entries detail the party's encounters with the Indian tribes of the Rocky Mountains and Pacific Northwest. In the following excerpt, Lewis describes his first, awkward encounter with a Shoshone Indian in what is now Montana.]

[Lewis]   Sunday August 11th. 1805.—

I discovered an Indian on horse back about two miles distant coming down the plain towards us. with my glass I discovered from his dress that he was of a different nation from any that we had yet seen, and was satisfyed of his being a Sosone; his arms were a bow and quiver of arrows, and was mounted on an eligant horse without a saddle, and a small string which was attatched to the under jaw of the horse which answered as a bridle. I was overjoyed at the sight of this stranger and had no doubt of obtaining a friendly introduction to his nation provided I could get near enough to him to convince him of our being whitemen. I therefore proceeded towards him at my usual pace. when I had arrived within about a mile he mad[e] a halt which I did also and unloosing my blanket from my pack, I mad[e] him the signal of friendship known to the Indians of the Rocky mountains and those of the

Missouri, which is by holding the mantle or robe in your hands at two corners and then th[r]owing [it] up in the air higher than the head bringing it to the earth as if in the act of spreading it, thus repeating three times. this signal of the robe has arrisen from a custom among all those nations of spreading a robe or skin for ther gests to set on when they are visited. this signal had not the desired effect, he still kept his position and seemed to view Drewyer an[d] Shields who were now comiming in sight on either hand with an air of suspicion, I wo[u]ld willingly have made them halt but they were too far distant to hear me and I feared to make any signal to them least it should increase the suspicion in the mind of the Indian of our having some unfriendly design upon him. I therefore haistened to take out of my sack some b[e]ads a looking glas and a few trinkets which I had brought with me for this purpose and leaving my gun and pouch with McNeal advanced unarmed towards him.

he remained in the same stedfast poisture untill I arrived in about 200 paces of him when he turn[ed] his ho[r]se about and began to move off slowly from me; I now called to him in as loud a voice as I could command repeating the word *tab-ba-bone*, which in their language signifyes *white-man*. but l[o]king over his sholder he still kept his eye on Drewyer and Sheilds who wer still advancing neither of them haveing sagacity enough to recollect the impropriety of advancing when they saw me thus in parley with the Indian. I now made a signal to these men to halt, Drewyer obeyed but Shields who afterwards told me that he did not obse[r]ve the signal still kept on the Indian halted again and turned his hor[s]e about as if to wait for me, and I beleive he would have remained untill I came up whith him had it not been for Shields who still pressed forward. whe[n] I arrived within about 150 paces I again repepeated the word tab-ba-bone and held up the trinkits in my hands and striped up my shirt sleve to give him an opportunity of seeing the colour of my skin and advanced leasure towards him. but he did not remain until I got nearer than about 100 paces when he suddonly turned his ho[r]se about, gave him the whip leaped the creek and disapeared in the willow brush in an instant and with him vanished all my hopes of obtaining horses for the preasent.

[As Jefferson had instructed, Lewis took detailed notes about the new flora and fauna he encountered. The following entry is typical.]

Friday September 20th. 1805.

This morning my attention was called to a species of bird which

I had never seen before [a Steller's jay]. It was reather larger than a robbin, tho' much it's form and action. the colours were a blueish brown on the back the wings and tale black, as wass a stripe above the croop ¾ of an inch wide in front of the neck, and two others of the same colour passed from it's eyes back along the sides of the head. the top of the head, neck brest and belley and butts of the wing were of a fine yellowish brick reed [red]. it was feeding on the buries of a species of shoemake or ash which grows common in [this] country & which I first observed on 2d. of this month. I have also observed two birds of a blue colour both of which I believe to be of the haulk or vulter kind. the one of a blue shining colour with a very high tuft of feathers on the head a long tale, it feeds on flesh the beak and feet black. it's note is chă-ăh, chă-ăh. it is about the size of a pigeon, and in shape and action resembles the jay bird.

[Lewis and Clark endured many hardships on their two-and-a-half-year journey, not the least of which was the winter of 1805–1806, which they spent at Fort Clatsop near present-day Tongue Point, Oregon. In the following entries, Clark writes of the dreariness and hunger that characterized this part of the expedition.]

Wednesday 11th. December 1805
rained all the last night moderately we are all employed putting up huts or Cabins for our winters quarters, Sergeant Pryor unwell from a dislocation of his sholder, Gibson with the disentary, Jo. Fields with biles on his legs, & Werner with a Strained Knee. The rain Continued moderately all day.

Monday 23rd. December 1805
Rained without intermition all the last night and to day with Thunder and Hail the fore and after part of this day. Capt. Lewis and my self move into our hut to day unfinished.

Christmas Wednesday 25th. December 1805
we would have Spent this day the nativity of Christ in feasting, had we any thing either to raise our Sperits or even gratify our appetites, our Diner concisted of pore Elk, so much Spoiled that we eate it thro' mear necessity, Some Spoiled pounded fish and a fiew roots.

Frank Bergen, ed., *The Journals of Lewis & Clark*. New York: Penguin, 1989.

Document 4: The Benefits of Acquiring Oregon

Beginning in 1830, thousands of settlers migrated to the Pacific Northwest. One of the most famous Oregon boosters was Hall J. Kelley, a Boston schoolteacher who organized societies for the colonization of the new territory. In the 1831 promotional pamphlet excerpted below, Kelley extols the virtues of Oregon and urges Congress to take permanent possession of the territory.

The American Society, for encouraging the Settlement of the Oregon Territory, instituted in A.D. 1829, and incorporated by the Commonwealth of Massachusetts, actuated by a faithful regard to duty, have cheerfully engaged in the work of opening to a civilized and virtuous population, that part of Western America, called *Oregon*.

They are convinced, that if that country should be settled under the auspices of the Government of the United States of America, from such of her worthy sons, who have drank of the spirit of those civil and religious institutions which constitute the living fountain, and the very perennial source of her national prosperity, great benefits must result to mankind. They believe, that there, the skilful and persevering hand of industry might be employed with unparalleled advantage; that there, Science and the Arts, the invaluable privileges of a free and liberal government, and the refinements and ordinances of Christianity, diffusing each its blessing, would harmoniously unite in meliorating the moral condition of the Indians, in promoting the comfort and happiness of the settlers, and in augmenting the wealth and power of the Republic.

The uniform testimony of an intelligent multitude have established the fact, that the country in question, is the most valuable of all the unoccupied parts of the earth. Its peculiar location and facilities, and physical resources for trade and commerce; its contiguous markets; its salubrity of climate; its fertility of soil; its rich and abundant productions; its extensive forests of valuable timber; and its great water Channel diversifying, by its numerous branches the whole country, and spreading canals through every part of it, are sure indications that Providence has designed this last reach of enlightened emigration to be the residence of a people, whose singular advantages will give them unexampled power and prosperity.

These things have excited the admiration of every observer, and have settled in the policy of the British nation the determined purpose of possessing and enjoying them, as their own; and have induced their Parliament to confer on the Hudson's Bay Company, chartered privileges for occupying with their settlements the fertile banks of the Columbia; which settlements have been made; and are flourishing, in rapid growth, under the culture secured by the provisions of a Colonial Government.

The Society conceive it clearly deduced, from all the facts in the case, that the right of sovereignty over the Oregon Territory, is invested in the government of the United States of America, consequently, in her is the exclusive right of colonizing that country, and of introducing into it the various business and benefits of civilized life.

The expense and labor necessary to the accomplishment of this work, planned by Providence, made easy by nature, and urged and encouraged by the persuasive motives of philanthropy, are, in no degree, commensurate with the national blessings to be derived from it; among which are enumerated the following; viz:

The moral condition of the *Aborigines*, if blessed by the influences of a refined and religious community, will be improved. The attempt to enlighten the minds and to dignify the nature of this unfortunate race, may no longer be defeated by injudicious plans.

Their unjust and unequal alliances with *another nation* may be broken, and their friendship secured to *this*.

By means, thus honorable, that valuable territory would be held from the possession of an unfriendly power.

Ports of Entry, and Ship and Navy Yards, might be established with great advantage, on the waters of Oregon, and thereby, the trade and commerce of both the Pacific and Atlantic Oceans would become extended and enriched. Capitalists and Mariners might pursue, with more profit and safety, the whale and other fisheries in the Western Seas, and the salmon trade on the Columbia.

A portion of the virtuous and enterprising, but not least faithful population, whom misfortunes have thrown out of employment, and who throng our villages and sea-ports, and seek a better home, might there find opportunities, under the paternal kindness of the government, to succeed to a happier condition, and to greater usefulness to themselves and to their country.

These are objects so obvious, so vast and valuable, as need not be urged by your memorialists, and seem necessarily embraced within the scope of a wise policy. They are yet deemed practicable. Another season—their possession will be thought expedient—but not so easily wrested from the grasp of British power.

The Society view with alarm the progress, which the subjects of that nation have made, in the colonization of the Oregon Territory. Already, have they, flourishing towns, strong fortifications, and cultivated farms. The domicile is made the abode of domestic comforts—the social circle is enlivened by the busy wife and the prattle and sport of children. In the convention of 1818, England secured for her subjects, the privilege of a free trade, that of buying furs of the Indians; but, at first, they practised trapping and hunting; now, they practice buying and improving lands, and assiduously pursue the business of the farmer and mechanic. Their largest town is Vancouver, which is situated on a beautiful plain, in the region of tide water, on the northern bank of the Columbia. At this place, saw and grist mills are in operation. Three vessels have been built, one of about 300 tons, and are employed in the lumber trade. Numerous herds and flocks of horses, horned cattle, and sheep, of the best European breeds, are seen grazing in their ever verdant fields. Grain of all kinds, in abundant crops, are the productions of the soil.

Everything, either in the organization of the government, or in the busy and various operations of the settlements, at this place, at Wallawalla, at Fort Colville, and at De Fuca, indicate the intentions of the English to colonize the country. Now, therefore, your memorialists, in behalf of a large number of the citizens of the United States, would respectfully ask Congress to aid them in carrying into operation the great purposes of their institution—to grant them troops, artillery, military arms, and munitions of war, for the defence and security of the contemplated settlement—to incorporate their Society with power to extinguish the Indian title, to such tracts and extent of territory, at the mouth of the Columbia, and at the junction of the Multnomah with the Columbia, as may be adequate to the laudable objects and pursuits of the settlers, and with such other powers, rights and immunities, as may be, at least, equal and concurrent to those given by Parliament to the Hudson's Bay Company; and such as are not repugnant to the stipulations of the Convention, made between Great Britain and the United States, wherein it was agreed, that any country on the Northwest Coast of America, to the westward of the Rocky Mountains, should be free and open to the citizens and subjects of the two powers, for a term of years; and to grant them such other rights and privileges, as may contribute to the means of establishing a respectable and prosperous community.

Hall J. Kelley, *A General Circular to All Persons of Good Character, Who Wish to Emigrate to the Oregon Territory.* Charlestown, SC: R.P. & C. Williams, 1831.

Document 5: The Place of Indians in the Republic

As early as 1803 President Jefferson proposed a plan for offering Indian tribes unsettled western prairie land in exchange for their traditional holdings east of the Mississippi. On May 28, 1830, Congress passed the Indian Removal Act, which authorized the president to carry out the removal plan. In his 1835 message to Congress, President Andrew Jackson defends the act and promises that white settlers will not encroach farther into Indian lands.

. . . The plan of removing the aboriginal people who yet remain within the settled portions of the United States to the country west of the Mississippi River approaches its consummation. It was adopted on the most mature consideration of the condition of this race, and ought to be persisted in till the object is accomplished, and prosecuted with as much vigor as a just regard to their circumstances will permit, and as fast as their consent can be obtained. All preceding experiments for the improvement of the Indians have failed. It seems now to be an established fact that they can not live in contact with a civilized community and prosper. . . . In the discharge of this duty an extensive region in the West has been assigned for their permanent residence. It has been divided into districts and allotted among them. Many have already removed and others are preparing to go, and with the exception of two small bands living in Ohio and Indiana, not exceeding 1,500 persons, and of the Cherokees, all the tribes on the east side of the Mississippi, and extending from Lake Michigan to Florida, have entered into engagements which will lead to their transplantation.

The plan for their removal and reestablishment is founded upon the knowledge we have gained of their character and habits, and has been dictated by a spirit of enlarged liberality. A territory exceeding in extent that relinquished has been granted to each tribe. Of its climate, fertility, and capacity to support an Indian population the representations are highly favorable. To these districts the Indians are removed at the expense of the United States, and with certain supplies of clothing, arms, ammunition, and other indispensable articles; they are also furnished gratuitously with provisions for the period of a year after their arrival at their new homes. In that time, from the nature of the country and of the products raised by them, they can subsist themselves by agricultural labor, if they choose to resort to that mode of life; if they do not they are upon the skirts of the great prairies, where countless herds of buffalo roam, and a short time suffices to adapt their own habits to the changes which a change of the animals destined for their food may require. Ample arrangements have also been made for the support of schools; in some instances council houses and churches are to be erected, dwellings constructed for the chiefs, and mills for common use. . . . And besides these beneficial arrangements, annuities are in all cases paid, amounting in some instances to more than $30 for each individual of the tribe, and in all cases sufficiently great, if justly divided and prudently expended, to enable them, in addition to their own exertions, to live comfortably. . . .

Such are the arrangements for the physical comfort and for the moral improvement of the Indians. The necessary measures for their political advancement and for their separation from our citizens have not been neglected. The pledge of the United States has been given by Congress that the country destined for the residence of this people shall be forever "secured and guaranteed to them." A country west of Missouri and Arkansas has been assigned to them, into which the white settlements are not to be pushed. No political communities can be formed in that extensive region, except those which are established by the Indians themselves or by the United States for them and with their concurrence. A barrier has thus been raised for their protection against the encroachment of our citizens, and guarding the Indians as far as possible from those evils which have brought them to their present condition.

Andrew Jackson, Seventh Annual Message to Congress, Washington, DC, December 7, 1835.

Document 6: The Annexation of Texas

The phrase "Manifest Destiny" was coined by John L. O'Sullivan, editor of the Democratic Review, *in an essay justifying the annexation of Texas. O'Sullivan's essay was first published in the July/August 1845 issue of his magazine; he used the term again in an editorial in the* New York Morning News, *and by 1846 the phrase was a popular slogan among expansionists.*

It is time now for opposition to the Annexation of Texas to cease, all further agitation of the waters of bitterness and strife, at least in connexion with this question,—even though it may perhaps be required of us as a necessary condition of the freedom of our institutions, that we must live on for ever in a state of unpausing struggle and excitement upon some subject of party division or other. But, in regard to Texas, enough has now been given to Party. It is time for the common duty of Patriotism to the Country to succeed;—or if this claim will not be recognized, it is at least time for common sense to acquiesce with decent grace in the inevitable and the irrevocable.

Why, were other reasoning wanting, in favor of now elevating this question of the reception of Texas into the Union, out of the lower region of our past party dissensions, up to its proper level of a high and broad nationality, it surely is to be found, found abundantly, in the manner in which other nations have undertaken to intrude themselves into it, between us and the proper parties to the case, in a spirit of hostile interference against us, for the avowed object of thwarting our policy and hampering our power, limiting our greatness and checking the fulfilment of our manifest destiny to overspread the continent allotted by Providence for the free development of our yearly multiplying millions. This we have seen done by England, our old rival and enemy; and by France, strangely coupled with her against us, under the influence of the Anglicism strongly tinging the policy of her present prime minister, Guizot. The zealous activity with which this effort to defeat us was pushed by the representatives of those governments, together with the character of intrigue accompanying it, fully constituted that case of foreign interference, which Mr. Clay himself declared should, and would unite us all in maintaining the common cause of our country against the foreigner and the foe. We are only astonished that this effect has not been more fully and strongly produced, and that the burst of indignation against this unauthorized, insolent and hostile interference against us, has not been more general even among the party before opposed to Annexation, and has not rallied the national spirit and national pride unanimously upon that policy. . . .

It is wholly untrue, and unjust to ourselves, the pretence that the Annexation has been a measure of spoliation, unrightful and unrighteous—of military conquest under forms of peace and law—of territorial aggrandizement at the expense of justice, and justice due by a double sanctity to the weak. This view of the question is wholly unfounded, and has been before so amply refuted in these pages, as well as in a thousand other modes, that we shall not again dwell upon it. The independence of Texas was complete and absolute. It was an independence, not only in fact but of right. No obligation of duty towards Mexico tended in the least degree to restrain our right to effect the desired recovery of the fair province once our own—whatever motives of policy might have prompted a more deferential consideration of her feelings and her pride, as involved in the question. If Texas became peopled with an American population, it was by no contrivance of our government, but on the express invitation of that of Mexico herself; accompanied with such guaranties of State independence, and the maintenance of a federal system analogous to our own, as constituted a compact fully justifying the strongest measures of redress on the part of those afterwards deceived in this guaranty, and sought to be enslaved under the yoke imposed by its violation. She was released, rightfully and absolutely released, from all Mexican allegiance, or duty of cohesion to the Mexican political body, by the acts and fault of Mexico herself, and Mexico alone. There never was a clearer case. It was not revolution; it was resistance to revolution; and resistance under such circumstances as left independence the necessary resulting state, caused by the abandonment of those with whom her former federal association had existed. What then can be more preposterous than all this clamor by Mexico and the Mexican interest, against Annexation, as a violation of any rights of hers, any duties of ours?

. . . The country which was the subject of Annexation in this case, from its geographical position and relations, happens to be— or rather the portion of it now actually settled, happens to be—a slave country. But a similar process might have taken place in proximity to a different section, of our Union; and indeed there is a great deal of Annexation yet to take place, within the life of the present generation, along the whole line of our northern border. Texas has been absorbed into the Union in the inevitable fulfilment of the general law which is rolling our population westward; the connexion of which with that ratio of growth in population which is destined within a hundred years to swell our numbers to the enormous population of *two hundred and fifty millions* (if not more), is too evident to leave us in doubt of the manifest design of Providence in regard to the occupation of this continent. It was disintegrated from Mexico in the natural course of events, by a process perfectly legitimate on its own part, blameless on ours; and in which all the censures due to wrong, perfidy and folly, rest on Mexico alone. And possessed as it was by a population which was in truth but a colonial detachment from our own, and which was still bound by myriad ties of the very heartstrings to its old relations, domestic and political, their incorporation into the Union was not only inevitable, but the most natural, right and proper thing in the world—and it is only astonishing that there should be any among ourselves to say it nay.

California will, probably, next fall away from the loose adhesion which, in such a country as Mexico, holds a remote province in a slight equivocal kind of dependence on the metropolis. Imbecile and distracted, Mexico never can exert any real governmental authority over such a country. The impotence of the one and the distance of the other, must make the relation one of virtual independence; unless, by stunting the province of all natural growth, and forbidding that immigration which can alone develop its capabilities and fulfil the purposes of its creation, tyranny may retain a military dominion which is no government in the legitimate sense of the term. In the case of California this is now impossible. The Anglo-Saxon foot is already on its borders. Already the advance guard of the irresistible army of Anglo-Saxon emigration has begun to pour down upon it, armed with the plough and the rifle, and marking its trail with schools and colleges, courts and representative halls, mills and meeting-houses. A population will soon be in actual occupation of California, over which it will be idle for Mexico to dream of dominion. . . .

Away, then, with all idle French talk of *balances of power* on the American Continent. There is no growth in Spanish America! Whatever progress of population there may be in the British Canadas, is only for their own early severance of their present colonial relation to the little island three thousand miles across the Atlantic; soon to be followed by Annexation, and destined to swell the still accumulating momentum of our progress. And whatsoever may hold the balance, though they should cast into the opposite scale all the bayonets and cannon, not only of France and England, but of Europe entire, how would it kick the beam against the simple solid weight of two hundred and fifty or three hundred millions—and American millions—destined to gather beneath the flutter of the stripes and stars, in the fast hastening year of the Lord 1845?

John L. O'Sullivan, "Annexation," *United States Magazine and Democratic Review*, July/August 1845.

Document 7: The Destiny of the Race

Thomas Hart Benton was a Democratic senator from Missouri and a powerful proponent of western expansion. In this 1846 speech before Congress excerpted below, Benton argues for the acquisition of Oregon territory from Great Britain. Using arguments that were popular at the time, Benton maintains that it is the destiny of the white race to spread throughout the New World.

Since the dispersion of man upon earth, I know of no human event, past or present, which promises a greater, a more beneficent change upon earth than the arrival of the van [first appearance] of the Caucasian race (the Celtic-Anglo-Saxon division) upon the border of the sea which washes the shore of eastern Asia. The Mongolian, or Yellow race, is there, four hundred million in number, spreading almost to Europe; a race once the foremost of the human family in the arts of civilization, but torpid and stationary for thousands of years. It is a race far above the Ethiopian, or Black—above the Malay, or Brown (if we must admit five races)—and above the American Indian, or Red; it is a race far above all these, but still, far below the White; and, like all the rest, must receive an impression from the superior race whenever they come in contact. It would seem that the White race alone received the divine command, to subdue and replenish the earth! for it is the only race that has obeyed it—the only one that hunts out new and distant lands, and even a New World, to subdue and replenish. Starting from western Asia, taking Europe for their field, and the Sun for their guide, and leaving the Mongolians behind, they arrived, after many ages, on the shores of the Atlantic, which they lit up with the lights of science and religion, and adorned with the useful and the elegant arts. Three and a half centuries ago, this race, in obedience to the great command, arrived in the New World, and found new lands to subdue and replenish. For a long time, it was confined to the border of the new field (I now mean the Celtic-Anglo-Saxon division); and even fourscore years ago the philosophic [Edmund] Burke was considered a rash man because he said the English colonists would top the Alleghenies, and descend into the valley of the Mississippi, and occupy without parchment if the Crown refused to make grants of land.

What was considered a rash declaration eighty years ago, is old history, in our young country, at this day. Thirty years ago I said the same thing of the Rocky Mountains and the Columbia: it was ridiculed then: it is becoming history to-day. . . . The van of the Caucasian race now top the Rocky Mountains, and spread down to the shores of the Pacific. In a few years a great population will grow up there, luminous with the accumulated lights of European and American civilization. Their presence in such a position cannot be without its influence upon eastern Asia. The sun of civilization must shine across the sea: socially and commercially, the van of the Caucasians, and the rear of the Mongolians, must intermix. They must talk together, and trade together, and marry together. Commerce is a great civilizer—social intercourse as great—and marriage greater. The White and Yellow races can marry together, as well as eat and trade together. Moral and intellectual superiority will do the rest: the White race will take the ascendant, elevating what is susceptible of improvement—wearing out what is not. The Red race has disappeared from the Atlantic coast: the tribes that resisted civilization, met extinction. This is a cause of lamentation with many. For my part, I cannot murmur at what seems to be the effect of divine law. I cannot repine that this Capitol has replaced the wigwam—this Christian people, replaced the savages—white matrons, the red squaws—and that such men as Washington, Franklin, and Jefferson, have taken the place of Powhattan, Opechonecanough, and other men, howsoever respectable they may have been as savages.

Civilization, or extinction, has been the fate of all people who have found themselves in the track of the advancing Whites, and civilization, always the preference of the Whites, has been pressed as an object, while extinction has followed as a consequence of its resistance. The Black and the Red races have often felt their ameliorating influence. The Yellow race, next to themselves in the scale of mental and moral excellence, and in the beauty of form, once their superiors in the useful and elegant arts, and in learning, and still respectable though stationary; this race cannot fail to receive a new impulse from the approach of the Whites, improved so much since so many ages ago they left the western borders of Asia. The apparition of the van of the Caucasian race, rising upon them in the east after having left them on the west, and after having completed the circumnavigation of the globe, must wake up and reanimate the torpid body of the old Asia. Our position and policy will commend us to their hospitable reception: political considerations will aid the action of social and commercial influences. Pressed upon by the great Powers of Europe—the same that press upon us—they must in our approach see the advent of friends, not of foes—of benefactors, not of invaders. The moral and intellectual superiority of the White race will do the rest: and thus the youngest people, and the newest land, will become the reviver and the regenerator of the oldest.

Thomas Hart Benton, "The Destiny of the Race," *Congressional Globe*, May 28, 1846.

Document 8: A Description of Rocky Mountain Trappers

George Frederick Ruxton was an English adventurer and member of the Royal Geographic Society. He wrote the following description of the Rocky

Mountain fur trappers after spending the winter of 1847 at a trading post in Colorado.

The trappers of the Rocky Mountains belong to a "genus" more approximating to the primitive savage than perhaps any other class of civilized man. . . . Strong, active, hardy as bears, daring, expert in the use of their weapons, they are just what uncivilized white man might be supposed to be in a brute state, depending upon his instinct for the support of life. Not a hole or corner in the vast wilderness of the "Far West" but has been ransacked by these hardy men. From the Mississippi to the mouth of the Colorado of the West, from the frozen regions of the North to the Gila in Mexico, the beaver-hunter has set his traps in every creek and stream. All this vast country, but for the daring enterprise of these men, would be even now a *terra incognita* to geographers, as indeed a great portion still is; but there is not an acre that has not been passed and repassed by the trappers in their perilous excursions. The mountains and streams still retain the names assigned to them by the rude hunters; and these alone are the hardy pioneers who have paved the way for the settlement of the western country.

Trappers are of two kinds, the "hired hand" and the "free trapper:" the former hired for the hunt by the fur companies; the latter, supplied with animals and traps by the company, is paid a certain price for his furs and peltries.

There is also the trapper "on his own hook;" but this class is very small. He has his own animals and traps, hunts where he chooses, and sells his peltries to whom he pleases.

On starting for a hunt, the trapper fits himself out with the necessary equipment, either from the Indian trading-forts, or from some of the petty traders . . . who frequent the western country. This equipment consists usually of two or three horses or mules—one for saddle, the others for packs—and six traps, which are carried in a bag of leather called a *trap-sack*. Ammunition, a few pounds of tobacco, dressed deer-skins for mocassins, &c., are carried in a wallet of dressed buffalo-skin, called a possible-sack. His "possibles" and "trap-sack" are generally carried on the saddle-mule when hunting, the others being packed with the furs. The costume of the trapper is a hunting-shirt of dressed buckskin, ornamented with long fringes; pantaloons of the same material, and decorated with porcupine-quills and long fringes down the outside of the leg. A flexible felt hat and mocassins clothe his extremities. Over his left shoulder and under his right arm hang his powder-horn and bullet-pouch, in which he carries his balls, flint and steel, and odds and ends of all kinds. Round the waist is a belt, in which is stuck a large butcher-knife in a sheath of buffalo-hide, made fast to the belt by a chain or guard of steel; which also supports a little buckskin case containing a whetstone. A tomahawk is also often added; and, of course, a long heavy rifle is part and parcel of his equipment. I had nearly forgotten the pipe-holder, which hangs round his neck, and is generally a gage d'amour, and a triumph of squaw workmanship, in shape of a heart, garnished with beads and porcupine-quills.

Thus provided, and having determined the locality of his trapping-ground, he starts to the mountains, sometimes alone, sometimes with three or four in company, as soon as the breaking up of the ice allows him to commence operations. Arrived on his hunting-grounds, he follows the creeks and streams, keeping a sharp look-out for "sign." If he sees a prostrate cotton-wood tree, he examines it to discover if it be the work of beaver—whether "thrown" for the purpose of food, or to dam the stream. The track of the beaver on the mud or sand under the bank is also examined; and if the "sign" be fresh, he sets his trap in the run of the animal, hiding it under water, and attaching it by a stout chain to a picket driven in the bank, or to a bush or tree. A "float-stick" is made fast to the trap by a cord a few feet long, which, if the animal carry away the trap, floats on the water and points out its position. The trap is baited with the "medicine," an oily substance obtained from a gland in the scrotum of the beaver, but distinct from the testes. A stick is dipped into this and planted over the trap; and the beaver, attracted by the smell, and wishing a close inspection, very foolishly puts his leg into the trap, and is a "gone beaver."

When a lodge is discovered, the trap is set at the edge of the dam, at the point where the animal passes from deep to shoal water, and always under water. Early in the morning the hunter mounts his mule and examines the traps. The captured animals are skinned, and the tails, which are a great dainty, carefully packed into camp. The skin is then stretched over a hoop or framework of osier-twigs, and is allowed to dry, the flesh and fatty substance being carefully scraped (grained). When dry, it is folded into a square sheet, the fur turned inwards, and the bundle, containing about ten to twenty skins, tightly pressed and corded, and is ready for transportation.

At a certain time, when the hunt is over, or they have loaded their pack-animals, the trappers proceed to the "rendezvous," the locality of which has been previously agreed upon; and here the traders and agents of the fur companies await them, with such assortment of goods as their hardy customers may require, including generally a fair supply of alcohol. The trappers drop in singly and in small bands, bringing their packs of beaver to this mountain market, not unfrequently to the value of a thousand dollars each, the produce of one hunt. The dissipation of the "rendezvous," however, soon turns the trapper's pocket inside out. The goods brought by the traders, although, of the most inferior quality, are sold at enormous prices. . . .

The "beaver" is purchased at from two to eight dollars per pound; the Hudson's Bay Company alone buying it by the pluie, or "plew," that is, the whole skin, giving a certain price for skins, whether of old beaver or "kittens."

The rendezvous is one continued scene of drunkenness, gambling, and brawling and fighting, as long as the money and credit of the trappers last. Seated, Indian fashion, round the fires, with a blanket spread before them, groups are seen with their "decks" of cards, playing at "euker," "poker," and "seven-up," the regular mountain games. The stakes are "beaver," which here is current coin; and when the fur is gone, their horses, mules, rifles, and shirts, hunting-packs, and *breeches*, are staked. Daring gamblers make the rounds of the camp, challenging each other to play for the trapper's highest stake,—his horse, his squaw (if he have one), and, as once happened, his scalp. There goes "hos and beaver!" is the mountain expression when any great loss is sustained; and, sooner or later, "hos and beaver" invariably find their way into the insatiable pockets of the traders. A trapper often squanders the produce of his hunt, amounting to hundreds of dollars, in a couple of hours; and, supplied on credit with another equipment, leaves the rendezvous for another expedition, which has the same result time after time; although one tolerably successful hunt would enable him to return to the settlements and civilised life, with an ample sum to purchase and stock a farm, and enjoy himself in ease and comfort the remainder of his days.

George F. Ruxton, *Adventures in Mexico and the Rocky Mountains*. New York: Harper & Brothers, 1848.

Document 9: The Discovery of Gold in California

Thomas O. Larkin was a merchant and land speculator in California in the 1840s. In 1846 and 1847 he also served as a U.S. consul and secret agent in the region. Larkin was the first to give confirmation to the fed-

eral government about the discovery of gold at Sutter's Mill in what is now Sacramento, California. In letter to Secretary of State James Buchanan, which arrived in September 1948, Larkin describes the beginnings of the "gold fever" that took hold first in California and later throughout the nation.

I have to report to the State Department one of the most astonishing excitements and state of affairs now existing in this country, that, perhaps, has ever been brought to the notice of the government. On the American fork of the Sacramento and Feather river, another branch of the same, and the adjoining lands, there has been, within the present year, discovered a placer, a vast tract of land containing gold, in small particles. This gold, thus far, has been taken on the bank of the river, from the surface to eighteen inches in depth, and is supposed deeper, and to extend over the country. On account of the inconvenience of washing, the people have, to this time, only gathered the metal on the banks, which is done simply with a shovel, filling a shallow dish, bowl, basket, or tin pan with a quantity of black sand, similar to the class used on paper, and washing out the sand by movement of the vessel. It is now two or three weeks since the men employed in these washings have appeared in this town with gold, to exchange for merchandise and provisions. I presume near twenty thousand dollars . . . of this gold has, as yet, been so exchanged. . . . I have seen the written statement of the work of one man for sixteen days, which averaged twenty-five dollars ($25) per day; others have, with a shovel and pan, or wooden bowl, washed out ten to even fifty dollars in a day. There are now some men yet washing, who have five hundred to one thousand dollars. As they have to stand two feet deep in the river, they work but a few hours in the day, and not every day in the week. A few men have been down in boats to this port, spending twenty to thirty ounces of gold each—about three hundred dollars. . . . I am confident that this town (San Francisco) has one-half of its tenements empty, locked up with the furniture. The owners—storekeepers, lawyers, mechanics, and laborers—all gone to the Sacramento with their families. Small parties, of five to fifteen men, have sent to this town and offered cooks ten to fifteen dollars per day for a few weeks. Mechanics and teamsters, earning the year past five to eight dollars per day, have struck and gone. Several United States volunteers have deserted. United States barque Anita, belonging to the army, now at anchor here, has but six men. One Sandwich island vessel in port lost all her men. . . .

Common spades and shovels, one month ago worth one dollar, will now bring ten dollars at the gold regions. I am informed fifty dollars has been offered for one. Should this gold continue as represented, this town, and others, will be depopulated. Clerks' wages have rose from six hundred to one thousand dollars per annum, and board; cooks', twenty-five to thirty dollars per month. This sum will not be any inducement a month longer, unless the fever and ague appears among the washers. The "Californian," printed here, stopped this week. The "Star" newspaper office . . . has but one man left. A merchant, lately from China, has even lost his China servants. Should the excitement continue through the year, and the whale-ships visit San Francisco, I think they will lose most all their crews. . . . I have seen several pounds of this gold, and consider it very pure, worth, in New York, seventeen to eighteen dollars per ounce. Fourteen to sixteen dollars, in merchandise, is paid for it here. What good or bad effect this gold region will have on California, I cannot foretell. It may end this year; but I am informed that it will continue many years. Mechanics now in this town are only waiting to finish some rude machinery, to enable them to obtain the gold more expeditiously and free from working in the river. Up to this time, but few Californians have gone to the mines, being afraid the Americans will soon have trouble among themselves, and cause disturbance to all around.

Thomas O. Larkin to James Buchanan, *House Executive Document 1*, 30th Congress, 2d session.

Document 10: The Need for a Transcontinental Railroad

William Gilpin had made his living as a lieutenant in the Seminole War, a newspaper editor, and a lawyer before heading to Oregon to promote and organize settlement in 1843. He later served in the Mexican War and was appointed governor of the Colorado Territory. In 1859 he wrote a book called The Central Gold Region *in which he argued that Colorado would become the center of world civilization and commerce. Part of his vision was that Denver would be the center of a network of railroads connecting all of the United States. The following excerpts from Gilpin's book are reprints of a speech he gave in Independence, Missouri, in 1849.*

Up to the year 1840, the progress whereby twenty-six States and four Territories had been established and peopled, had amounted to a solid strip of twenty-five miles in depth, added annually, along the western face of the Union from Canada to the Gulf. This occupation of wild territory, accumulating outward like the annual rings of our forest trees, proceeds with all the solemnity of a Providential ordinance. It is at this moment sweeping onward to the Pacific with accelerated activity and force, like a deluge of men, rising unabatedly, and daily pushed onward by the hand of God. . . .

. . . From this very spot [Independence] had gone forth a forlorn hope to occupy Oregon and California; Texas was thus annexed, the Indian country pressed upon its flanks, and spy companies reconnoitering New and Old Mexico. . . . Thus, then, *overland* sweeps this tide-wave of population, absorbing in its thundering march the glebe, the savages, and the wild beasts of the wilderness, sealing the mountains and debouching down upon the seaboard. Upon the high Atlantic sea-coast, the pioneer force has thrown itself into ships, and found in the ocean-fisheries food for its creative genius. The whaling fleet is the *marine* force of the pioneer army. These two forces, by land and sea, have worked steadily onward to the North Pacific. They now reunite in the harbors of Oregon and California, about to bring into existence upon the Pacific a commercial grandeur identical with that which has followed them upon the Atlantic. . . .

To the American people, then, belongs this vast interior space, covered over its uniform surface of 2,300,000 square miles, with the richest calcareous soil, touching the snows towards the north, and the torrid heats towards the south, bound together by an infinite internal navigation, of a temperate climate, and constituting, in the whole, the most magnificent dwelling-place marked out by God for man's abode. As the complete beneficence of the Almighty has thus given to us, the owners of the continent, the great natural outlets of the Mississippi to the Gulf, and the St. Lawrence to the North Atlantic, so is it left to a pious and grateful people, appreciating this goodness, to construct through the gorge of the Sierra Madre [Rockies], a great artificial monument, an iron path, a NATIONAL Railway to the *Western* Sea. . . .

This central railroad is an essential domestic institution, more powerful and permanent than law, or popular consent, to thoroughly complete the great systems of fluvial arteries which fraternize us into one people; to bind the two seaboards to this one nation, like ears to the human head; to radicate the foundations of the UNION so broad and deep, and render its structure so solid, that no possible force or stratagem can shake its permanence; and to secure such scope and space to progress, that prosperity and equality shall never be impaired or chafe for want of room.

What, sirs, are these populous empires of Japan and China, now become our neighbors? They are the most ancient, the most highly civilized, the most polished of the earth. It was from Sinim [China] that the Judean king Solomon imported the architects, the mechanics, the furniture of his gorgeous temple. . . . Hence came the climax of all human inventions, *letters and figures*, which fix language and numbers, making them eternal . . . Tea, sugar, the peach produced from the wild almond, the orange from the sour lime, the apple from the crab, the fruits, the flowers, the vegetables of our gardens, are the *creations* of Chinese *horticultural* science. The horse, cattle, the swine and poultry of our farms, come to us from thence. . . . Hence also came gunpowder, the magnetic needle, and calomel. The paints, varnish, and tools of the art have come, and the remedies used in pharmacy.

. . . Such as *Progress* is to-day, the same has it been for ten thousand years. It is the stream of the human race flowing from the east to the west, impelled by the same divine instinct that pervades creation. . . .

. . . It is by the rapid propagation of new States, the immediate occupation of the broad platform of the continent, the aggregation of the Pacific Ocean and Asiatic commerce, that inquietude will be swallowed up, and the murmurs of discontent lost in the onward sound of advancement. Discontent, distanced, will die out. The immense wants of the Pacific will draw off, over the Western outlets, the overteeming crops of the Mississippi Valley. Thus will the present seaboard States resume again their once profitable monopoly of the European market, relieved from the competition of the interior States. The cotton and rice culture of Georgia and the Carolinas will revive. The tobacco of Virginia and Maryland will again alone reach Europe. Ships withdrawn from the Northern States to the Pacific, will regenerate the noble business of nautical construction in New England and New York. The established domestic manufactures of clothing and metals will find, in our great home extension, that protection which they in vain seek to create by unequal legislation, nocuous and impracticable in our present incomplete and unbalanced geographical form. Thus calmly weighed and liberally appreciated, does this great Central Railroad minister to the interests, and invite the advocacy and cooperation of every section of our territory, and every citizen of our common country.

William Gilpin, *The Central Gold Region: The Grain, Pastoral, and Gold Regions of North America with Some New Views of Its Physical Geography; and Observations on the Pacific Railroad*. Philadelphia, Sower, Barnes & Co., 1860.

Document 11: The Sod-House Frontier

On the plains of Kansas and Nebraska, where trees were scarce, settlers who could not afford lumber built sod-houses. These primitive shelters were made by pressing soil and sod into building blocks. The description of one such dwelling below was written by Sara T.L. Robinson, wife of the first governor of Kansas, in 1856.

Take a walk down to the town, [Lawrence, Kansas,] and call upon one of our fellow-travellers. We find her in a little cabin of mud walls, cotton-wood roof, and with cloth covering the inside. It is tent-shaped, and very small. There is an earthy smell and a stifled feeling as I enter the low door, and, as I at a glance see the want of comfort pervading all, I scarcely can find courage to ask how she likes Kansas. A bed, standing crosswise, fills up one entire end of the cabin, leaving only about eight feet square of space for the family, consisting of father, mother, and four little girls under six years of age. Two rough benches, about two feet in length, and two rude tables, make up the furniture. The cooking is done out of doors, after camp fashion.

Sara T.L. Robinson, *Kansas: Its Interior and Exterior Life.* Boston: Crosby, Nichols, and Company, 1856.

Document 12: The Frontier as Melting Pot

Horace Greeley, who founded the New York Tribune *in 1841 and edited it until his death in 1872, was considered the most outstanding newspaper editor of his time. He was very interested in western expansion and is credited with coining the phrase "Go West, young man, go West!" In the following account of his 1859 journey to San Franscisco, Greeley is struck by the cosmopolitan make-up of the frontier populace.*

The first circumstance that strikes a stranger traversing this wild country is the vagrant instincts and habits of the great majority of its denizens—perhaps I should say, of the American people generally, as exhibited here. Among any ten whom you successively meet, there will be natives of New England, New York, Pennsylvania, Virginia or Georgia, Ohio or Indiana, Kentucky or Missouri, France, Germany, and perhaps Ireland. But, worse than this; you cannot enter a circle of a dozen persons of whom at least three will not have spent some years in California, two or three have made claims and built cabins in Kansas or Nebraska, and at least one spent a year or so in Texas. Boston, New York, Philadelphia, New Orleans, St. Louis, Cincinnati, have all contributed their quota toward peopling the new gold region. The next man you

meet driving an ox-team and white as a miller with dust, is probably an ex-banker or doctor, a broken merchant or manufacturer
from the old states, who has scraped together the candle-ends
charitably or contemptuously allowed him by his creditors on settlement, and risked them on a last desperate cast of the dice by
coming hither. Ex-editors, ex-printers, ex-clerks, ex-steamboat
men, are here in abundance—all on the keen hunt for the gold
which only a few will secure. One of the stations at which we slept
on our way up—a rough tent with a cheering hope (since blasted)
of a log house in the near future—was kept by an ex-lawyer of
Cincinnati and his wife, an ex-actress from our New York Bow-
ery—she being cook. Omnibus-drivers from Broadway repeatedly
handled the ribbons; ex-border ruffians from civilized Kansas—
some of them of unblessed memory—were encountered on our
way, at intervals none too long. All these, blended with veteran
Mountain men, Indians of all grades from the tamest to the
wildest, half-breeds, French trappers and *voyageurs* (who have generally two or three Indian wives apiece) and an occasional negro,
compose a medley such as hardly another region can parallel.
Honolulu, or some other port of the South Sea Islands, could
probably match it most nearly.

Horace Greeley, *An Overland Journey, from New York to San Francisco in the Summer of 1859*.
New York: C.M. Saxton, Barker & Co., 1860.

Document 13: Arguments for the Homestead Act

*On May 29, 1862, President Abraham Lincoln signed the Homestead
Act, which granted free land in the Midwest, the Great Plains, and the
West to people willing to settle and cultivate it. Westerners in general
greatly favored passage of the act, and the May 5 remarks of Senator
Samuel Pomeroy of Kansas are typical of western enthusiasm for the law.*

It may be thought to be an unfavorable time to introduce a bill to
dispose of the public lands, or a bill that puts the lands out of the
reach of our Government to sell or to pledge for the purpose of
raising revenue. I know full well the anxiety of every Senator to devise every means to raise money for the necessities of the Treasury
in this hour of extreme anxiety for the public credit. . . . The rebellion with which we are contending is not so much a question of
arms as of money. . . .

 If then this Homestead Bill is to weaken materially the resources of the Government in this crisis, then I am not for this Bill.

 But what are the facts? Are the public lands under our system of management likely to yield us any income during the war, or have they yielded any net profits during the past five years? That the land offices do nothing at present is perfectly evident. There is not land enough now selling to keep up the expenses of the offices. . . .

This, then, Mr. President, is the question I propose to discuss, involved in the passage of this homestead bill, namely, that the speedy settlement of the country by actual occupants of the land, though they be "small-fisted farmers," taking a homestead without expense or benefit to the Government, will produce more revenue to the country, and vastly more increase its wealth and productiveness, than any present or prospective sale, even though $1.25 can be realized for every acre. For my own part, I believe it should not be the policy of the Government to derive a revenue from the sale of the land, any more than from the sale of the air or the sunshine. These natural elements and auxiliaries of human life are God's great gifts to man, and the Government may as well bottle up the one as deed away the other. . . . Monopolizing great tracts, having estates embracing townships and counties, though, perhaps, gratifying to the individual, is always destructive of the general good. The indiscriminate sale of the public lands opens the door to the wildest speculations and the most unprincipled land monopolies. The greatest curse to a new country, and, indeed, to all countries, is to have large tracts of unoccupied lands held by non-residents, and non-occupants. . . .

I am, sir, for opening these lands for the landless of every nation under heaven. I care not whether he comes to us from the populous cities of our older States, or from the enlightened though oppressed nations of Europe. . . . To me he is an American, if he has an American heart in his bosom; if he be inspired with American impulses and American hopes, and yields himself joyfully to the moulding influence of American civilization. . . .

Now, then, I ask, how can the public lands be used so as to best increase the wealth of the country, and so be the better able to consume the imports of the country . . . as well also, as to meet the taxes imposed by the Government? And here let it be observed that the wealth of a nation does not consist in the money paid into its treasury, exacted, as it often is, from half-paid toiling millions, nor in an endless unoccupied public domain, running to waste with wild men and wild buffaloes. But wealth consists in flocks and herds, cultivated fields, in well paid labor, and well directed energy. . . .

I need not disguise the fact that while this system of small farms of a quarter section of land each will greatly promote the wealth, strength and glory of the Republic . . . it will secure the entire public domain to human freedom forever! . . .

This bill, enacted into a law, shall give civilization and life throughout the silent gorges and gentle sleeping valleys, far away into the deep recesses of the continent. Where it leads the way there shall go in triumph the American standard, the old flag of the Union. And when once thus planted, it shall never again be trailed in the dust. The proudest bird of the mountain is upon the American ensign, and not one feather shall fall from plumage here. She is American in design, and an emblem of wilderness and freedom. I say again she has not perched herself upon American standards to die here. Our great western valleys were never scooped out for her burial place. Nor were the everlasting, untrodden mountains piled for her monument. Niagara shall not pour her endless waters for her requiem; nor shall our ten thousand rivers weep to the ocean in eternal tears. No, sir; no. Unnumbered voices shall come up from river, plain and mountain, echoing the songs of our triumphant deliverance, while lights from a thousand hill tops will betoken the rising of the sun of freedom, that shall grow brighter and brighter until a more perfect day.

Samuel Pomeroy, *Smoky Hill and Republican Union*, May 29, 1862.

Document 14: The Frontier as a Land of Opportunity

Even as it was being settled the frontier was romanticized as a land of abundance, where hard work was rewarded and where able-bodied men and women could make new lives for themselves. This image of the frontier was fostered by "boosters" (including the railroad companies and western merchants and landowners) who circulated pamphlets encouraging western emigration. Below is the text of one such pamphlet, an 1868 tract describing the benefits of life in Colorado.

Those who can do well in the west, are the producing class, the farmer, stock-raiser, wool-grower, dairyman, miner, and laborer. The natural wealth is there, but a great drawback, common to all our mining countries, has been the want of a permanent class of settlers, who will go, prepared to stay and build up homes. All are fast finding out that the climate, resources and advantages, more than repay for the privations attendant on settling in a new country. Those who wish to settle in a new country, and grow up with it, and have a location that is pleasant to live in, with good society and the comforts of a life in the east, can find it now among the towns of Colorado. Doctors are not in demand, the climate is too healthy; from its great elevation and distance from large bodies of water, it cannot be otherwise. Many who have left the east, despairing and hopeless, have soon recovered, and rejoiced in restored health, renewed energies and prospects. Politicians are plenty, as in all new countries, and of legal talent there is no lack; few states, old or new, can boast a better standard class of legislators or members of the bar.

School teachers are well paid, and good ones are always in demand, as the rising generation are increasing very rapidly, the country being exceedingly productive in young ideas to be taught how to shoot.

Servant girls get from $10 to $12 per week, and if steady and reliable, find good homes among the best families. These prices should, and probably will be reduced somewhat, but from the lightness of the air, dryness of the atmosphere, and various other causes, servant girls seem to get in the notion of setting up housekeeping, and thus vacancies are frequent, and often hard to fill. 1000 could probably now obtain good situations or husbands in Colorado.

Mining labor is always in demand, and at better prices, considering cost of living, than any other mining country so easily reached.

Fortune-hunters, who expect to get rich in a month, will likely be disappointed; if getting rich was so easy, there are sharp men there to take advantage of it. Whoever goes to Colorado or any other mining country, with an idea that gold digging is not labor, had better get that idea out of their heads at once, and those who expect to live without work, will find poor encouragement in that country.

Fast young men who are only useful in carrying a gold-headed cane, will not find it a paying business.

Rogues and light-fingered gentry do not thrive. They seem to become afflicted with a throat disease, caused by too close contact with a rope.

But there is a constant demand for honest labor, and those who have no capital but their muscle, cannot do better than in Colorado. If they do not get above their business when they arrive, they need not starve, as they are doing by thousands in our large cities and in Europe. Cooperative clubs might be formed in every settlement in the east, of 10 or 20 persons, assessing the members enough to pay the expenses of one or two of the party, who could go ahead and select a location for the balance. This would be a saving of time and expense on the part of many, who can ill afford to spend a hundred dollars and their time for the trip, but could work and help pay for some one else to go in their stead.

"Nothing ventured nothing gained." Thousands in our Eastern States, millions in Europe, would be glad to have a home in the west, if they only *knew* they would have no bad luck. Of course all cannot succeed in everything; some failures will occur, but those who are struggling for a mere living, and have families to feed, should seek the west, put all together they can, and move on before all the best chances are taken, somewhere, anywhere out of the crowded cities. The great west has a plenty, and room for all; the poorest may be a peer if the stuff is in him; as a boy once wrote from the west to his father in the east, "some very small men get elected to office here; you better come on."

• • • • •

Thousands are led to go to new countries, on account of stories of fabulous wealth just discovered, where all can get rich. Don't rush. Just reflect a little, and remember there are other men as smart as you already on the ground, and prepared to pick up all the big things. If you go west, prepared to work for what you get, go ahead. If you are doing well, stay at home, but if you are out of business, no opening offers, you are desperate, bound to go somewhere, or commit suicide, don't do it. Go west, by all means, and give your spirit vent; a live man in the west, is worth a half dozen dead ones anywhere.

Ned E. Farrell, *Colorado, the Rocky Mountain Gem, as It Is in 1868*. Chicago Western News Company, 1868.

Document 15: An Army Officer's View of the Indian Question

Wars between American Indians and the U.S. Army became more frequent in the 1860s and 1870s, as farmland, gold, and other natural resources induced white settlers to move into the Great Plains, the Southwest desert regions, and California. In the following excerpt from an 1878 treatise on "the Indian question," an army officer describes the Indians as an inferior people and an obstacle to progress.

What qualities then does this American Indian lack, that he is so little impressed by the efforts which have been put forth for his amelioration? He has the same physical properties, the same senses, the same elementary mental powers which we possess, but here the parallel ceases. Although equally if not more skilled in the use of the senses than the white man, he lacks the faculty of abstraction, and consequently his imagination, reason and understanding, are of a very low order. He is almost entirely destitute of the moral qualities, and his religious nature is of that kind which presumes the existence of a Supreme Being, simply to account for facts and occurrences beyond his comprehension. His conceptions of that Divinity are extremely vague and uncertain. It may be one and indivisible, or it may exist in many and antagonistic forms. . . . His Divinity has none of the attributes of goodness, for he, in his utter ignorance of virtues, is unable to imagine their existence. It is only propitiated by substantial material gifts, and may be persuaded to assist in enterprises of the most wicked character.

Like all savage people, the Indian has not the slightest conception of definite law as a rule of action. He is guided by his animal desires. He practices all forms of vice, and even to a great extent those crimes which are pronounced as against nature. He takes little thought except for the present, knows nothing of property in the abstract, and has not therefore any incentive to labor further than to supply immediate wants. Instead of making an effort for moral improvement he strives to strengthen his vicious propensities. He eats the raw liver of ferocious beasts to augment his ferocity, wounds and bruises his person to increase his animal courage, boasts in council of his brutalities, parades them as deeds of approved valor and as examples worthy of imitation. . . .

It is well known that no portion of the Indian population can much longer maintain itself after its old customs of life, for wild game can only be found in sufficient quantities for its subsistence in small sections of the country. It is well known that it is impossible to improve the Indian while in a nomadic state, and that in such condition he is a constant source of menace to pioneers, and to the frontier settlements. It is also well known that much of the country now rendered insecure and unrenumerative because roamed over by irresponsible tribes, is sought by our citizens for occupation, and that it is desirable that routes of travel be opened through the same which can be safely journeyed over by the public. In fine, it is well understood that imperative necessity and the interests of both races demand, that the entire Indian population shall be permanently located either individually by tribes or collectively, and that it be compelled to conform to the laws of the country. It might also be stated as a fact, that this population must be compelled to work for its food, which must in future be largely gained through agricultural toil, for neither charity, gratitude, nor justice, requires the Government to feed it in idleness, and its own well-being and prosperity calls upon it to labor for its own maintenance and support.

The question of the future relationship of the white and red races to each other, cannot be satisfactorily determined. Very likely, the idea that a large civilized Indian nation might be created, and preserved, within the country, has been entirely abandoned. That has given way to the hope that Indian communities may be perpetuated, and made similar, in action and intention, to white societies. Speculation, however, based upon tendencies as shown in the past, might lead to the belief that such a hope cannot be realized.

We have in mind more particularly, that gradual absorption of the Indian stock, which has been in progress since the discovery of America, and which is even more noticeable in Mexico, and in some of the South American provinces, than in the United States. But even with us, it has been so rapidly progressing, as to raise a strong presumption, that the Indian race will, in a few generations, be practically absorbed. In eighteen hundred and seventy-six, the Commissioner of Indian Affairs reported, that nearly one-sixth of the Indian population of the United States, exclusive of Alaska, was made up of mixed bloods; and his figures show, that only about one half of the Cherokees, Creeks, Choctaws, Chickasaws and Seminoles are of pure extraction. These estimates are approximative, and really enumerate the mixed bloods at too low a rate. At many of the agencies, a large number of the half and quarter breeds there dwelling seem to be almost entirely ignored.

The gradual absorption of our Indian stock will assuredly continue, and it is probable, that it will be finally merged in the great body of our white population. The question whether the unity of the two races will produce vigorous physical organisms, is still debatable; and the psychological inquiry, whether the product will be mentally and morally of an inferior order, is still unsettled in the minds of many. Our own opinions upon the latter subject are decided. . . . The cross will be an inferior being, both in mind and morals, when viewed in the light of our civilization, or rather, when measured by the rules prescribed by our civilization, as tests of nature and quality.

However much such an ultimate result is to be deplored, the effect will scarcely be perceptible upon our institutions, except in those sections of country where the Indians shall have been collected in masses. They are now in numbers, only as one to ninety of our entire white population; and indeed as one to twelve of our colored population. In nineteen hundred, the ratio of Indians to whites, even if the two races can be restrained from much intermingling, will be about as one to one hundred and seventy-five. Whatever view therefore, may be taken of this social problem no decided effect can be produced upon our national character. It is only in the event that Indians are collected in large bodies (which certainly, in so far as attempted, seems to have encouraged amalgamation,) that any danger is to be apprehended. Should a course of action, having for its object the concentration of the tribes, be persistently and successfully prosecuted, we shall have, within the heart of the United States, an element which will there prolong social disorder for generations to come. If scattered throughout the interior, its evil effects will, in a short time, be neutralized.

Elwell S. Otis, *The Indian Question*. New York: Sheldon and Company, 1878.

Document 16: An Indian's View of Indian Affairs

In 1875 the U.S. Army went to war with the Nez Percé Indians of eastern Oregon, who were led by Young Joseph. Chief Joseph and most of his tribe were captured in 1877 and forced onto a reservation in Oklahoma. In 1879, Chief Joseph made a trip to Washington, D.C., where he made a speech calling on the government to rethink its Indian policies.

My friends, I have been asked to show you my heart. I am glad to have a chance to do so. I want the white people to understand my people. Some of you think an Indian is like a wild animal. This is a great mistake. I will tell you all about our people, and then you can judge whether an Indian is a man or not. I believe much trouble and blood would be saved if we opened our hearts more. I will tell you in my way how the Indian sees things. The white man has more words to tell you how they look to him, but it does not require many words to speak the truth. What I have to say will come from my heart, and I will speak with a straight tongue. . . .

We did not know there were other people besides the Indian until about one hundred winters ago, when some men with white faces came to our country. They brought many things with them to trade for furs and skins. They brought tobacco, which was new to us. They brought guns with flint stones on them, which frightened our women and children. Our people could not talk with these white-faced men, but they used signs which all people understand. These men were Frenchmen, and they called our people "Nez Percés," because they wore rings in their noses for ornaments. Although very few of our people wear them now, we are still called by the same name. These French trappers said a great many things to our fathers which have been planted in our hearts. Some were good for us, but some were bad. Our people were divided in opinion about these men. Some thought they taught more bad than good. An Indian respects a brave man, but he despises a coward. He loves a straight tongue, but he hates a forked tongue. . . .

For a short time we lived quietly. But this could not last. White men had found gold in the mountains around the land of winding water. They stole a great many horses from us, and we could not get them back because we were Indians. The white men told lies for each other. They drove off a great many of our cattle. Some white men branded our young cattle so they could claim them. We had no friend who would plead our cause before the law councils. It seemed to me that some of the white men in Wallowa were doing these things on purpose to get up a war. They knew that we were not strong enough to fight them. I labored hard to avoid trouble and bloodshed. We gave up some of our country to the white men, thinking that then we could have peace. We were mistaken. The white man would not let us alone. We could have avenged our wrongs many times, but we did not. Whenever the Government has asked us to help them against other Indians, we have never refused. When the white men were few and we were strong we could have killed them all off, but the Nez Percés wished to live at peace. . . .

On account of the treaty made by the other bands of the Nez Percés, the white men claimed my lands. We were troubled greatly by white men crowding over the line. Some of these were good men, and we lived on peaceful terms with them, but they were not all good. . . .

Year after year we have been threatened, but no war was made upon my people until General Howard came to our country two years ago and told us that he was the white war-chief of all that country. He said: "I have a great many soldiers at my back. I am going to bring them up here, and then I will talk to you again. I will not let white men laugh at me the next time I come. The country belongs to the Government, and I intend to make you go upon the reservation."

I remonstrated with him against bringing more soldiers to the Nez Percés country. He had one house full of troops all the time at Fort Lapwai.

General Howard replied: "You deny my authority, do you? You want to dictate to me, do you?"

Then one of my chiefs—Too-hool-hool-suit—rose in the council and said to General Howard: "The Great Spirit Chief made the world as it is, and as he wanted it, and he made a part of it for us to live upon. I do not see where you get authority to say that we shall not live where he placed us."

General Howard lost his temper and said: "Shut up! I don't want to hear any more of such talk. The law says you shall go upon the reservation to live, and I want you to do so, but you persist in disobeying the law" (meaning the treaty). "If you do not move, I will take the matter into my own hand, and make you suffer for your disobedience."

I said in my heart that, rather than have war, I would give up my country. I would give up my father's grave. I would give up everything rather than have the blood of white men upon the hands of my people.

General Howard refused to allow me more than thirty days to move my people and their stock. I am sure that he began to prepare for war at once. . . .

There were bad men among my people who had quarreled with white men, and they talked of their wrongs until they roused all the bad hearts in the council. Still I could not believe that they would begin the war. I know that my young men did a great wrong, but I ask, Who was first to blame? They had been insulted a thousand times; their fathers and brothers had been killed; their mothers and wives had been disgraced; they had been driven to madness by whisky sold to them by white men; they had been told by General Howard that all their horses and cattle which they had been unable to drive out of Wallowa were to fall into the hands of white men; and, added to all this, they were homeless and desperate.

I would have given my own life if I could have undone the killing of white men by my people. I blame my young men and I blame the white men. I blame General Howard for not giving my people time to get their stock away from Wallowa. I do not acknowledge that he had the right to order me to leave Wallowa at any time. I deny that either my father or myself ever sold that land. It is still our land. It may never again be our home, but my father sleeps there, and I love it as I love my mother. I left there, hoping to avoid bloodshed. . . .

When I think of our condition my heart is heavy. I see men of my race treated as outlaws and driven from country to country, or shot down like animals.

I know that my race must change. We can not hold our own with the white men as we are. We only ask an even chance to live as other men live. We ask to be recognized as men. We ask that the same law shall work alike on all men. If the Indian breaks the law, punish him by the law. If the white man breaks the law, punish him also.

Let me be a free man—free to travel, free to stop, free to work, free to trade where I choose, free to choose my own teachers, free to follow the religion of my fathers, free to think and talk and act for myself—and I will obey every law, or submit to the penalty.

Whenever the white man treats the Indian as they treat each other, then we will have no more wars. . . .

For this time the Indian race are waiting and praying. I hope that no more groans of wounded men and women will ever go to the ear of the Great Spirit Chief above, and that all people may be one people.

[Hin-mah-too-yah-lat-keht] has spoken for his people.

Young Joseph, "An Indian's View of Indian Affairs," *North American Review*, April 1879.

Document 17: "The Typical Cowboy"

The image of the cowboy as a rugged, independent western hero is not a twentieth-century invention. In the 1880s, as the era of the cattle drive was coming to an end, the popular press had already developed an idealized image of cowboy life, as this piece from the Denver Times *(reprinted in the* Kansas Cowboy) *attests.*

The typical cowboy, according to the . . . correspondents of Eastern papers is a cross between a bear and wild cat, a sort of a man-eating son of a seacook, who isn't comfortable until he has been permitted to chew somebody's ear off and establish his reputation as a wild horse from Texas. There may have been cowboys of that character . . . but the breed has run out. . . .

Last winter I had occasion to visit a cow camp. . . . A dozen cleanly built, muscular men, with intelligent faces and gentlemanly manners, were seated about the room. As I looked about me I wondered if they were all cowboys. They were, every one of them. . . .

I have never met with a class of men more worthy of confidence and respect. . . .

A peculiarity of the class is its independence. They recognize no superior except the foreman of an outfit, or the ranch superintendent, and then only when on duty on the range. . . . If a call for the night relief is not answered speedily the persons of the offenders are liable to become acquainted with the foreman's boot, but if at any other time the foreman should take such a liberty, he takes chances that few, understanding the situation would care to. . . .

Thrown together so far away from civilization it follows as a matter of course that mutual confidence is a necessity. . . . A lie is not glossed over as in fashionable society. It is promptly branded as such in plain terms, and the habitual liar is tolerated only when he is a sufficiently skillful and diligent workman to hold his own with his fellows on the range, while no one cares to conceal his contempt for the man whose word cannot be taken. . . .

The duties of the position are arduous and not infrequently dangerous. Hot or cold, rain or shine, the work must be done and shrinking cannot be tolerated, for that increases the work of others. As a consequence the men who stand the severe test are not only self-reliant but reliable. . . .

The cowboy is a character developed by circumstances, and his development is a credit to himself no less than to the industry which brought him into existence. . . . He is no longer permitted to kill a beef regardless of the capacity to consume the carcass . . . but he manages to maintain his usefulness on bacon and flour, and is, taken all in all, a manly, industrious, energetic fellow . . . a credit to the country.

Kansas Cowboy, "The Cowboy of the Day," February 7, 1885.

Document 18: Frederick Jackson Turner's Frontier Thesis

College professor Frederick Jackson Turner was the first to develop a formal theory of how the American frontier influenced the development of the nation. Below are excerpts from a paper Turner submitted to the American Historical Society in 1893. He argues that the experience of taming the frontier made the first Americans more independent from Europe and led later generations to prize individual freedom and limited government. Turner further developed his thesis in books such as 1926's The Frontier in American History. *Many historians have since challenged Turner's views, but his central hypothesis remains a provocative interpretation of frontier history.*

In a recent bulletin of the Superintendent of the Census for 1890 appear these significant words: "Up to and including 1880 the country had a frontier of settlement, but at present the unsettled area has been so broken into by isolated bodies of settlement that there can hardly be said to be a frontier line. In the discussion of its extent, its westward movement, etc., it can not, therefore, any longer have a place in the census reports." This brief official statement marks the closing of a great historic movement. Up to our own day American history has been in a large degree the history of the colonization of the Great West. The existence of an area of free land, its continuous recession, and the advance of American settlement westward, explain American development. . . .

At first, the frontier was the Atlantic coast. It was the frontier of Europe in a very real sense. Moving westward, the frontier became more and more American. As successive terminal moraines result from successive glaciations, so each frontier leaves its traces behind it, and when it becomes a settled area the region still partakes of the frontier characteristics. Thus the advance of the frontier has meant a steady movement away from the influence of Europe, a steady growth of independence on American lines. . . .

At the Atlantic frontier one can study the germs of processes repeated at each successive frontier. We have the complex European life sharply precipitated by the wilderness into the simplicity of primitive conditions. The first frontier had to meet its Indian question, its question of the disposition of the public domain, of the means of intercourse with older settlements, of the extension of political organization, of religious and educational activity. And the settlement of these and similar questions for one frontier served as a guide for the next. . . .

· · · · ·

But with all these similarities there are essential differences, due to the place element and the time element. It is evident that the farming frontier of the Mississippi Valley presents different conditions from the mining frontier of the Rocky Mountains. The frontier reached by the Pacific Railroad, surveyed into rectangles, guarded by the United States Army, and recruited by the daily immigrant ship, moves forward at a swifter pace and in a different way than the frontier reached by the birch canoe or the pack horse. . . .

The most important effect of the frontier has been in the promotion of democracy here and in Europe. As has been indicated, the frontier is productive of individualism. Complex society is precipitated by the wilderness into a kind of primitive organization based on the family. The tendency is anti-social. It produces antipathy to control, and particularly to any direct control. . . .

· · · · ·

The frontier individualism has from the beginning promoted democracy.

The frontier States that came into the Union in the first quarter of a century of its existence came in with democratic suffrage provisions, and had reactive effects of the highest importance upon the older States whose peoples were being attracted there. An extension of the franchise became essential. It was *western* New York that forced an extension of suffrage in the constitutional convention of that State in 1821; and it was *western* Virginia that compelled the tide-water region to put a more liberal suffrage provision in the constitution framed in 1830, and to give to the frontier region a more nearly proportionate representation with the tidewater aristocracy. The rise of democracy as an effective force in the nation came in with western preponderance under Jackson and William Henry Harrison, and it meant the triumph of the frontier—with all of its good and with all of its evil elements. . . .

So long as free land exists, the opportunity for a competency exists, and economic power secures political power. But the democracy born of free land, strong in selfishness and individualism, intolerant of administrative experience and education, and pressing individual liberty beyond its proper bounds, has its dangers as well as its benefits. Individualism in America has allowed a laxity in regard to governmental affairs which has rendered possible the spoils system and all the manifest evils that follow from the lack of a highly developed civic spirit. In this connection may be noted also the influence of frontier conditions in permitting lax business honor, inflated paper currency and wild-cat banking. . . .

• • • • •

From the conditions of frontier life came intellectual traits of profound importance. The works of travelers along each frontier from colonial days onward describe certain common traits, and these traits have, while softening down, still persisted as survivals in the place of their origin, even when a higher social organization succeeded. The result is that to the frontier the American intellect owes its striking characteristics. That coarseness and strength combined with acuteness and inquisitiveness; that practical, inventive turn of mind, quick to find expedients; that masterful grasp of material things, lacking in the artistic but powerful to effect great ends; that restless, nervous energy; that dominant individualism, working for good and for evil, and withal that buoyancy and exuberance which comes with freedom—these are traits of the frontier, or traits called out elsewhere because of the existence of the frontier. Since the days when the fleet of Columbus sailed into the waters of the New World, America has been another name for opportunity, and the people of the United States have taken their tone from the incessant expansion which has not only been open but has even been forced upon them. He would be a rash prophet who should assert that the expansive character of American life has now entirely ceased. Movement has been its dominant fact, and, unless this training has no effect upon a people, the American energy will continually demand a wider field for its exercise. But never again will such gifts of free land offer themselves, For a moment, at the frontier, the bonds of custom are broken and unrestraint is triumphant. There is not *tabula rasa*. The stubborn American environment is there with its imperious summons to accept its conditions; the inherited ways of doing things are also there; and yet, in spite of environment, and in spite of custom, each frontier did indeed furnish a new field of opportunity, a gate of escape from the bondage of the past; and freshness, and confidence, and scorn of older society, impatience of its restraints and its ideas, and indifference to its lessons, have accompanied the frontier. What the Mediterranean Sea was to the Greeks, breaking the bond of custom, offering new experiences, calling out new institutions and activities, that, and more, the ever retreating, frontier has been to the United States directly, and to the nations of Europe more remotely.

Frederick Jackson Turner, "The Significance of the Frontier in American History," American Historical Association, *Annual Report for 1893*. Washington, DC: Government Printing Office, 1894.

Chronology

1787

July 13—Congress passes the Northwest Ordinance, which sets guidelines for settlement of the frontier.

1803

In April, France agrees to sell the Louisiana Territory to the United States for $15 million.

1804

On May 14, Meriwether Lewis and William Clark begin their expedition to discover a direct water route across the continent.

1806

Zebulon Pike sets out on an expedition to trace the source of the Mississippi River and instead discovers the peak that bears his name.

September 23—Lewis and Clark return to St. Louis, Missouri.

1808

John Jacob Astor founds the American Fur Company.

1812

The United States and Great Britain clash in the War of 1812, which ends with the Treaty of Ghent on December 24, 1814.

1817

Construction of the Erie Canal begins in New York. The canal will become a significant artery in the westward movement of Americans from the East Coast.

1820

Explorer Stephen Long leads an expedition across Kansas to the Rocky Mountains. He labels the area east of the Rockies the "Great American Desert," steering settlers away from the region for decades.

February 17—Congress passes the Missouri Compromise, which prohibits slavery north of latitude 36°30'. There are now twelve slave and twelve free states.

1821

January 17—The Spanish governor of Texas Moses grants Moses Austin permission to settle three hundred families in the region.

August 24—Mexico rebels against Spain and wins independence with the signing of the Treaty of Córdoba.

November—Trader William Becknell blazes the Santa Fe Trail between Independence, Missouri, and Santa Fe, Mexico. The trail becomes the principal avenue for manufactured goods and emigrants bound for Santa Fe and the Southwest.

1822

St. Louis trader William Ashley places an advertisement in the *St. Louis Gazette* asking for "one hundred enterprising young men" to join him in a trapping and trading venture in the trans-Mississippi west. This signals the beginning of the "mountain man" era.

1825

The federal government adopts a policy of exchanging Indian lands in the east for public land in the west and establishes an Indian territory in the region known as the Great American Desert.

1826

Fur trapper Jedediah Smith leads the first party of Americans overland to California.

1834

Congress establishes the Department of Indian Affairs.

1835

Samuel F.B. Morse invents the telegraph. October: Texas declares its independence from Mexico; war between Texas and Mexico follows.

1837

March 3—President Andrew Jackson officially recognizes the Republic of Texas.

1838

Over eighteen thousand Cherokee Indian people are forcibly relocated to Indian Territory from Georgia, Alabama, and Tennessee along the "Trail of Tears."

1839

The last fur trade rendezvous is held at Fort Bonneville. Several factors, including the change in men's fashions from beaver to silk top hats and the exhaustion of the beaver supply, have led to the decline of the fur industry.

1841

Congress passes the Pre-Emption Act to encourage settlement of the frontier. The act gives "squatters" the right to purchase federal land at a minimum price.

1843

Over one thousand settlers participate in the Great Migration via the Oregon Trail to the Pacific Northwest. It becomes an annual event, with thousands more following each year.

1845

March 1—Lame-duck president John Tyler signs a resolution annexing the Republic of Texas. In his March 4 inauguration speech, President James Polk calls for the acquisition of Oregon and California as U.S. territories. The phrase "manifest destiny" is coined by John L. O'Sullivan.

1846

May 13—After a clash between Mexican and U.S. troops along the Rio Grande, the United States declares war on Mexico. The Mexican War continues until February 1848.

1847

April 16—Brigham Young leads a small group to the Great Salt Lake Basin. The following year, thousands of Mormons follow and begin building Salt Lake City.

1848

January 24—Gold is discovered at Sutter's Mill near Sacramento, California. In the next two years, tens of thousands of "Argonauts" journey to California.

1849

The Pacific Railroad Company is chartered and begins construction of the first railroad west of the Mississippi River, from St. Louis to Kansas City.

1853

In the Gadsden Purchase, Mexico sells the United States a strip of land running along Mexico's northern border between Texas and California for $10 million.

1854

Congress approves the Kansas-Nebraska Act, which repeals the Missouri Compromise of 1820. The Republican Party is born out of opposition to the act and to slavery in general.

1858
Gold is discovered at Pike's Peak in Colorado. The '59ers pour into the state the following year.

1859
The first major silver strike in the United States, the Comstock Lode, is discovered in Nevada.

1860
Republican Abraham Lincoln is elected sixteenth president of the United States. In response, South Carolina secedes from the Union. Severe drought leads to an exodus of thirty thousand settlers, the "Exodusters," from Kansas.

1861
Mississippi, Florida, Alabama, Georgia, Louisiana, and Texas join South Carolina to form the Confederate States of America. The Civil War begins in April with the clash between Confederate and Union troops at Fort Sumter, South Carolina.

1862
The Homestead Act is passed, which allows citizens to acquire 160 acres of land in the public domain by settling on them for five years and paying a small fee.

1865
The Civil War ends, and the Thirteenth Amendment, which abolishes slavery, is ratified.

1867
The United States purchases Alaska from Russia for $7,200,000. The Kansas Pacific Railroad reaches Abilene, Kansas, and the first cattle drive from Texas up the Chisholm Trail to Abilene marks the beginning of the cattle driving era.

1869
March 10—The first transcontinental railroad is completed as the Union Pacific Railroad joins the Central Pacific Railroad at Promontory Point in Utah Territory.

1871
Congress passes the Indian Appropriations Act, which ends the practice of treating Indian tribes as sovereign nations. Instead, Indians are legally designated as wards of the federal government.

1881
The second transcontinental railroad is completed. Helen Hunt Jackson publishes *A Century of Dishonor*, the first detailed examination of the atrocities committed against American Indians.

1887
The free delivery of mail is provided in all communities with a population of at least ten thousand.

1889
Congress establishes the Oklahoma Territory on unoccupied lands in the Indian Territory, breaking a sixty-year-old pledge to preserve this area exclusively for American Indians forced from their lands in the east. In the Oklahoma Land Rush on April 22, thousands of settlers stake their claims on almost 2 million acres of land.

1890
After the 1890 census, the federal government declares that the frontier is now settled.

1896
The discovery of gold at Bonanza Creek, a tributary of the Klondike River near Dawson City, Alaska, sparks the "Klondike Stampede," the last great western gold rush. Henry Ford completes the assembly of the first American automobile for sale to the public.

1898
The United States annexes Hawaii. After a short war with Spain, the United States also acquires Cuba, Puerto Rico, Guam, and the Philippine Islands.

1902
Owen Wister publishes *The Virginian*, a novel romanticizing cowboy life. It introduces the climactic "showdown," further expanding the growing myth of the American West.

For Further Research

General Histories of Frontier Expansion

Ray Allen Billington, *America's Frontier Heritage*. Albuquerque: University of New Mexico Press, 1974.

———, *The Far Western Frontier, 1830–1860*. New York: Harper, 1956.

———, *Westward to the Pacific: An Overview of America's Westward Expansion*. St. Louis, MO: Jefferson National Expansion Historical Association, 1979.

Ray Allen Billington and Martin Ridge, *Westward Expansion: A History of the American Frontier*. New York: Macmillan, 1982.

Dee Alexander Brown, *Bury My Heart at Wounded Knee: An Indian History of the American West*. New York: Holt, Rinehart, and Winston, 1970.

Thomas D. Clark, *Frontier America: The Story of the Westward Movement*. New York: Scribner's, 1959.

Dale Van Every, *The Final Challenge: The American Frontier*. 1804–1845. New York: Quill, 1988.

William H. Goetzmann, *Exploration and Empire: The Explorer and the Scientist in the Winning of the American West*. New York: Norton, 1978.

———, *Mountain Men*. Cody, WY: Buffalo Bill Historical Center, 1978.

Robert V. Hine, *The American West: A New Interpretive History*. New Haven, CT: Yale University Press, 2000.

Wilbur R. Jacobs, *Dispossessing the American Indian: Indians and Whites on the Colonial Frontier*. New York: Scribner's, 1972.

Mary Ellen Jones, *Daily Life on the 19th-Century American Frontier*. Westport, CT: Greenwood Press, 1998.

Nelson Klose, *A Concise Study Guide to the American Frontier*. Lincoln: University of Nebraska Press, 1964.

Gerald F. Kreyche, *Visions of the American West*. Lexington: University Press of Kentucky, 1989.

S.L.A. Marshall, *Crimson Prairie: The Wars Between the United States and the Plains Indians During the Winning of the West*. New York: Scribner's, 1972.

Walter T.K. Nugent, *Into the West: The Story of Its People*. New York: A.A. Knopf, 1999.

Arthur King Peters, *Seven Trails West*. New York: Abbeville Press Publishers, 1996.

Sanford Wexler, ed., *Westward Expansion: An Eyewitness History*. New York: Facts On File, 1991.

Compendiums of Primary Documents

William F. Deverell and Anne F. Hyde, eds., *The West in the History of the Nation: A Reader*. Boston: Bedford/St. Martin's, 2000.

Robert V. Hine and Edwin R. Bingham, eds., *The Frontier Experience: Readings on the Trans-Mississippi West*. Belmont, CA: Wadsworth, 1963.

Robert W. Richmond and Robert W. Mardock, eds., *A Nation Moving West: Readings in the History of the American Frontier*. Lincoln: University of Nebraska Press, 1966.

Clark C. Spence, ed., *The American West: A Source Book*. New York: Thomas Y. Crowell, 1966.

The Lewis and Clark Expedition

Stephen E. Ambrose, *Undaunted Courage: Meriwether Lewis, Thomas Jefferson, and the Opening of the American West*. New York: Simon & Schuster, 1996.

———, *Lewis & Clark: Voyage of Discovery*. Washington, DC: National Geographic Society, 1998.

Frank Bergon, ed., *The Journals of Lewis & Clark*. New York: Penguin, 1989.

Sally Senzel Isaacs, *America in the Time of Lewis and Clark: 1801 to 1850*. Des Plaines, IL: Heinemann Library, 1998.

Donald Jackson, *Thomas Jefferson & the Stony Mountains: Exploring the West from Monticello*. Norman: University of Oklahoma Press, 1993.

Donald Jackson, ed., *Letters of the Lewis & Clark Expedition with Related Documents, 1783–1854*. Chicago: University of Illinois Press, 1978.

Bill and Jan Moeller, *Lewis and Clark: A Photographic Journey*. Missoula, MT: Mountain Press, 1999.

Daniel P. Thorp, *Lewis & Clark: An American Journey*. New York: MetroBooks, 1998.

Manifest Destiny

William H. Goetzmann, *When the Eagle Screamed: The Romantic Horizon in American Expansionism*. Norman: University of Oklahoma Press, 2000.

Norman A. Graebner, ed., *Manifest Destiny*. Indianapolis: Bobbs-Merrill, 1968.

Frederick Merk, *Manifest Destiny and Mission in American History: A Reinterpretation*. Westport, CT: Greenwood Press, 1983.

Robert Sobel, *Conquest and Conscience: The 1840s*. New York: Crowell, 1971.

The California Gold Rush

Peter J. Blodgett, *Land of Golden Dreams: California in the Gold Rush Decade, 1848–1858*. San Marino, CA: Huntington Library, 1999.

Mary Hill, *Gold: The California Story*. Berkeley: University of California Press, 1999.

J.S. Holliday, *Rush for Riches: Gold Fever and the Making of California*. Berkeley: University of California Press, 1999.

Malcolm J. Rohrbough, *Days of Gold: The California Gold Rush and the American Nation*. Berkeley: University of California Press, 1997.

The Transcontinental Railroad

Stephen E. Ambrose, *Nothing Like It in the World: The Men Who Built the Transcontinental Railroad, 1863–1869*. New York: Simon & Schuster, 2000.

Dee Alexander Brown, *Hear That Lonesome Whistle Blow*. New York: Simon & Schuster, 1994.

John F. Stover, *American Railroads*. Chicago, IL: University of Chicago Press, 1997.

Index

DATE DUE
